FIRSTHAND

WRITERS ON WRITING
Jay Parini, Series Editor

A good writer is first a good reader. Looking at craft from the inside, with an intimate knowledge of its range and possibilities, writers also make some of our most insightful critics. With this series we will bring together the work of some of our finest writers on the subject they know best, discussing their own work and that of others, as well as concentrating on craft and other aspects of the writer's world.

Poet, novelist, biographer, and critic, Jay Parini is the author of numerous books, including *The Apprentice Lover* and *One Matchless Time: A Life of William Faulkner*. Currently he is D. E. Axinn Professor of English & Creative Writing at Middlebury College.

Firsthand

How I Solved a Literary Mystery and Learned to Play Kickass Tennis while Coming to Grips with the Disorder of Things

A Comic Memoir

KEITH GANDAL

University of Michigan Press
Ann Arbor

For questions or permissions, please contact um.press.perms@umich.edu

Published in the United States of America by the
University of Michigan Press
Manufactured in the United States of America
Printed on acid-free paper
First published July 2024

A CIP catalog record for this book is available from the British Library.

Library of Congress Cataloging-in-Publication Data

Names: Gandal, Keith, author. | Michigan Publishing (University of Michigan), publisher.
Title: Firsthand : how I solved a literary mystery and learned to play kickass tennis while
    coming to grips with the disorder of things : a comic memoir / Keith Gandal.
Other titles: Writers on writing (Ann Arbor, Mich.)
Description: Ann Arbor [Michigan] : University of Michigan Press, [2024] |
    Series: Writers on writing | Includes bibliographical references (pages 261–277).
Identifiers: LCCN 2024002373 (print) | LCCN 2024002374 (ebook) |
    ISBN 9780472076956 (hardcover) | ISBN 9780472056958 (paperback) |
    ISBN 9780472221813 (ebook)
Subjects: LCSH: Gandal, Keith. | Literature—Research—Methodology. |
    Literature—Research. | Creation (Literary, artistic, etc.) | Tennis.
Classification: LCC PN73 .G36   2024 (print) | LCC PN73 (ebook) |
    DDC 807.2—dc23/eng/20240229
LC record available at https://lccn.loc.gov/2024002373
LC ebook record available at https://lccn.loc.gov/2024002374

FOR J.L.V.

*I know we're not saints or virgins or lunatics; we know all the lust and lavatory jokes,
and most of the dirty people; we can catch buses and count our change and
cross the roads and talk real sentences. But our innocence goes awfully deep,
and our discreditable secret is that we don't know anything at all,
and our horrid inner secret is that we don't care that we don't.*

—Dylan Thomas

Everyone has a plan until they get punched in the mouth.

—Mike Tyson

Contents

Acknowledgments

This book has been a dozen years in the making, and I've had invaluable assistance along the way.

Dan Andries, Gavin Jones, and Amy Newman read early versions of it. John Wilkins and Alex Siskin helped develop the book and give it form. Jonathan Holland fine-tuned it stylistically at a middle stage. Eric Sundquist, who was my dissertation adviser and has gone on to read everything I've written, gave support all the way along. And Albert LaFarge helped me streamline and condense it, whereby it assumed its final form.

PSC-CUNY, the Professional Staff Congress of the City University of New York, supported the editing of the book with a grant.

The unwavering belief and support of Elizabeth Sherburn Demers, the editorial director of University of Michigan Press, and Albert LaFarge have quite simply made this publication possible.

Most of all, I'd like to thank my wife, Jen Voris, who was endlessly supportive as I wrote, revised, and struggled with this sometimes very recalcitrant book.

Author's Note and Disclaimer

Basically, the last thing Michel Foucault said to me, a few months before his death: "What was the New Man of the 1920s?"

Huh? What the fuck? Why the 1920s? (Why not the sixties, or forties? So many good decades.) And "the New Man"? What in the world does that mean?

I had no idea what he was talking about. Do you? This book is the story of my attempt to understand and answer the question. I think after all this time, I know. Stick with me.

As they say, this book is based on actual events. None of the characters are invented (while some names are); all of the actions and exchanges took place. Although some details have been altered for rhetorical purposes, it should be regarded in essence as true.

Well, actually this whole book concerns the susceptibility to self-delusion, the tyranny of viewpoint, and the difficulty of knowing anything, so it's more accurate to say: this memoir is a good-faith attempt at a factual narrative, which inevitably turns out to be fictional—given the human limits of memory, perspective, and honesty with oneself; the selectivity of events necessitated by a finite page count; and their organization into some kind of dramatic structure that makes a book readable. There is another insoluble problem involved in writing autobiography before your life ends, which entails, for me at least, a need to refer in only the most abstract terms to tangential events that, while necessary background for understanding the story, are by no means finished and thus do not belong to memoir but to the present and future. Writing about them publicly may very well change that future in undesirable ways.

Given the above caveats and also that some of my ways of seeing things are unusual at the very least, and most people would say "dead wrong," my disclaimer is this: I believe everything I say here, but any number of things may very well be false, and so I do not stand by the truth of any part of this memoir that attributes intentions, words, or actions to other people. My mental and psychological limitations, as well as my not-exactly-neutral presence, necessarily affect not only my perception of others, but their actual behavior. This is something like the "uncertainty principle" in physics: looking at an electron, that is, casting light particles or light waves on it, affects the electron and changes it. But with human interaction, there is more than mere observation having an effect on the other, especially when the human observing is not behaving very well himself.

In other words, I make no claims to accuracy when it comes to the depiction of other people I don't know well. The representations of those people—almost all of the characters, that is—are not objective portraits but rather accounts of the author's perceptions of them in the course of limited interactions. (The exceptions to this rule are the author's wife Beth, his brother, his mother, his father, his grandmother, Foucault, a tennis mentor named Bobby, and another called Chong.) I only stand by what I myself perceived, reasoned out, felt, and did. This includes my scholarly research, but it was, in the end, unlike everything else in this book, submitted to official peer review.

Such is the nature of a memoir written by someone who, for better or worse (many would say mostly worse), has spent so much of his life reading, thinking, questioning, researching, and trying things out—including one thing or another that seems very unwise on its face—and ultimately trusting only what he learns, or believes he learns, firsthand.

Prologue

JUNE 26, 1984: *TRUTH IS THE WIDOW*

I guess you could say I wasn't in the mood to pay a bribe.

Otherwise, I wouldn't have been standing in some unkempt back room in the Mexico City airport, remonstrating with a large police official who sat at his metal desk with a porno magazine open in his hands. To be fair, he'd lowered it slightly when I was brought in. In a limited nod to politeness, he'd stopped "reading."

"You lost your visa," said the heavy-set man.

"I believe I were not losing it," I replied in a Spanish that very well may have been correct, but felt wrong to my gringo ears. "No visa was given to me."

"But your wife has hers. Why don't you?"

"She is not my wife. We come here on different airplanes," I added, messing up the tense. She'd flown from New York, and I from Washington, DC, where I'd been doing research in the National Archives.

"You need a visa to show that you came in on a flight."

It was news to me that there was a little yellow form without which one could not leave the country, a "visa" everyone supposedly got on their way in. I sensed that this little peccadillo, like so many others committed in this country, could be instantly resolved with a couple hundred pesos changing hands, but the standard of professionalism exhibited by this police person created the strong impression that he was a thug and this was a shakedown.

More to the point, I was pissed off already. I'd rather liked my month in Mexico on the whole, but I had certain beefs. I wasn't a fan of the subjunctive, which I'd learned played an enormous role in the language here, though it hadn't in my Spanish classes back in the US. Then there was the minor inconvenience of having spent the first two days in the vicinity of the bathroom in our hotel room. Meanwhile, the otherwise pictur-esque streets were filled with Chiclet sales-boys, two of whom begged me to take them to the US—and whose exposure of the desperation of the poverty problem left me with a feeling I found hard to shake. These nine-year-old kids were very likable and swore they had *no problema*, if I'd have them, to leave their families that day.

I was saved from thinking very seriously about fulfilling their wish because taking two of them home was just out of the question, and I obviously couldn't leave one on his own. I was a graduate student barely supporting myself, and I was about to be even less moneyed when my relatively well-to-do girlfriend and I broke up, as agreed, upon hitting American soil at Kennedy Airport. One of my few ethical resolves at age twenty-four was never to break up with a woman while in a foreign country. You had no idea what kind of horrible shit might befall her, even in the departure airport, an ethic whose relevance had now been sort of pointedly demonstrated by my consultation with the cops.

That was another thing—though I couldn't blame this entirely on Mexico: we'd been traveling with this guy she was fucking (or I was con-vinced she was) and, it seemed to me, clearly in love with. I'd liked him well enough myself at the beginning of the trip.

I obviously bore some responsibility for the bad mood I was in. For starters, I'd been cheating on my girlfriend too, as she well knew: I wasn't exactly a victim even though I hadn't gone so far as to invite the woman I'd been sleeping with to join us on the trip. Part of my problem was my emulation of Ernest Hemingway, whose *Sun Also Rises* had provided me the blueprint for this kind of vacation. It turned out that reading a novel about a trip to a bullfighting country in which the narrator's girl-friend's lover will participate, and going on such a jaunt yourself, are not remotely the same thing.

Another part of my problem, which I wouldn't understand until years later, was my then mysterious fascination with the confidence and pol-ish of the tall, handsome guy my girlfriend was involved with: it was tied up with the fact that his parents were wealthy, highly cultured, intellectual, and still together, while mine were barely middle class, and my mother had had three divorces by the time I was eighteen. My girlfriend's upbringing was similar to his.

But I was damned if I was going to cap off my insanely misguided visit to Mexico by handing over a bribe to a uniformed officer who didn't feel there was anything wrong with hectoring me in his official capacity while holding smut between us. Whether you're for porn or against it, I think you'll agree that there are times and places it's just not appropriate. As much as I didn't like my girlfriend at the moment, I was very glad she'd been issued a little yellow card.

Truth be told, I wasn't too broken up about our impending split. I wasn't even very concerned about the hardly deniable psychological problems that might lead someone to think it might be a worthwhile experience, as I had, to participate in a monthlong carnival ride through the Tunnel of Dejection. There would be other women, maybe even someone who wouldn't want to travel abroad with me and another guy she was involved with.

But more than that, something extraordinary had befallen my young life, and I was looking only forward. I didn't even feel the urge to write a novel based on this Mexican misadventure à la Hemingway. Come the fall, I'd be working on a book project with the French philosopher and historian Michel Foucault and a couple other Berkeley grad students, one in history and the other in anthropology. Foucault's magnetic presence had created the small beginnings of an interdisciplinary revolution around him—there were a dozen departments represented in our larger circle of male and female students. The barbed wire between fields was being snipped, and some of the chairpersons of our respective departments, including mine, were not happy. That's why I, a literature student, had been at the National Archives, looking at, of all things, the US military papers concerned with the army's mobilization and organization in World War I.

After being let off with a solemn warning that seemed out of keeping with the atmosphere of the police lounge, I returned to the airport proper, picked up my favorite Spanish-language paper, and boarded the plane with a woman I was barely speaking to, in English or any other language.

I opened up the daily as soon as we were airborne. As chance would have it, there was a huge feature article on Foucault. Wow. Another reason to like Mexico: that would never happen in a major US newspaper.

The piece had a weird title, *La viuda es la verdad*. Viuda? That sent me to the Spanish dictionary I'd always had on my person for the last month (except when in a hotel-room toilet). "Truth Is the Widow." Poetic, but what in the hell does that mean? I was unnerved. I started the article—and here I didn't need the dictionary.

Foucault had died the day before.

I was blindsided. Yes, I knew he was a bit sick when I saw him a couple of months ago in the spring, but . . . It was even harder to believe it in a foreign language.

They were saying the cause was "septicemia," and the dictionary translation was unhelpfully "septicemia." Which probably meant AIDS. I hadn't known he had the retrovirus.

My eyes were watery all the way to JFK; I hadn't cried like this since age eight, my first day at sleepaway camp—where I'd lost my innocent beliefs that the world was just and I was a good kid. I had no choice but to communicate something to the woman sitting next to me whom I didn't want to be talking to. She was very nice about it.

In addition to Foucault having provided the most thrilling intellectual experience of my short life, he and I had also shared a lot of inane jokes, my favorite kind. Like the time I took him to Bette's Oceanview Diner down near the Berkeley marina, and I insisted he give me his honest opinion of the French toast, not sparing my (American) feelings. Or the day he came to my house, and I showed him my room, which, maybe a tad messier than usual, looked like it had been ransacked, and he nodded and said in German, "All is in order."

My idea of a good time is to exchange really dumb jokes with truly brilliant people—or anyone at all, really. Which begins to explain my having consented to this absurd vacation: my travel companions were extraordinarily bright and witty, if also not particularly interested in my well-being (though in retrospect maybe I'd been wrong and *she* was).[1]

---

1. I could, but I'm not going to, pepper the book with parentheticals of this kind, as it will make the book unreadable, and it is most likely unnecessary, as you get the idea.

But none of that mattered now. I had been catapulted from the life I knew. There was nothing but thin air beneath the floor, and I was flying into the emptiness of outer space.

At JFK, where my girlfriend and I had planned, a week ago—in some previous, now decimated existence—to break up, I was offered a new job.

Inside the arrivals gate, we ran into two men who were colleagues of my girlfriend's uncle. She introduced me. They said some things, maybe even asked me something. She must have thoughtfully explained to them why I was in a daze. They were lawyers, one senior, one junior, waiting for a flight south. The older attorney was a special master charged by a federal court order to bring the prison system of the State of Texas into compliance with the US Constitution, which famously forbade "cruel and unusual punishment."

The special master knew who Foucault was, a rarity for an American outside of academia. This was because the Frenchman's most famous book was on the history of the prison, called *Discipline and Punish.*

"How would you like to join our team?" the special master asked me. He understood I had no legal training. But he could use someone like me to assist with the investigation, documenting the situation.

"Someone interested, and smart," he said. "And who knows something about this stuff." He looked to his younger partner. "I imagine you might be wanting to do something meaningful . . ."

"I don't mean to be unresponsive," I finally said. "I . . ."

He nodded sympathetically. "It's not dangerous," he added. "The prisoners want us there. They're living in horrific conditions. The biggest peril is to your shoes. I've ruined a couple pairs walking through corridors with human shit two inches deep . . . You can come with us right now, if you're up for another flight. Or come in a few weeks. We'll be at this for months."

"I appreciate it," I said. "I just don't know."

"Of course. You don't have to decide now. Think it over."

Anytime I claim anything concerning anyone else for which I do not provide overwhelming evidence and of which one reasonably might ask, "Do you know this for certain?" the answer is, "No, I don't. And I may very well be wrong."

He gave me his card, and we shook hands.

As my girlfriend and I waited at baggage claim, I wondered. The coincidence seemed ordained by the universe. I could continue Foucault's work. One of the coolest things about him was that he wasn't just a thinker: he not only wrote about the penitentiary but was an activist for prison reform.

And I had my problems with academia—without Foucault in it. Maybe the shit there didn't get on your shoes, but there was plenty that got between your ears. It wasn't that the academic world was singularly an ivory tower; the same label could be pasted on politics, medicine, Hollywood, and professional sports, for starters; and if hermeticism was bad, it could also have its good side. Academia felt—well, "unmanly" clearly wasn't the right word because women I knew felt this way too—it felt slavish. Feudal. And divided into fiefdoms. But, again, maybe all professions felt that way. I'd been an adult for exactly three years; what did I know?

In any case, my closest friends in grad school were already making noises about leaving. I too had considered dropping out before Foucault showed up. And now that he was gone . . . It wasn't that I'd hoped to ride his coattails to academic success; things didn't work that way. Something else, something larger than me had been afoot. And without him, the magic was drained out.

Yes, Mexico, intellectual neighbors of Europe and not the United States, could comprehend: truth *was* the widow. And, even at the tender age of twenty-four, I understood she wouldn't be remarrying anytime soon. This was the end of an era. I was tremendously lucky to have caught the last couple years of it, its beautiful last breaths, but it was absolutely over as of the day before, June 25, 1984. Things would quietly return to the old, artificial Balkanization of inquiry. And I, well, still red-eyed over Foucault's early death, I hardly gave a fuck about myself at that point . . .

PART I

AN AUTHENTIC MYSTERY

The biggest danger, that of losing oneself, can pass off in the world as quietly as if it were nothing; every other loss, an arm, a leg, five dollars, a wife, etc. is bound to be noticed.

—Kierkegaard, *The Sickness unto Death*

CHAPTER 1

Twenty-One Years Later

MY FATHERS' GHOSTS

My father drove up in a dark 1920s car, like you saw in old gangster movies.

"Pops," I yelled. "I thought you were dead." We'd had a funeral.

He stopped, and the car burped and chugged.

"Is that really you?" I asked.

"You betcha," he said. It was perhaps his favorite phrase.

"Thank God," I said.

I leaned on the driver's side door.

I saw past my pops that Foucault was in the passenger seat.

"Oh, Jesus," I said. "This is bullshit symbolism," I barked.

"It's a 1928 American coupe," Foucault said. The year of my dad's birth.

I wasn't going to play along. "You guys don't know each other; you weren't born the same year, so there's no way you're in the same car." Foucault was born in 1926.

"Hop in, Son," said my pops.

"No room," I said.

"There's a convertible seat in the back, just for you," he said.

Then I was riding in the open rumble seat. "This isn't real," I yelled over the wind.

"Reality, in that sense, is a social construction," remarked Foucault.

My dad laughed.

"You don't even know what that means, Pops."

3

Now they were smiling at each other.

"All right, you two, enough," I said. "Where're we going?"

"You don't recognize it?" Foucault asked.

"It's Berkeley," my pops said.

"You were never there," I said.

I looked from side to side. We were driving up University Avenue. The campus loomed above us. "This is ridiculous."

"You never finished," Foucault said.

"You died before we could start."

"'What is the New Man of the 1920s?'"

"I don't even understand the question," I said. "To be honest, Michel, I never understood a goddamn thing about that project of yours."

"Hmm," my dad said. "Have you ever thought that maybe you'll learn something important about yourself?"

"What? No. I can't fuck around again on this. It almost caused me to flunk out of graduate school all those years ago. I need a score now."

"You've already started. On twenties writers and the war," said Foucault.

"Hemingway, Faulkner—" my dad piped up.

"Pops, you didn't read novels. Michel, nobody in my field is interested in white male authors. Or in war for that matter."

My father shook his head. "You always did things your own way, Son."

I woke up. It was just after nine on a mild Saturday morning in the early spring. My head was throbbing. I must have had another exasperating dream about my father.

I awkwardly scooted down the bed to the bottom, trying not to bump and awaken my wife, Beth. This was the only way out of bed as our "master" half-bedroom just fit our king-size mattress. It filled the entire floor space except for a narrow strip in front of the closet, and so was bordered on the other three sides by walls. It was as if the snug room were custom-made for people who had a terror of falling out of bed in their sleep.

My dad had just died a few weeks ago. My anger was not at death, which was bad enough. My pops had died in surgery during a so-called routine procedure. In other words, he'd been accidentally slaughtered. This was my second parent—of two—to die on the operating table.

The circumstances of my father's death—an accidental slip of the doctor's knife hand during a tune-up of his pacemaker, a procedure supposedly so low-risk that my pops wouldn't think twice about having it[1]—had left me carrying around a monumental rage.

Making matters worse, my brother and sister weren't interested in pursuing a malpractice case. When I'd told my brother on the phone I was in contact with a law firm, he said to me, "It won't bring him back."

That was not news to me. "But we have to do right by him. They carelessly took his life."

"What if the hospital countersues us?" he asked. I could hear something all too familiar in his voice I really didn't like.

"They won't do that," I said, as calmly as I could.

In addition, given probate, and the fact that a fantastically rich "party" was, despite no mention in the will, claiming a large chunk of my dad's money was hers—as well as an unrelated, ongoing, unavoidable legal case of a personal nature that cannot be detailed here[2]—I had four separate lawyers and sometimes spoke to all of them in the course of a couple of days. The wealthy female "party" had said to me, "I'm obviously not lying. Your father knew nothing about markets." My brother and sister didn't want a conflict and were ready to hand over the money. I was not.

And though I'd never before tried to sue anyone, this surgical murder of my father wasn't something I could take lying down. I was consciously attempting to throw off a legacy of fear and fatalism I'd inherited from my family, which my brother's comments that day typified.

---

1. According to a study conducted by Johns Hopkins medical researchers and published in May 2016 in the *British Medical Journal*, hospital death, not included on death certificates or in rankings of mortality causes, was, before Covid, the third-leading cause of death in the United States, after heart disease and cancer, responsible for around 250,000 per year, or nearly 10 percent of all fatalities in the nation. What we generally think of as "medical error" accounts for only a portion of these deaths, which also include, for example, wound infection and adverse drug reactions.

2. Though crucial background information, this is an ongoing story and, as such, is in its entirety a subject that cannot be broached.

CHAPTER 2

My Better Half

I took some aspirin and drank a quart of water. I was blankly staring out the window when a low-riding sedan zoomed around the nearby corner at something like seventy miles an hour. There was no way you could possibly pull off a turn on a regular city street at that velocity, I was thinking. Then the vehicle slammed into a parked minivan so hard it was sent airborne, and landed with a second bang on the sidewalk, some ten feet from where it was hit. The dog in the flat below began barking like mad.

"What the hell?" It was Beth's voice from the bedroom.

I caught a glimpse of the driver as he sped off, burning rubber, his automobile somehow still functioning despite its now bashed-in left front end. Judging by the slicked-back hair, the thick gold necklaces, and the car, it was most likely a member of one of the gangs that operated in our Humboldt Park neighborhood.

"Don't go out there," I heard Beth say sleepily.

Fifteen minutes later I was in the street talking to a Chicago police officer through an open window on the passenger side, as he sat in his cruiser.

While the husky, young white officer was typing on his computer in laborious two-finger style, another low-rider slunk around the corner and headed toward us. As it got closer, I had a good view of the driver: it was the same guy, in a different car, this time going maybe seven miles an hour. Without pointing, I said in a low voice to the policeman, "That's the driver, coming by us right now."

"Oh, yeah?" the cop said. He didn't look up and went right on tapping a key here and there.

The driver and I got a good look at each other.

He sighted down the "barrel" of his finger at me, his thumb out. "Muerto," said his lips.

Great. The day was off to an excellent start. When had kids started imitating a gun held sideways, instead of straight up?

"He's driving away," I said to the cop.

"Hmm," he mumbled, still focused on his computer screen. "So, what was the color of the car?"

"Adios," I said to the officer and walked away. I sat down on our front stoop.

I was going to turn forty-five in a few months, and I wasn't where I wanted to be in life.

I wanted to be in a different job, in a different part of the country, making a different amount of money even. At an institution that was not, well, moribund. Various deep-set problems that dragged down my workplace might be enumerated, but it is probably more meaningful to say, as Beth had done around the time we first met, "People come to this place to die."

My father's death had dramatically sharpened this perception. I think most of us feel the thresher of mortality encroaching as we enter midlife, even if we haven't just lost our one remaining parent.

But dwarfing all of this was a pressing reason for our needing to move. My ongoing (unmentionable) legal battle was taking a toll on both of us, and our relationship. We simply had to get away. I had gotten myself involved in this mess, but it wasn't fair to Beth. It was dreadful to see her in pain that was my fault. Neither of us could live like this indefinitely. She'd already shared two years of it, and the case was far from over. We needed to distance ourselves geographically.

I was a professor, at the rank of "full." And if I wanted to get out of here and keep my career, into which I'd sunk half my life and essentially all my economic prospects, I needed to write another book, and one so good that it could be parlayed into a new job. It wasn't so easy to move at the senior level in my line of work. Literature departments are not exactly a growth industry.

I went inside and poured myself a cup of vodka. I sat back down by the window. Though it was a bit early, it was Saturday. Maybe I was having a midlife crisis. I couldn't be sure because I lived pretty much from crisis to crisis, without a lot of downtime. A vague sense of dread was my norm.

I was so used to a feeling of dread that I now accepted it, and rationalized it as part of the human condition. But probably most people did not wake up mornings with a seemingly causeless sense of impending doom. Maybe most people didn't sit most days at the breakfast table, having coffee, juice, and toast in near panic, their hair standing on end.

At this point, I was long past wondering why I was this way—I was far too preoccupied with my current midlife crisis for idle thoughts. But maybe I shouldn't have waited for my "orphaning" to reopen this question, which I'd certainly had about myself as a young man.

I'd had plenty of therapy, and I understood, for example, the significance of my biological father having taken off when I was a toddler. I also thought I knew what it meant that, when I was twelve, my adopted father, the one who'd recently died—who I simply thought of as my dad because he always treated me like a son—was divorced by my mother, moved out, and withdrew into himself. My mother had the next year married a man I didn't get along with. Before his verbal hammering, I'd apparently endured another sort of "psychological abuse" from a mother who was, in today's parlance, manic-depressive. "Emotional incest," one therapist had called it. The effects of these things too I thought I grasped. My home, fractured in multiple ways, had left me, in the terminology of a couple of these clinical experts, "post-traumatic"—and thus vulnerable, not to flashbacks exactly, but emotional hallucinations of a sort.

Yet there are things therapy tends not to address. And though I practiced a historical approach to literature, it'd never occurred to me to turn that analytic lens squarely on myself. I hadn't tried to understand myself the way I understood the authors I interpreted for a living, as historically specific individuals whose mentalities and psychic lives were to a large degree shaped by their class, gender, and ethnic status—along with the opportunities and obstacles that followed from these.

But a series of events, starting with my father's completely unexpected "medical death," was about to set me on a course of scholarly and personal detection that would change my life in fundamental ways. Which, if it isn't clear already, was not altogether a bad thing.

Beth was up, making coffee. "How'd it go?"

"Good," I said. "The officer is going to hunt this guy down if it's the last thing he does."

"Really?"

"It's hard to say."

"So, he basically didn't give a shit." She shook her head. "He probably took one look at you and thought, 'another dumbass middle-aged white hipster who's moved into a ghetto neighborhood with violent gangs because he thinks it's cool. We got bigger problems than some reckless driving.'"

"But we're not hipsters," I said, pushing my hair out of my eyes, glancing down at my attire, and stroking my stubbly chin. At that moment I had long, unwashed, stringy locks, hadn't shaved in a week, and was wearing torn clothing. Okay, maybe I still looked it, but my bohemian days were well over.

The fact was, we were hard up for money. We were trying to live in Chicago on my rural-university professor's salary, and Beth having gone back to school also meant tuition bills. Cheap rent was the entire reason we were living in this part of town in seven hundred square feet.

"Okay. It was stupid," I said.

"But probably no harm done. As long as no gang members saw you." There was a small silence.

She looked me in the eyes. "No gang members saw you, right?"

We drove out Interstate 88 toward Beth's parents' house, where she'd grown up, some two hours outside of Chicago.

She wanted me to talk to her father, who'd also lost both of his parents.

I was going to ask him about self-defense. I was pretty sure nothing would happen: this gang member had no good reason to shoot anyone, as he'd gotten away with his car "accident."

But it was remotely possible the guy was a psychopath or would get hopped up on PCP, and come looking for me precisely for no good reason. Say, because of macho pride. Or a sense of neighborhood ownership. Or the hell of it.

Beth's father was a Vietnam vet. I also kind of wanted to get a weapon; the best I had was an old tennis racket with a cracked frame. But I thought I'd keep that intention to myself until we got there.

Beth hated violence.

Generally I felt secure when Beth was around. I would pity the person who made the mistake of getting into a fight with her—unarmed. While she detested violence, she was tall and unusually strong, and had "anger-management problems," as she sometimes, somewhat sheepishly, confessed. Though she was against killing and had often told me so—maybe too often, as many people take the prohibition on murder for granted—she would have little problem, physically, in beating a thug within an inch of his life if he came looking for me. Of course, she'd cry a lot afterward because violence was horribly "intimate," as she'd put it. But I could comfort her.

All bets were off, however, if this gang member was really touchy *and* had a real gun.

CHAPTER 3

Scholarly Detective Story I

NOTICING ANOMALIES IN THE LIT-CRIT PARADIGM

While my father's death had for the moment displaced our pressing problem—our need to move—I knew it would return front and center soon enough, provided I wasn't whacked.

I luckily had this sabbatical semester coming up in a couple months, in which I could theoretically write that great book I hadn't yet conceived of. It was imperative that I come up with a topic soon. Sabbaticals didn't roll around all that often. Generally, you get a half or full year off from work every seven. (It's an old biblical idea that somewhere along the line lost its original meaning and purpose.) This was my first-ever such opportunity, after fifteen years of university teaching.

Time off from work with pay is everyone's dream, even if, as in academia, it typically involves a salary cut. A professorial sabbatical also means you have to carry out a research and writing project that's been approved by the institution.

Never having had one before, I vaguely wondered if I'd go crazy with months of unstructured time in which I was supposed to be writing. Did I need something else to do? What could that something else be? I assured myself I knew one thing: I wasn't going to spend part of my time training maniacally for a sport, as I knew some guys did in similar situations. I had no interest in tests of physical prowess. And no time for such nonsense.

Most people, quite sanely, would rather dig ditches or shelve bodies in a morgue than produce an academic monograph. I needed to write another one if I hoped to advance professionally, which was theoretically fine. Though I too could hate research, I loved it in the right circumstances.

I found scholarship repulsive and impossible when I had a sense in advance of what the conclusions would be. I could only do it when I'd stumbled across an authentic literary-historical mystery, and I didn't know what I'd find. Then it had all the thrill of cracking a case. It smacked of a detective story—only you weren't the spectator but the private eye.

It wasn't really that I had no idea about a project. Rather, I had a risky one, which had a fair chance of failing.

I wanted to research Hemingway, Fitzgerald, Faulkner—the "big three" American "modernist" writers—and World War I. After teaching their books for ten years to no avail, I'd stumbled on a legitimate question.

A successful project on this subject was not only a huge undertaking but perhaps doomed from the start. I'd never written about any of these writers or about war. For the previous twenty years, I'd confined myself to writing about less-studied American authors. How could I possibly discover anything new about the big three? They were some of the most written-about writers of all times: a critic named John Aldridge, who'd pretty much created what became the established take on the Lost Generation, had already declared, twenty years ago, of Fitzgerald and Faulkner, that "the fundamental interpretations have been made," and "very little of much surprise or value remains to be discovered about them." Meanwhile, he'd estimated that there was by the late 1980s "a seven-story mountain of critical literature" on Hemingway alone.

Another challenge to the project was that I knew next to nothing about World War I, a pretty big topic.

I wondered if I were setting myself up for failure. But I didn't have anything else that drew me.

Though at a younger age I'd been infatuated with Hemingway especially, I was no longer suffering from what a British college friend of mine and I called "Hemingitis": the desire to feel like one is Hemingway. Yes, we'd wanted to be like Hemingway because he was not only one of the most famous male writers, but one of the most *male* male writers. I'd visited Pamplona, and seen with this friend, whom I'd met on a junior year abroad, the running of the bulls as well as a few bullfights, and I'd visited some of the hundred bars in northern Spain that proudly displayed signs reading, "Hemingway drank here" (and even one in Madrid that advertised, "Hemingway never drank here").

Though we made fun of our fascination with him because he was too macho to be believed, there seemed to be something undeniably cool about Hemingway. We weren't into war or shooting animals, like he'd been, but we subscribed to his cult of experience, and it was still possible to admire his blend of toughness and sensitivity. Gregory Clark, a writer who knew the twenty-year-old Hemingway, had said of him, "A more weird combination of quivering sensitiveness and preoccupation with violence surely never walked this earth."

A few years later, in the mid-1980s (not too long after Foucault died), I did after all end up trying my hand at an entire novel based loosely on Hemingway's *The Sun Also Rises*, and not at all loosely on my masochistic trip to Mexico. *Sun* is about a sick, codependent, even infernal, but somehow romantic relationship, between a guy who's had his genitals blown away in the war and a beautiful female nymphomaniac, who was initially his nurse. It also involves a love triangle that includes a Jewish man who didn't serve.

That juvenilia was all behind me. What interested me now in these writers was the seedling of a research question that had, I guess, grown out of my teaching their modernist novels for years on end and believing less and less in what I was saying about them.

I was presenting a version of what had been taught to me by my high school and college teachers, who'd in turn been informed by the critics of a previous generation. Namely, that these most famous American writers, especially Hemingway, had been disillusioned, alienated by the experience of the horrors of World War I. As young, impressionable men, they'd been thrown into the ugly, brutal, and insane slaughter of machine-gun and trench warfare by benighted governments and militaries equipped with beautiful, empty ideas and slogans from a bygone age. Consequently, they were, as Hemingway put it, borrowing a phrase from Gertrude Stein that she supposedly got from a French car mechanic, who perhaps came up with it himself, "a lost generation."

To take perhaps the most dramatic example I encountered of an ideology of heroism divorced from the reality of modern technological war, the US Army in the early 1900s—before the experience of World War I—taught officers that a soldier with the right fighting spirit, with his "blood up," could prevail over machine-gun fire. Could run through it and keep going. With ideas like that prevailing at the start of the war, disillusionment was bound to be extreme.

In Hemingway's most renowned pronouncement about World War I, from *A Farewell to Arms*, he rejected "the words sacred, glorious, and sacrifice. . . . There were many words that you could not stand to hear, and finally only the names of places had dignity." A well-known scholarly book on the subject, *World War I and the American Novel* (1967), declared: "Total violence, machine civilization, futile terror, and mass death. . . . The impact of World War I was unparalleled; it shattered a cultural universe." Aldridge wrote way back in 1951: "The generation that had fought in the war felt urgently the need . . . to redefine the terms of existence." That's why they were called modernists.

These renowned writers' prominent postwar novels, which many of us read in high school or college, famously symbolized the feelings of injury and loss caused by the terrible war. There is, in *The Great Gatsby*, Jay Gatsby's prewar romantic dream of Daisy Fay, from the richest family in Louisville, that cannot be recaptured in the postwar world. There is, in *Sun*, Jake Barnes's combat wound—*the* wound—that leaves him impotent and unable to be with his true love, Lady Ashley.

I was having trouble believing what I was saying in class because, after teaching these authors for a decade, I began to notice niggling little discrepancies between the established take and what was actually in their novels—anomalies in the paradigm, to use the language of science. The critics agreed that the emasculating horrors of World War I were experienced in the trenches, where soldiers hunkered down and huddled while being bombed, machine-gunned, and gassed, and as a result could not, in this modern, technological war, participate in the brave and individualized encounters of martial combat available in past wars.

So it was strange that Hemingway didn't have poor old emasculated and alienated Jake Barnes wounded in the trenches but instead made him a pilot injured in flight, where, in the much-ballyhooed and romanticized "dogfights" in the sky, the brave and individualized encounters of traditional martial combat were singularly carried on in World War I, despite the unprecedentedly technological quality of that war. We still know the names of some of these American, Canadian, and German aces who shot down dozens of enemy planes in one-on-one aerial combat— well, I didn't yet know their names, but I was to learn them—Baron von Somebody-or-Other, for example, the *Red Baron*. As in Snoopy and the Red Baron: that guy.

Another major anomaly was that these postwar novels of Hemingway and Fitzgerald, though they were supposed to be shaped by the trauma of World War I slaughter and indeed expressed disillusionment, didn't seem disillusioned with war. On the contrary, their narrators seemed pretty enthusiastic about the combat, were kind of sorry it was over, and had nostalgic memories of serving in it. In *Gatsby*, Nick Caraway "enjoyed [it] so thoroughly that [he] came back restless."

True, Hemingway's narrator in *A Farewell to Arms* in its most famous passage expresses disgust with bullshit official propaganda about death on the battlefield (as "sacred," etc.). But when you read his novels, you're left feeling that while Hemingway is antimilitary, he's not antiwar.

This anomaly was more than niggling because World War I, the first large-scale mechanized war in which tens of thousands could get wiped out in minutes and in which something like nine million men died and over twenty-one million were wounded, was supposed to have awakened the Western world to the unprecedented horrors of industrial warfare. And a decisively antiwar attitude was precisely what was supposed to characterize interwar literature, European and American alike.

Oh, and there was one other thing that bothered me. Critics had noticed that these novels featured a "new woman" of the 1920s, a more independent, sexually liberated, and empowered woman—familiarly figured in the image of the short-haired, short-skirted flapper who fast-danced, smoked, drank, and had flings. This woman was a first step to closing the gender gap, though of course there was still a long way to go in terms of achieving equality with men: that's the way the critics talked.

But when you read *Sun*, the main female character, Lady Brett Ashley, is—though still dependent for money on men who were lining up to give it to her—the most powerful figure in the book, a person that none of the major male characters in the story, not even the fiancé who is supporting her, have the ability to stand up to, no matter how outrageous her actions. And how many affairs she has. She is answerable to no one.

I could hardly feel that these were brilliant, sharp-eyed observations, since it had taken me ten years of teaching the books to make them. These anomalies weren't particularly subtle either. I was finally clearly seeing what might have been evident in ten minutes to anyone who hadn't been indoctrinated at a young age with the established take.

It wasn't only my indoctrination and mental slowness that were to blame. The real-world obligation to teach these books also got in the way of thinking about them. I had to go into class with something to impart.

To come up with fruitful questions, as I'd finally done, even if the questions were obvious once you saw them, was not a trivial thing. As Isaac Asimov said, "The most exciting phrase to hear in science is not 'Eureka! I've found it!' but, 'that's funny ...'" If I still emulated the scientific method, it was because in college, unrealistically hopeful that I could successfully pursue a career as a doctor or scientist, I'd taken more math and physics courses than humanities ones.

My parents had had high hopes for me. But they failed to understand that the financially and emotionally unstable home environment they provided tends not to produce doctors and scientists—or businessmen or lawyers or military officers. Yes, I'd gotten all As in high school and nearly the same in college, and I was very good with numbers. Maybe I had the brains to have any number of lucrative careers and live out various American Dream scenarios. My parents felt I was wasting my talents becoming, of all things, a literature professor. I was choosing a field that required an inordinate number of years of training (at least six and usually more like eight, nine, or ten at Berkeley) and was highly competitive: every "tenure track" position I would try for, regardless of rank, had had at least 250 applicants, and a couple had more than 1,000. But at the same time it offered "no real money" relative to other careers. To my elders, what I was doing was tantamount to killing the goose that laid golden eggs, not in the impatient hope of finding a large store of gold inside, but so I could dissect it and learn bird anatomy just for the hell of it.

But people with backgrounds and childhoods like mine don't have the ongoing functionality and evenness to hold down regular, high-stress jobs, month after month, year after year. Sure, I'd done a lot of nine-to-five jobs, but only for temporary durations. Given the levels of mental distress I experienced day in and day out, I sometimes thought my parents were lucky I'd found any career I could handle and wasn't a homeless drug addict or a gang member and thief.

The point being, though my literary project wasn't science, I was nonetheless going to try to proceed as if it were.

CHAPTER 4

Guns, Guard Dogs, and Yoga

When we swung onto the main street of the little town Beth had grown up in, I suggested we stop by the gun store.

"Not that I think we should buy a gun," I said. "I just would like to hold one for a second."

She looked at me cockeyed.

"Come on, indulge me. I've had a hard day—and month."

I'd never been in the gun shop before, though the shabby, decaying storefront was familiar since we passed it every time we visited Beth's folks. I'd also never contemplated owning a firearm. I couldn't buy one now; I didn't have a license. But I picked up an application for a permit.

"It doesn't commit us to anything," I said to Beth.

She shook her head.

I still felt the need to arm myself immediately somehow. So I bought a mean-looking hunting knife with a long serrated blade, though it wasn't actually practical for stabbing someone, and was really intended to skin animals.

As I shook hands with Beth's dad in the living room of their rural home, which he was constantly in the process of rebuilding in one way or another, I marveled again at his size.

Beth's father had seen a lot of combat as a Ranger in Vietnam, a member of what was initially called a long-range reconnaissance patrol or "LRRP," a small, heavily-armed, highly-trained group that ventured into enemy territory.[1] He'd luckily come through the war without

---

1. Michael Herr called men in these patrols Lurps, in his *Dispatches*. The Ranger designation replaced that of LRRP or Long-Range Reconnaissance Patrol, in 1969. Fourth

a physical scratch. It wasn't entirely luck. You might pity the man who crossed Beth, but pity would not begin to describe what you would feel for the man who crossed Curt. With Curt, who was the reason Beth was tall and strong, and was himself gigantic and Herculean, anger management was a way of living civilian life—after a few decades had gone by and his PTSD got to manageable levels. Though I might have felt angry enough to try to kill someone who came after me, I had no idea how to do it. Curt, though he never talked about it, had undoubtedly killed a number of people in the Vietnam War and knew any number of ways to do it.

"Not a bad idea to have a gun," he said.

I completed the Illinois application for a firearm license, and he took my picture and produced on his computer a passport-size photo. I asked him if he would teach me how to shoot, which I'd never done—I knew from Beth that he had a sawed-off shotgun somewhere on the premises.

Curt kind of grunted.

I deduced from his manner that he was reluctant to discuss it. So I let it go for the moment.

"Will you show me how to use a knife?" I said. "I just bought one, and I've got it right here in this bag."

He shook his head but corralled Beth and me into the bedroom where he and his wife slept and closed the door. I took out the new knife.

He demonstrated how to hold it and thrust it. "The important thing is that the flat side of the blade is horizontal," he said. (Maybe this was how gang members learned to hold a gun?)

"So it won't get stopped by the ribs and can slip in between them," he explained.

This was adequately graphic. "Thanks," I said.

Division commander General William R. Peers in 1968 enumerated the abilities that qualified a soldier for LRRP service: "[A]n individual must be qualified both physically and psychologically.... Physically, because ... you never know when you are going to have to cover 10 or 15 kilometers on the ground in very short order.... The psychological qualifications.... You need somebody out there who has nerves of steel, who can stay in there along the side of a trail, can sit there and watch that trail with a large enemy formation going by and not have the slightest inclination to stand up and fire a rifle or even move."

I asked him again about the gun. "All right," he snapped. "We'll go off in the morning to a spot out in the fields."

It then occurred to me that Curt simply hadn't wanted to discuss deadly weaponry within earshot of his wife.

Around midnight, Beth and her mom had gone to bed. I was in the basement with my father-in-law, watching an action movie on DVD. Framed photos of him as a young man in Vietnam, in uniform or with camouflage face paint, decorated the room.

We talked a little bit about my father. Yes, he'd been in the army too, in between World War II and Korea.

"Where was he posted?" Curt asked.

"Fort Knox. He helped guard the gold."

We talked about our jobs. Neither of us had imagined as kids doing what we came to do.

"Yeah, academia's pretty weird," I said.

"Maybe not as screwed up as the electric company," he said, chuckling.

I told him how I almost dropped out of grad school at one point, when I thought seriously about working with the special master for prison reform.

"You didn't want to be a lawyer?" he asked.

"Not really. But it's more like I don't like quitting until . . ."

He nodded. "I decided not to stay in the army because, after the war, they wouldn't make me sergeant. Never told me why officially, but heard I wasn't enough of a team player. After what we'd done in the field as a group, I just said, 'Fuck this.' Guess I could walk away—"

"—because you'd proved what you set out to," I finished.

He nodded.

"Wait a second," I said. "You thought about staying in the army after Vietnam?"

"Oh, yeah. I thought I'd have a military career."

"But before you got drafted, what did you imagine for yourself?"

"Oh, I wasn't drafted. I enlisted," he said.

"Ah." I'd heard about that. During Vietnam, guys enlisted to get their choice of the armed services, with the hope of a less dangerous assignment and ideally a posting outside the war zone. The poor guy had ended up in combat anyway.

"I had the darnedest time getting the army to send me to Vietnam,"
Curt added. "But finally they did."
"*What?*"

I went up to join Beth in bed. I was surprised to find her awake. There
was an old photo of her in a frame, in a red baseball uniform and cap
holding a bat. She must have been eight or nine years old.

When I was that age, I'd had to stop playing sports for a while. I'd
gone through a serious illness—the Hong Kong flu. I'd nearly died.

This event hadn't popped into my consciousness for about three
decades. And it felt like something else buried away was about to come
to the surface.

"We've got to talk," she said. She put down the book she was reading
called *The Nature of Personal Reality*.

"Okay." I sat down on the edge of the bed.

"You're a bit out of control. You're actually beginning to do things that
endanger us. I told you not to go out there and talk to the cops."

"Yeah. Sorry."

"I don't mind about the knife, and you can get a gun license if that
answers a need you have right now. But we're not getting a gun," she said,
"and you're not going out in the fields tomorrow to shoot with my dad."

A freight train roared past on the nearby tracks.

She waited until the sound was dying away. "I don't want a gun
around. I have problems with impulse control. They're illegal in Chicago
anyway."

"Okay."

"We're gonna do what our landlords have done."

"What's that?"

"Get a guard dog."

They lived below us, in our dodgy neighborhood, and I'd never before
thought about their German shepherd as such.

"I'm not really a pet-lover," I said. "And a dog takes a lot of time."

"The dog can also be an emotional-support animal. It calms you
down. Two birds . . . We're getting a dog."

"Really?"

"I know you're really angry about your dad, and your case—"

"I'm trying to—"

"You have every right to be angry. And I know you want to move away. I know I need to as much as you do."

I looked down and nodded.

"But your anger is spilling out in all directions. You're courting a fight. If you keep going this way, you *will* bring violence into our lives. And I can't stay around for that."

"Okay."

"Look, I don't pretend to know what it's like to be a man in our culture. I know there's tremendous pressure to prove your masculinity. You have to deal with other men posturing all the time. And right now you want to push back. Hard. Maybe you feel you missed out on something because your generation never had to go to war. Or protest the government—"

"What's happening to me is very circumstantial—"

"Wait. Let me say my piece." She reached out and touched my shoulder. "I can't stand most men because they've let themselves regress to some atavistic, apelike state. But you're not like that." She sat back.

"Well, that's something, I guess." I forced a smile. "So, what do you suggest I do? I'm trying to fight back in the socially acceptable way. I'm lawyered up to the max. I'm trying to get another job, so we can get the hell out of here . . ."

"I know. And we have to believe it's gonna happen. But that doesn't quite deal with the emotional fallout right now."

I thought about that.

"Can we enjoy a little the good fortune we've got?" she said. "We haven't even celebrated your making full professor."

"I know. Since my dad's death I'm not—"

"You never celebrate anything. Name something you've celebrated since we've been together."

I couldn't.

"You don't even see that that's no way to live," she said.

"You think maybe I need therapy."

"Definitely. But I think there's something more pressing. You need an outlet. A spiritual practice. Someplace to channel your anger while we're stuck here. Something safe."

"That sounds good. Like what?"

Beth herself played this video game that allowed her avatar to put on armor and kill adversaries and monstrous beasts with swords and maces in an alternative medieval world.

"I don't know what's right for you. You know yoga works for me. And running. And horror movies. A lot of men play online war games."

"I used to work out. Could take that up again. Isn't yoga too peaceful?"

She shook her head. "No. What about your tennis?"

"It's doubles: a friendly game. More of a social thing."

"Couldn't it be competitive? Singles?"

"You have to be in really good shape for singles."

"So?"

"It's time consuming to get that fit."

She shrugged. "Well, you gotta find something you can get into."

A dog and a visit to the gym a few times a week? That ought to provide me with some structure.

At that moment in our bedroom, I was saying goodbye to my time being entirely my own during my precious semester off from work. Very soon, we would be on dog time. From the pound, we would bring home a pit bull, who apparently had been at least briefly employed as a fighting dog, and got the name Quilty on account of his scars and stitch marks. He would need three walks a day, minimum. And Lazarus, our new German shepherd, would as well.

We had intended to get one dog, and we both liked Quilty on first sight. He was spirited and rambunctious and took to us even before he was out of the cage, trying to thrust a paw between the bars to make our acquaintance. But the blue-coated worker in charge there said, "You don't want that one." When we inquired, "Why not?" he refused to answer and simply insisted. "Trust me. You want this other one; he's much calmer and nicer," indicating a German shepherd that was lying down in the back corner of his unit and didn't move or make a sound as we stood in front of him. In fact, the guy wouldn't allow us to adopt Quilty on the spot. "If you still want him tomorrow, you can get him then." He shrugged when we protested. "I'm not letting you have him today."

This was baffling, and, when we came back the next day still set on Quilty, the guy now told us that if we took Quilty, we had to take Lazarus too. They couldn't be separated since they'd been "together" so long, as next-door neighbors in adjacent cages. Intent on Quilty, we took them both. Upon getting her home, Lazarus went under our bed and wouldn't come out. It turned out that the German shepherd wasn't by nature quiet and docile, but near death. We took her the very same day back to the veterinary clinic at the animal shelter, where she stayed for the next month and where we visited her twice a week.

There would be no question now of panicking at the expanse of empty months that lay before me, with nothing to do but write, because the oncoming expanse had suddenly contracted. Even if I couldn't research, because I had no project, I could still be plenty busy with the dogs. And with talking to my sister, who was the executor of our dad's will, going through his papers, filing various forms, and making calls to banks and probate lawyers. And with speaking to malpractice attorneys. And then there was the ongoing case that never ended. I'd be on the phone sometimes for several hours a day.

If Beth hadn't been there, well, I could have kissed my sabbatical, not to mention my sanity, goodbye. Instead, totally exhausted maybe, almost out of my mind with rage—as it was becoming apparent that there was no malpractice, just a gross but perfectly legal slip of the scalpel, and so no even small relief to be had—I was relatively okay. I was even becoming more confident that I'd be able get somewhere with my research on Hemingway, Fitzgerald, Faulkner, and World War I—although I was also concerned that I'd have little time in which to do it.

If I felt basically fine, it was most of all because for the first time in my life when faced with a hard thing, I was not alone.

I'd had several long-term relationships, but I'd always previously felt essentially on my own. No doubt this was partly or even entirely my own doing, and I'd finally grown up some in my late thirties and early forties, but it was also because I'd never before met anyone I could be entirely comfortable with.

When it came to core things philosophical or spiritual—not quite sure how to categorize them—Beth and I overlapped to a startling degree. She took her incorporeal development as a human being seriously, an idea many people don't even bother to pay lip service to.

Beth's internal journey was very much her own. And she was willing to pay for it, with whatever capital it demanded. It shaped her life choices. She would even forfeit our relationship if I didn't respect her development. I knew that she would leave me if I became either an "ape-like" bully, who pressed her to abandon that undertaking, or a weasel-like "tool" (also her word), who himself came to care only about money and status.

Though derived from no recognized religious tradition, Beth's ideas were closer to Native American beliefs than Christian ones. She put great stock in her dreams, essentially following their "instructions" in great matters. And also in small. Sometimes our houseplants let her know in her sleep when they needed water, or "perhaps," as she put it, her "other self" knew when they did. She sometimes had out-of-body experiences at night, meeting others in the dreamscape, something I'd never believed in until the first night we spent together (after knowing each other for a year) when we had the *same* dream in which we said the *same* things to each other, essentially communicating something on the unconscious network that felt way premature to say with our mouths while awake.

It was Beth's being there that was making the other things possible as well. I believed I could take on a huge project about some major American writers. With Beth, I had a solid home life for the first time since my parents' divorce when I was twelve—which was, ominously when I thought about it, the last year of my life when I still had a healthy disinterest in reading and writing.

Moreover, Beth was an inspiration. Here was a twenty-nine-year-old literature BA and MA, who'd gone back to school at the University of Illinois, Chicago, to do a premed course. She was also working in a lab on experiments with cancer in chicken cells. She'd just finished an EMT course. It was ballsy on just about every level. If she could jump the chasm between the humanities and sciences—not to mention come in contact with blood and gore in ambulances and ICUs—then I could hardly be intimidated by taking on some famous authors and a new subject more or less in my own discipline.

But she was also right about my need to make an adjustment. No matter how much support our relationship was giving me, there was no getting around the fact that I was on edge. I wasn't sleeping well. Got headaches. Swore almost constantly while driving, which, living in Chicago and commuting seventy miles to work, I did a good deal of my waking time. Had the urge to hurl certain people I worked with against a wall.

I tried the weight room on campus a few times, but it left me cold. And I stopped going.

Though it would require even more time away from my research and further eat into my precious sabbatical, I clearly needed an outlet.

PART II

PRETTY UGLY RIVALRIES

It is the theory which decides what we can observe.

—Albert Einstein

CHAPTER 5

Midlife Athletic Crisis

I guess I should have seen it coming. Sure, I found the whole idea of training maniacally for a sport during my sabbatical to be repugnant. But why was I thinking about it at all?

I'd heard many stories about adult men who used time off from work to train for decathlons, or ski, or swim across a channel. To realize some unfulfilled athletic dream. I was also hearing about it from Hemingway and Fitzgerald. Well into his thirties Fitzgerald rued the fact that he hadn't been good enough or big enough to play football in college. Cohn, in *Sun*, imagines going back and playing football again, this time with the adult knowledge he has about handling himself. At which point another character authoritatively and understandably calls him a "moron."[1]

I liked sports and had played them competitively through high school. I continued to have dreams—actually nightmares—about secondary-school soccer well into my thirties. While in grad school, I even entertained the fantasy that I could redshirt on the Cal soccer team since I hadn't used up any of my college eligibility, though I knew I wouldn't try to do it, putting aside the fact that I probably wasn't good enough to do it. The whole concept struck me as overly macho, kind of pathetic, and, yes, moronic.

I now considered intense physical training to be some kind of

---

1. Some Hemingway critics might say that these references are related, as they argue that Cohn was partly based on Hemingway's literary frenemy, Fitzgerald. In earlier drafts of *Sun*, the Cohn character's first name was Gerald.

compensation—for failed dreams in other, more important, domains, like one's profession or love life, or life. A salve for masculine self-doubt. My professional dreams weren't failed; they were only in process. Perhaps a little stalled was all. Or so I reassured myself a dozen times a day.

But surely my masculinity didn't need any bolstering by proofs of athletic accomplishment and physical victories over other men. I'd been through a long, tortuous auto-da-fé in my thirties when I lived on the Lower East Side of New York and tried to be a novelist. It had involved enough meatheaded demonstrations of masculinity to last a lifetime.

Moreover, the last thing I thought I needed to do during my sabbatical was to become obligated with some sport that was going to use up loads of my free time. Sure, I could use a bit of structure: but no obligations whatsoever. I wanted to be able to work crazily for a day and a half and then sleep the next fifteen hours if that's what I felt like. I wanted to be inspired and to follow my inspirations. My writing, and only my writing—and helping taking care of Quilty and Lazarus, and spending time with Beth, and dealing with the aftermath of my father's death, and also handling that never-ending, unnamable legal case—had to set the tone for this extraordinary and important period in my life, this first sabbatical in which I was going to write a successful academic book. Nothing, or nothing unnecessary and embarrassing, could interfere with it.

I had a lot of work ahead of me. It might even be necessary in the end to take up a different topic and start over. Yes, I had real questions about these novels of Hemingway, Fitzgerald, and Faulkner, but maybe they were unanswerable and would not yield in the least to research. These were some of the most studied books on the entire planet: probably other critics had already asked themselves these very questions and failed to get anywhere.

The next thing I knew I was involved in a grueling exercise regimen, as I hungrily looked forward to amateur tennis competitions with other grown men. It occurred to me that the whole reason I'd been thinking, "I'm not going to do this," was because privately I was feeling, "I'm going to do this." If I really hadn't been wanting to throw myself into training for a sport, it wouldn't have been on my mind; instead, I was almost daily thinking about not doing it.

I set myself a goal. I wanted was to play at a level I'd long ago dreamed of, a 4.0 USTA or United States Tennis Association rating. I planned to be in an official amateur tournament at that level nine months from then: in September, when I had to return to work and my research book had better be finished.

Could a middle-aged guy, with a very limited childhood background of tennis competition, who hadn't played in college or even high school, improve to the point at which he could play serious competitive amateur tennis?

Tennis would siphon off my anger and give me a break from the intellectual pursuit. This was the entirety of what I thought I was in it for. But something was unconsciously drawing me to the tennis court, something much more intangible and mysterious, which had nothing in particular to do with tennis, or even sports.

Did I need to engage in a sport to do my research project? Though I didn't think about it at the time, enacting things physically, putting one's body on the line or into the mix, can have surprisingly powerful results in the nonphysical realm. Tennis is not ultimately about hitting a ball over a net with a racket, just as kneeling for prayer is not about knee bends. All religions seem to take for granted the spiritual importance of ritual: physical actions performed in a prescribed order.

Much later it would occur to me that tennis might be considered a physical pantomime of research. There are various shots to take at any moment, but not all will succeed, even in the short term. A return that neither goes out of bounds nor hits the net is not necessarily fruitful. One's opponent, the documentary evidence as it were, pushes back, sometimes decisively, unless one chooses an adversary, a subject of inquiry, with little resistance (say, where one sort of knows what one's going to "find"). One has a limited freedom if one desires to play by the rules of the game, or those of evidence and logic. Sometimes one has the sensation of knocking one's head against a wall, and, to move forward, one has to rethink, get a fresh perspective. It is often necessary to be willing to change tactics, innovate on one's feet. A great shot requires great risk, unless one is playing a weaker competitor, a dead horse, or a straw dog.

John McPhee, in his masterpiece of sports journalism *Levels of the Game*, finds that the contrasting styles of play of Arthur Ashe and Clark Graebner, in their 1968 Forest Hills match, reflect the players' backgrounds, personalities, and even politics. Ashe is a thoroughly Democratic player; Graebner plays Republican tennis. If you want some quick self-analysis—if you want to know just who you are at the present moment—get on a tennis court and compete in singles matches.

I had an old friend who confirmed this. "Oh, yes," he said. "My matches go just like my life. I get ahead in a set, then slack off, get nervous or distracted, and I let the guy catch up, until I find myself in a dramatic situation with my back to the wall. I do the same thing with work, health, relationships. Everything in my life goes to a tiebreak."

Tennis, like other sports, like the battlefield, say, in Stephen Crane's imagination of it in *The Red Badge of Courage*, or Hemingway's in *A Farewell to Arms*, like any competition or confrontation, involves a large psychological component. One's body being involved makes the encounter that much more visceral. How tennis singles differs from most other sports is that, like boxing or badminton as well, it is particularly revealing of this component since there is no team to buoy up, absorb, or obscure an individual player's mental state. Two psyches are bruisingly bare and exposed out there on the singles court.

And in thus being revealed to another and to oneself, one opens up the possibility of real change, something relatively rare for adults because it's so difficult. The tennis court isn't only a forum for therapeutic diagnosis; it's also a venue for working through emotional problems: learning to deal with difficult people, including oneself. I'd later meet a man who took up tennis after his divorce to process his sadness and rage, and a woman who went onto the court the very day her husband died after a very long illness. When she told me this, I was initially appalled by what I took to be a monstrous insensitivity and a psychotic investment in a racket sport; later, I realized she'd used the court to grieve, and exorcise years of pain and frustration.

When Cohn at the beginning of *Sun* expresses his desire to take up football again because he thinks that, as an adult, he's learned to handle himself and will thus perform better, his comment *is* pretty moronic because he has things backward. Playing football a decade and a half after high school isn't simply stupid because one will probably end up in the hospital after a single quarter. Cohn's comment is dumb because he drastically overestimates his knowledge about handling himself. But playing football would teach him just how little he knows.

I knew I was very angry about my father's medical assassination. But I didn't realize that *I* needed to change. If people had suggested to me at the start that tennis, a mere sport and a minor one to boot—something seemingly so insignificant and peculiar—might be a road to profound, even mystical, discovery, that it could alter me in some deep way, I'd have laughed in their faces.

As fall moved into winter, tennis players moved from outdoors to indoors, and the sabbatical was only two months away, I signed up for an eight-week, round-robin tournament. I hadn't played a singles match in a third of a century. Yes, I did play doubles twice a week, but doubles is not physically demanding, except maybe for eighty-year-olds.

I was playing doubles mainly because the organizer of the games, a curly-haired man in his late sixties named Bobby Lewis, who spoke with a distinctive Southside Italian American accent and ran some check-cashing stores, had adopted me as a pet project. Bobby had found me a couple years before when I'd gone up to some public courts to get exercise and fresh air after hours at the computer. He told me he was always on the lookout for new players to mix into his doubles game that'd been going on since the 1970s. He was under the impression that I had natural athletic talent and a lot of potential in tennis.

Singles can only be fun when you're in decent shape. When you're not, it's more torture than pleasure. Playing even a single game of singles, I felt like an animal trapped in a cage, without food or water, while being jolted with electrical shocks.

CHAPTER 6

Scholarly Detective Story II

IDENTIFYING THE LITERARY MYSTERIES
TO BE SOLVED

"Aren't these Lost Generation guys done to death?" said Mary.

"What do you know about them?" added Jerry, who knew a lot. "I should probably tell you that nobody studies modernism and war anymore. It's passé."

"It's not even your period of expertise," pointed out Larry, whose period it was.

I was sitting at lunch with a few colleagues I didn't hate, wishing I hadn't just opened my mouth about my plans. So I took a bite of my turkey sandwich, as if putting a stopper in it.

Notwithstanding these little obstacles my coworkers were good enough to remind me of, in the late fall, with my sabbatical fast approaching and my love of scholarship overwhelming my distaste for it, I found myself making headway with the Lost Generation and World War I.

I was once again teaching the 1920s masterpieces by Fitzgerald, Hemingway, and Faulkner: forget the books for a moment, the titles alone—
The Great Gatsby, *The Sun Also Rises*, and *The Sound and the Fury*—have become iconic, promising a quick trip to the heart of American experience and identity. I was relieved to be no longer repeating in class the hand-me-down interpretations I'd gotten from teachers, professors, and a Panzer division of literary critics. I found I had something new to say to my students because I'd begun to notice in these novels haunting sim-

ilarities in plot and character, analogous love triangles that seemed to have been lost in the mist of literary and political agendas. There were mysterious overlaps among these novels, which I couldn't explain. Unless the explanation was that I was imagining them.

For me not to be hallucinating, it would mean that decades of criticism on the most evaluated American writers somehow had missed something fairly large, and that the interpretative anomalies I'd noticed earlier were a sign of a bigger break with the critical tradition than I'd first imagined. As for the overlaps, Hemingway and Faulkner could have taken their cue from Fitzgerald, whose *Gatsby* came first, but even if they did, why were they enthralled enough with this love triangle to produce their own versions of it?

There *was* an unsolved mystery regarding Hemingway's work, or at least one important critic thought there was. The same Aldridge fellow who'd published a foundational study about the Lost Generation in the 1950s had more recently asserted that there was an untold story of Hemingway's life that shimmers in his novels, in particular *Sun*. And if anyone was in a position to know—or rather to see that there was something he didn't know—Aldridge was the man: he'd written about Hemingway for almost half a century.

"Hemingway managed through his complex artistry to use words in such a way that we are indeed allowed to see through them and to glimpse the outlines of the mysterious and probably tragic adventure that the words were not quite able to describe but were also not quite able to conceal." Less cryptically, he added, "Gertrude Stein, in one of her famous pronouncements . . . , said that there is in fact a real story to be told about Hemingway, one that he should write himself, 'not those he writes but the confessions of the real Hemingway.' Clearly, Hemingway did not write it and could not because the real story was too deeply disturbing to tell."

These were provocative claims, and they presented a challenge for the would-be literary detective. (It was also noteworthy for a literary critic to admit that he or she didn't know something. Especially after four decades of studying the subject. I find that kind of honesty to be almost breathtaking.)

But I was still unaware of Aldridge's suspicions. If I felt there were any mysteries about Hemingway at this point, my speculations were much cruder, more hostile, and less informed. Why had he been so freakin' obsessed with masculinity? Why so into ridiculously manly activities like bullfighting, deep-sea fishing, big-game hunting—and of course war? Also, why was he so damned racist and anti-Semitic? And were these various obnoxious things about Hemingway—his machismo and his racism—somehow related?

I no longer particularly liked Hemingway—or Fitzgerald or Faulkner, whom I also found racist and anti-Semitic. But I did like reading some Hemingway: especially *Sun*. That I liked the writing but not the writer was itself maybe a little mysterious—or perhaps it suggested I'd matured into an almost stable late adolescent.

None of these mysteries, however, presented a research question—at least not the kind my discipline recognized. But I did have the mysteriously repeating love triangle, or actually rectangle.

As I saw it, the books contained

1. An Anglo female from a "good family," who is sexually "promiscuous" and desired by more than one man.

    Gatsby's Daisy is born into money; *Sun*'s British Brett is Lady Ashley on account of her marriage; Caddy in *The Sound and the Fury* is from the southern aristocratic Compson family.

2. A social outsider male, sometimes ethnic American, who has a sexual relationship with the desirable Anglo female, much to the dismay of certain insider, Anglo males: an affair that is the primary conflict in the book.

    Gatsby, who has a wartime fling with Daisy and pursues her after the war, is born to poor parents in North Dakota and changes his name from Gatz to Gatsby to pass as Anglo. Hemingway's Robert Cohn is Jewish, and Brett sleeps with him. Faulkner's Dalton Ames, a stranger to the area where the Compsons live in *Sound*, impregnates Caddy.

3. An insider, Anglo, male narrator, who has a close, but nonsexual relationship with the central Anglo female—a special rapport that is nonsexual not by choice but because of an objective obstacle.

    The Anglo male is missing his penis—Hemingway's Jake—or

the Anglo female he loves is his sister, as is the case with Quentin Compson. *Gatsby*'s narrator Nick Carraway is likewise related to Daisy: they are cousins. This Anglo male has intensely mixed feelings about the outsider male who "gets the girl" he can't have, a combination of jealousy or awe and dislike.

4. A patriarchal Anglo male who badmouths ethnic Americans.

Racist bully Tom Buchanan, Daisy's husband, insinuates that Gatsby, given his ethnic background, isn't "white"—according to the standards of the era. Brett's English fiancé, Mike Campbell, repeatedly derides Cohn and, though tolerant generally of Brett's affairs, complains about her sleeping with a Jew. Jason Compson engages in familiar anti-Semitic rants about Wall Street moneymakers.

And as I became interested in this quite distinctive, repeating love triangle, which apparently no one else had noticed, I discovered that someone else had in fact done so, and not just an anonymous expert but someone I knew personally, Walter, an old mentor of mine in graduate school I was still in contact with who lived a mile away.

He'd attempted to explain this triangle in *Our America*, a relatively well-known book that I'd looked through but hadn't read. I asked him for a copy, and he dropped it off one evening on his way out to dinner. I should already have known what was inside it, not only because I'd known him for over twenty years and he lived a short drive away but because the ten-year-old book had actually been reviewed in the *New Yorker*. This discovery was at once relieving and disappointing.

I was relieved to know that my brain wasn't warped—that my possible hallucinations were probably based on old lessons I'd forgotten, undigested bits of someone else's thoughts. But I was disappointed that someone had beaten me to the punch. The book on the subject that I hoped would be my research project had evidently already been written.

I cursed at the dogs.

But after I calmed down a little, and reassured Quilty and especially Lazarus, who was very touchy and given to sulking, I realized I wasn't satisfied with Walter's explanation for this love triangle.

He'd said: well, Hemingway, Fitzgerald, and Faulkner were simply partaking of the common Anglo-American racist perspective, or what he called the "master discourse" of postwar nativism, which was alarmed about interbreeding between Anglos and ethnic Americans, and the threat this supposedly represented to the American identity, character, and intelligence. The authors' famous novels were part of a pervasive discourse—or cultural "conversation"—that included the texts of the unprecedented immigration restriction acts of the 1920s, notorious for having drastically reduced immigration from southern and eastern Europe. As Anglos (Fitzgerald was half Anglo, half Irish), these writers were shoring up their privilege. Protecting it against erosion, like the immigration acts that were basically excluding Jews, Italians, Poles, Turks, and so on.

What he was saying wasn't so different from what lots of critics of these famous American writers had said about their racism and anti-Semitism: namely, it was normal and to be expected for people of their class and background in this period. But Walter was also maintaining that their racism was central to their postwar books, as opposed to being marginal or a kind of unpleasant background static—"*white* noise"—that might be ignored, as most previous critics, and my professors back in college, had maintained.

Were these writers just shoring up Anglo privilege? I didn't buy it, as these books were intensely personal when it came to the subject of ethnic Americans. The alarm of these authors didn't seem abstract or intellectual, and their loss of privilege didn't seem like something looming in the future: it seemed all too immediate, and emotionally excruciating. These books weren't "cool" enough for me to buy my old mentor's explanation. They were too "hot" with ugly feeling.

In fact, their heat—or rather the awkwardness of that intensity—was one of the things that made their racism and anti-Semitism bearable. Though it kind of attempted to be cool, their prejudice was pathetically uncool. Maybe that helped explain why I could dislike Hemingway but enjoy reading him. He could mock his own prejudices.

Jake Barnes, the emasculated Anglo narrator of *Sun*, is never smugly anti-Semitic or racist or homophobic but always agonizingly, childishly, laughably so. He's always hating these outsiders and accusing them of acting "superior" and calling them names because of jealousy: they're obviously close in one way or another to his would-be girlfriend, Brett, with whom he can never be sexually intimate. This is true of the gay men he knows he's supposed to be "tolerant" of (as a resident of bohemian Paris) but who he wants to "swing on"—evidently because, as he notes over and over, to the point of a pathos that seems humorously demented, they're "very much with" Brett. And in very much the same capacity that he's with her: as nonsexual male company. It's entertaining precisely because Jake himself doesn't notice—as Hemingway and the reader do—that their being with Brett, and not the other reasons he gives for disliking them, is what largely makes him dislike them.

This is also true of his obvious rival in the book, the Jewish Cohn, of whom he says, after Cohn sleeps with Brett, "Why I felt that impulse to devil him I do not know. Of course I do know. I was blind, unforgivably jealous of what had happened to him. The fact that I took it as a matter of course did not alter that any. I certainly did hate him." This is pathetic, but it's also funny stuff, the way the narration wildly zigzags or trips up: staggering from a momentary attempt at detachment ("why I felt that impulse . . . I do not know") to an immediate failure of that pose ("of course I do know") and then to a passionate confession of vulnerability, envy, and hatred ("I was blind, unforgivably jealous. . . . I certainly did hate him").

It also seems true of the Black drummer at a bar called Zelli's, whom Jake calls by the N-word: "The nigger drummer waved at Brett." The reader wonders by this point in the novel if Jake would have used this racial slur if the drummer hadn't waved to Brett, if Jake isn't reflexively denigrating him precisely because the guy waves to her. Brett seems, unconsciously, or perhaps mock-unconsciously, which is to say, perhaps very purposefully, to want to wind Jake up. While he is mentally tossing out this slur and chewing on other racist insults, apparently to ease his resentment, Brett innocently, or mock-innocently, describes the drummer, and we can pleasurably feel Jake stewing as she does so, as "a great friend of mine." Brett's "friendships" with straight men tend to be sexual in nature.

So, if there was something intensely personal in Hemingway's self-conscious rivalry with and resentment of people he considered his social "inferiors," and Jews in particular, something akin to Jake's ugly competitiveness with the major character in the book whose Jewishness is insisted on at every turn, then what was it? Or to put it crudely and concretely: Jake is missing a dick, which Cohn without question possesses, so Cohn gets the girl and Jake doesn't; was Hemingway missing something that he felt some Jews had? What? And was this perhaps something that allowed certain Jews, and not him, to get the female attention he craved?

Though my discipline wouldn't have recognized these as legitimate research questions, I felt I had a real mystery on my hands.

CHAPTER 7

Secondhand Existence

I may not have known how to aim and shoot a gun, or hold and thrust with a knife, but I knew how to grip and swing a racket.

I'd taken up tennis at the age of nine, when my brother and I had happened one summer afternoon upon some free lessons at the nearby junior high school. I liked tennis for some reason; my brother quickly lost interest, and then I liked it intensely.

It is hard to have anything of your own at the age of nine when you have an older brother who claimed the world before you even knew it existed. Not only did I have secondhand clothes and books and pencil sets. My brother taught me first-grade math in our basement when I was four, so even school was to be drained of newness. It is hardly an exaggeration to say that I experienced life itself as a hand-me-down from my brother. I'd come down with a bad case of the Hong Kong flu at the age of eight, and it's no wonder: I was apparently so desperate to have an experience of my own that I'd even take sickness, hospitalization, and near death.

But my brother and I had discovered tennis together—he hadn't gotten there first—and his early departure from it gave it a special aura. It was not of this world, or at least not handed down from it. I was destined to be obsessed with tennis for the rest of my life.

What I was most of all fixated on at age nine was beating my brother. Though smaller, I soon had the distinct advantage of being much better at tennis. I joined a Junior Davis Cup team representing our little suburb and ended up captaining that squad. This was the one thing in life I could do better than my brother. It's hard to explain how important this was to me. My entire sense of self—the sheer possibility of having an independent self—depended on it. The only problem was I still couldn't beat him.

I'd jump ahead to a lead of several games, hardly losing a point. But then as I was coming close to winning the set, something else would kick in that had nothing to do with my skill, something I didn't understand at all and couldn't control in the least. I'd start to feel the wrongness of beating my older brother; I'd see his pained face and feel bad. And then I'd promptly, systematically, begin to lose.

Was it possible my desire for unmediated experience and understanding came from having an older brother? Had my place in the sibling order—strange as it sounded—determined not only my interest in tennis and my entire take on the world, but also my weird choice of profession?

I'd always felt the overwhelming desire to smash through "the collected drivel" of critics and historians, and just about everyone else, to some concealed, raw, complicated truth. I'd always felt, from my earliest schooling all the way through college, incredibly oppressed by nearly everything I was told and read. Most of the answers, the accounts, the histories struck me as too pat to be true. They seemed tired and worn out the first time I heard them. It was like being served cud for every meal when what you really wanted was unchewed food. Marxism the way it was taught: I mean, come on, could anybody buy this? And much of Freud: was he kidding? I felt I was being indoctrinated, not out of some purposeful conspiracy but because it was easier and more comfortable for all involved.

The "grand narrative" that cast light on my generation but also hung like a shadow over it was the history of the 1960s rebellion. That previous half-generation was for me like a grand "big brother" that had done it all, said it all, changed everything for the better—just before I came along. Much the same could be said about my actual brother and often was, in the smaller context of our family.

Growing up, I unconsciously idolized my brother and the great "big brothers" of the sixties antiwar protest, but as I got older I was also bored by them. And because some hungry, curious, distrustful part of me wanted and believed in a fresh understanding that would be truer and had to be tastier, I slowly developed a sneaking suspicion about everything he said and they said—even as everything they'd done and he did made me wildly jealous. He was too good to be true. ("Why can't you be more like your brother?" my mother would say. "Why can't I be?" I'd wonder.) And they were too good to be true. ("Why can't we be more like the rebels of the sixties?" my peers and I would say. "Why didn't we have a movement?" we'd wonder.)

As a young adult, I didn't believe he and they were entirely full of shit: I just felt after a while that he and they, like everything and everyone else I'd ever known, were holding back certain things in order to paint themselves in a more flattering light, which is to say they were partly full of shit.

But maybe it wasn't just boredom and resentment that had me wanting to smash through the drivel to some buried, unremembered, intricate reality. It was also possible that there really was something I needed to discover about my generation and myself, some hidden truth.

CHAPTER 8

Scholarly Detective Story III

FINDING CLUES IN THE LITERATURE

It was late November, and I should have been out doing the Thanksgiving shopping, but I was once again contemplating the literary love triangle that I was beginning to hate because I couldn't figure it out. Beth was at the lab; she had to replace a bunch of batches that an intern had accidentally contaminated, something that was hard to avoid. I wondered how she was doing. I was at my desk paging through these 1920s novels, as I had so many times before, when I finally noticed something. It was undeniable once you saw it, but it was for some reason hard to see.

The outsider male characters who got the desirable Anglo woman—Fitzgerald's Gatsby, obviously; much less clearly with Faulkner's Ames; and perhaps least obviously with Hemingway's Cohn—all had ties to the US military.

Gatsby was a decorated officer in World War I, and no one reading the novel could fail to notice that except by trying to—students I taught in college often didn't remember this about the novel because high school teachers didn't pay it much heed. Faulkner's Ames, Caddy's lover, "had been in the army" and "had killed men"—that was generally overlooked by critics (I later discovered that at least one other critic had discussed it). This and other related information about Ames's military experience was easy to miss because it was buried in the confusing stream-of-consciousness narrative. Hemingway's Robert Cohn had gone to military school—and though that was announced rather prominently, on the second page of the book, and that fact was presented as important in his personal development—it was, nonetheless, apparently easily passed over. I myself had done so, over and over.

It was easy to miss this information about Ames and Cohn only because earlier critics, who had established the basic readings of these books, had not noticed it or thought it important. How influenced we tend to be by these phantom readers who come before us. When I brought this discovery into class a few days later, I pointed out to my students that Ames had been in the army, and maybe that's why he's a crack shot with a revolver and why Caddy's brother, Quentin, is so intimidated by him. One PhD student, who had written a master's thesis on Faulkner, objected strongly.

"I can't accept that. Where does it say he'd been in the army? It doesn't directly say that. What definitive evidence do you have?"

I flipped pages. "Would you accept as definitive evidence the quotation 'had been in the army had killed men'?"

Oddly, he would not.

He insisted that the line in question was simply not in his version of the text. His copy was well thumbed; he declared he'd read it many times, and indeed there was underlining on just about every page. On some pages he'd underlined every line. He couldn't have missed it.

It took some time, but I eventually found the same phrase in his copy. Not surprisingly, these words weren't highlighted—in fact, they were just about the only ones on the page left untouched. He was stunned into silence. And I was finally able to continue on with class.

But like him (up to a point), I had trouble noticing this information because of my preconceived notions of these books.

Though I had no clear idea what it meant, I was onto something. And it was something my mentor Walter hadn't noticed, or considered significant; his book barely mentioned the war. Which meant—if this turned out not to be a red herring—that I'd finally wandered into original, uncharted territory, and I was on my way to an alternative answer to the mystery of the repeating love triangle.

One thing made me confident I was on the scent. As I'd started to educate myself about the World War I era, I'd read a book in which the historian Nancy Bristow had discussed the dramatic outpouring of sexual activity between local women and army recruits in and around military training camps during the war—a flood so dramatic it came to be seen as a threat to the war effort. The local women were called "charity girls" because, unlike prostitutes, who likewise swarmed the camps, they didn't charge for the sex they were "doling out."

The US government's wartime Commission on Training Camp Activities had reported:

> The "lure of the uniform" is more than a phrase; it is an actuality. Girls often lose their heads in a whirl of emotion brought about by these unusual conditions.
>
> In all towns, both large and small, in the vicinity of the camp [Dix, New Jersey] or accessible to the soldiers by jitney, trolley or train, there still is considerable volume of "charity" intercourse. There seems to be a psychological feature to this particular evil in that young girls between the ages of 14 and 20 are inordinately susceptible to any man in uniform whether he be an officer or one of lesser rank.

This was happening around all the camps. Later, I was to discover a similarly concerned—but more entertaining—report from an average citizen who resided near one in Pennsylvania. The man wrote, more colloquially and less coherently, to an officer in the army: "The girls of Scranton . . . have lost all the sentiment of decency that is proper of the sexes . . . hunting for men like a bunch of sea dogs in the season of love. Maybe they were sacrificing themselves on the altar of the fatherland, which I believe is not asking so much of the patriotism of their women. Never before [have] . . . I witnessed such a debauche [sic]."

I'd also heard a radio interview with 105-year-old Lloyd Brown, "the last living American World War I vet," who'd snuck into the service at age 16. Asked why he did so, he still remembered, some nine decades later, that it was because the war was "very popular with the ladies."

It wasn't hard to imagine why there was this sexual revolution. Thousands of young men were pouring into town, cut loose from the normal ties and surveillance of family members and neighbors. For the first time in the lives of the local girls and women, there were lots of available young men who were not only strangers but would not be hanging around long. Moreover, these guys might be going off to die. The possibilities for clandestine sex, and sex without consequences, were not only plentiful, but also highly romantic.

It was 1917: the majority of people had never ridden in a car; few had ever even seen an airplane; movies were silent; rock concerts did not exist, and TV had yet to be invented. In most of the towns and small cities where there were training camps, nothing so exciting had ever happened. It must have seemed that nothing so exciting might ever occur again. It was, for many women and soldiers, a once-in-a-lifetime moment not to be missed. Fitzgerald's wife Zelda remembered: before World War I, "There was scarcely a ripple in our lives. . . . Then the war came and we had the inescapable feeling that all this beauty and fun—everything—might be over in a minute. We couldn't wait, we couldn't afford to wait, for fear it would be gone forever, so we pitched in furiously, dancing every night."

A study of female adolescents put together by psychologists just after the war asserted that, when it came to the United States, the Great War "wrought its greatest influence . . . in the field of sexual relationships." It created "a vast emotional tension which tends to break conventionalities."

Meanwhile, the government considered the sexual outbreak a serious health and moral problem, mostly because it spread venereal disease, which could sideline soldiers. The military ended up cracking down on the females, imprisoning somewhere between fifteen and thirty thousand women and girls, who could be picked up, stripped of their civil rights, forced to undergo an invasive medical exam, and jailed simply for wearing supposedly provocative clothing within five miles of a training camp.

Given all this, it made sense in these postwar books to find the representation of liaisons between men with military connections and women. But most "charity girls" were working class, and these novels were focused on privileged Anglo women—who were getting together with social outsiders, men who were ethnic American or working class, or both, and so usually didn't have sexual access to desirable insider women.

Such liaisons would be especially noteworthy to insider men, and the narrators and authors of all three of the books I was considering were such. In *Sun*, Brett's fiancé, Mike, complains, "Brett's had affairs with men before. . . . But they weren't ever Jews."

The unusual nature of such a liaison is also obviously made a big deal of in *Gatsby*—there we have the affair between well-born Daisy Fay and the poor, ethnic American Gatz, who anglicizes his name. Daisy's husband Tom will be "damned" if he sees how Gatsby, this "Nobody from Nowhere," "got within a mile of [Daisy] unless [he] brought groceries to the back door." The novel makes clear that Gatsby went in the front door, as an officer at Camp Taylor.

Did such "cross-ethnic" as well as "cross-class" encounters actually take place because of World War I—or were they the invention of these novelists? If Fitzgerald's novel reflected reality in this regard, unusual liaisons were taking place between privileged Anglo woman and outsider men who made officer. This, too, made a certain kind of sense. After all, to be an officer in the army was officially to be deemed "an officer and a gentleman," a title extended to commissioned officers up until the Vietnam era.

But—and here was the key question—how would lower-class and ethnic American men have gotten officer commissions?

What Fitzgerald's novel doesn't make clear at all is how Gatsby, born Gatz, without money or Anglo family prestige, and most likely a German American, got to be a commissioned officer in the US Army, which was not only notoriously racist (witness its segregation of African Americans) but fighting Germany.

Gatsby implies to Nick that he was offered a commission when the war began, on the basis of his exalted family connections. I knew that the American military indeed had a strong tradition of nepotism; in the Civil War, I'd heard, one way to become a Union general was to have been a drinking buddy of Ulysses S. Grant. This wasn't so far-fetched. It was well known that governors doled out commissions in their state militias as political favors.

Gatsby's individual claim is obviously a lie, since his elite family name and background are inventions. But the book seems to suggest the possibility—at least it's been read this way—that Gatz managed to sneak into the officer class by passing himself off as a well-to-do son of a distinguished but fabricated Anglo family called Gatsby. If sixteen-year-olds could pass themselves off as eighteen (the minimum enlistment age), like the last living American World War I veteran, could the army brass, or state governors, also have been fooled about family backgrounds?

Or was something else going on: something historically significant but apparently little known? From the major historical literature on the period, I knew that, during World War I, ethnic Americans, especially German Americans, who suddenly hailed from an enemy nation, were treated with extreme prejudice.

How did Gatsby—from a poor Midwestern farming family and German American to boot—make lieutenant in the US Army? How did he then go on to make captain? The privileged Anglo narrator, the usually comprehensible Nick, who tells us exactly what gets Gatsby promoted to major on the battlefield, thinks it important enough to interject a seemingly trivial, and definitely vague, corrective piece of information late in the novel about his previous climb through the ranks. Nick revises Gatsby's account that he got catapulted from lieutenant to major, bypassing captain, on the basis of battlefield success. Nick reveals, "He was a captain before he went to the front."

Why does Nick mention this but not explain how Gatsby made it into officers' training in the first place? This is a piece of information that today's reader has little idea what to do with, and it seemed no critic had previously done anything with it.

But I thought it referred to something in the real world back then during the war, which the author wanted to mention but didn't want to get into. I thought this because Fitzgerald had experienced the World War I training camps himself and wanted badly to make captain but never did, stalling at the rank of lieutenant.

Was something new and unusual, in terms of the officer selection process, going on at the training camps? Or Camp Taylor in particular?

This seemed an apt question because, though Fitzgerald was at Taylor, he was also, supposedly more significantly in terms of his conception of the plot of *Gatsby*, at Camp Sheridan, which was in Montgomery, Alabama, where he met Zelda, the inspiration, according to many critics, for

Daisy. Why did Fitzgerald choose this other camp, Taylor, for Gatsby—and put Daisy in Louisville, Kentucky?

I was now coming to a surprising, possibly paranoid, research question. Was Fitzgerald's novel—along with Faulkner and Hemingway's—obliquely referring to a secret history of the US war effort in World War I? Were these hideously overanalyzed novels the repository of clues nobody else had ever noticed or managed to follow up on? Why would this history be secret? Why would these novels refer to it only indirectly—for example, in a book that's so detailed about Gatsby's past, devoted to telling his success story step-by-step, why not make it absolutely clear how the title character became an officer? Indeed, the entire plot of the novel hinges on the unusual fact that an ethnic American man from the lower classes manages to meet the richest Anglo girl in town on an equal footing as an officer, but the book doesn't bother to explain how he does so.

Why the reticence here, the odd discretion? Why did Fitzgerald not want to get into it?

And there was another thing that was making me feel paranoid. As my colleague Jerry had implied over lunch, the Lost Generation novelists were no longer labeled as such. Contemporary critics called them "modernists" and didn't anymore consider World War I to be important to "modernism." That was why Walter's 1995 book, though focused on American modernism, said almost nothing about the war. So I also began to wonder, why had this critical change happened?

It sounded totally ridiculous, but had there been some kind of cover-up of the military's role in our literary history? I thought the government and military did the covering up.

It was also dawning on me that this oversight might not be aberrational but part of a more regular pattern. I now realized that I'd never been taught any twentieth-century American war literature in college and graduate school, which was especially odd because at the latter I'd focused on US literature from the late nineteenth century to the middle of the twentieth: during which time period the country had fought some pretty major wars. The one American war novel I'd been assigned in college—Hemingway's *A Farewell to Arms*—was in a class I took on a junior year abroad in the UK. I'd had to travel to England to be assigned a work of twentieth-century US war literature.

Were these most famous American novels not only or not really about what they were ostensibly about—the "horror of modern warfare," the resulting "postwar malaise," the "Roaring Twenties"—but actually to a large extent, or even for the most part, a reaction to a secret history of the US Army in World War I?

Or was I nuts?

CHAPTER 9

A Farewell to Love Handles

I had for years looked askance at middle-aged men who trained for triathlons, took up deep-sea diving, or got serious about mountain biking. Now I was one of them. And while I thought Fitzgerald's lingering regrets in his midthirties about not being good enough or big enough to play football in college were pathetic, I was in my midforties and actually attempting to reignite the tennis career I'd abandoned in junior high because I hadn't been good enough or tall enough. My body simply hadn't finished growing yet.

I told myself that the closer the research sabbatical got and the more I felt my identity as a scholar reemerging, the more I needed to counteract this reality, though I wanted badly to succeed as a scholar again. Wanting to reestablish myself as a scholar and feeling like one weren't the same thing. And given the enduring emasculating stereotype of scholars in our culture, I was starting to feel the discomfort of being one (as I had once before, during my Bohemian Writer period). Thus, I thought, as my research project amped up, my training for tennis also went into high gear. But I was mistaken: that wasn't the real reason.

Two months earlier, I'd also felt disdain for the way men talked endlessly about tools, paraphernalia, cars, equipment, home repair. It was another thing I didn't like about Hemingway, and this time something I didn't like about his writing: the long and minute descriptions of fishing and bullfighting left me cold and irritated. I raced through them or skipped them entirely. It wasn't so much that it involved a pissing contest but that it was a dull one.

But these long-established feelings of repulsion didn't stop me from becoming suddenly involved in discussions of gear as I sought to equip myself effectively for my tennis comeback. I felt no embarrassment about my abrupt switch in attitude, mostly because I didn't notice it.

If I was gravitating to what I claimed I hated and quite easily embracing activities I detested, then at some deeper level I evidently needed these things badly.

I had this sanguine image of myself as someone who'd always liked tennis and now, after years of playing doubles, decided, for mental-health reasons, to take up singles and see what he could do. I told myself I simply wanted to channel some anger and raise my game, as I dealt with middle-age stresses and recommitted to scholarship. I'd busy both hands: my left, with which I wrote, and my right, with which I played sports. To put it classically, *mens sana in corpore sano.*

This was my image of myself: a picture of sanity and balance. The reality was monstrously different. My investment in tennis was just as feverish as everything else going on in my life, starting with my rocky, intense feelings about scholarship, which, though I was supposed to be focusing on it exclusively, now became arguably secondary to tennis.

I was playing almost every day, sometimes twice a day. As soon as the fall term ended, and thanks to coffee, electricity, and Beth's understanding, I kept ghoulish hours, often beginning my research and writing for the day at midnight and finishing at five in the morning—when I'd take the dogs out for a dawn walk.

The seriousness with which I took this amateur athletic undertaking was hard to imagine, harder still to exaggerate. I "test drove" a series of rackets from a tennis specialty store and eventually chose one.

As for a healthy body, well, it looked very healthy. I saw in the mirror definition in my muscles I hadn't seen for twenty years or more; I was reacquainted with secondary and tertiary muscles I'd forgotten were part of the human body, or at least mine. I was broader; my arms were bigger, and the veins on them stuck out even when I wasn't trying to make them pop, which I often was. My abdomen was hard and flat, and the love handles were gone.

My thighs, which had been bird's-leg thin my whole life except during high school soccer more than twenty-five years ago, and which I thus tended to keep disguised with baggy pants, were bulked up and therefore of almost normal size, and not mortally embarrassing. Also, for the first time in my life, I had an ass. I couldn't count the number of times in my life women and gay men had said to me, "God, you have no butt."

When I had my yearly physical, my doctor came into the office exclaiming about my off-the-chart "good cholesterol" score on my blood test: a score unheard of in adult men who aren't exercising to a compulsive degree.

But in many ways too numerous to count, I was physically anything but well. Tennis elbow? Yes, I had it. Anyone who plays any tennis at all, no matter how noncompetitive and lax it may be, can develop it—eighty-year-olds can get it. I had it, but I hardly noticed. That was because I also had tennis wrist, bicep, and shoulder; tennis knee, calf, ankle, and foot; tennis back and neck.

I had other kinds of injuries as well. For starters, I had tennis shin: I continuously had cuts and scabs on my legs from the occasional botched follow-through on a serve that drove my racket right into my flesh. Much worse than tennis shin, I had tennis toe and finger. My right hand was so grotesquely blistered that I started wearing a weightlifting glove when I played (tennis gloves are too thin for tennis).

That was after I'd had to burst the worst blister I'd ever seen. I had to have Beth do it—I was too squeamish about the thick, green pus underneath that erupted like a pimple.

Worse than the blister on my finger were the ones on my toes. I debated for days whether to burst them. But they proved too hard to penetrate, even with a needle.

I went to see a doctor since I could barely stand to be on my feet—and, more importantly, couldn't play tennis. The doctor took one look, gave me a referral slip for a podiatrist, and left.

I hate going to doctors and hate even more going to specialists, and I thought, "Oh, great; this is the end of my tennis comeback, if not my ability to walk."

But, as I was tying my shoes, the attending nurse, whose husband it turned out was a serious runner, sneaked into the examining room.

In a low voice, she gave me a piece of advice that saved my feet and my comeback. "Wear two pairs of socks, no matter how thick the first pair is."

This was the best possible outcome you could have from a doctor's visit for a problem of this kind. Somehow give the trained medical expert the slip, speak privately to the nurse, and get the insider, experiential, inductive information you needed.

Doctors irritate me with their tendency to refuse the inductive approach, which starts with observation and experiment, even when it's available. They favor deduction, which rushes recklessly to theory and is more glamorous intellectually and on which, because of their specialized training, they have a monopoly. It reminds me a lot of literary theory, which starts with an answer and forces a piece of art to speak that "truth," even as it's choking on the gag of deduction.

I'd begun to think that perhaps I understood how the long-standing take on American Lost Generation literature had apparently started off on, well, the wrong foot, how it came to be misapprehended as a horrified response to trench warfare. Wasn't it the reliance on deduction that had initially led the literary-critical world to the standard but maybe misguided ideas about post–World War I American fiction? Probably the characterization of Hemingway and Faulkner's novels as antiwar came out of studying European literature and then applying those observations to the US case—despite America's very different experience of the war.

Almost all commentators were aware of the most obvious differences. The European experience not only took place on European soil and lasted much longer (four-plus years as opposed to nineteen months), but many more soldiers from the major European combatant countries were killed. France lost more than 1.3 million men and England 900,000. Meanwhile, US deaths were about 125,000. That's a lot of dead too, but remember that the casualty differences between England and America, for example, were even more pronounced than the sheer numbers implied because the US population at the time (around one hundred million) was more than twice that of the United Kingdom and Ireland (around forty-six million). That meant that the per capita death rate in the UK was wildly greater than the American one: one out of fifty as opposed to one out of eight hundred for the United States.

The American involvement obviously came later in the war, a significance lost on many commentators but not on the military in 1917. The US Army had the examples of England and Canada—or, to put it more accurately, as counterexamples: America had the advantage of basing its own mobilization on avoiding what it saw as the catastrophic mistakes made by other nations.

I didn't know yet exactly what this meant—I knew I needed to learn a lot more about just what the Americans did differently—but I'd already come across a tantalizing quotation in a well-known book from the early 1980s called *Over Here*, by the historian David Kennedy: "England offered an especially compelling example" of how not to mobilize. "The British had refused until 1916 to resort to the draft. In the first two years of the war they had seen their best-educated and most talented young men rush willy-nilly to the colors and as quickly and haphazardly die in the mud in Flanders. That non-policy wrought a terrible loss of leadership cadres that seriously crippled the British military effort."

To avoid the British mistake, the United States instituted a draft from the beginning. That was well known. But there was nothing in Kennedy's book or the other, more recent histories I'd looked at to indicate how someone like Gatsby—that is, a poor, ethnic American—could have become an officer and then captain in the training camps. It occurred to me that maybe there were all kinds of distinctive policies that the US military instituted to avoid the British errors, moves that were long forgotten.

I was going to have to wade deep into the pretty obscure territory of military-mobilization history, and I seriously doubted the specialized information I needed would be available in books, where the whole subject tended to be treated in passing. I wondered if I was biting off more than I could chew.

CHAPTER 10

Meetings with Unbearable Men

To go along with my (completely deluded) perception of myself as someone reasonably involved in pursuing tennis, I had the impression that I was bringing a dignified maturity to the courts, much as Cohn in Hemingway's *Sun* imagines he'd like to play football again with his adult knowledge. This, too, was radically false. Like Cohn, I'd evidently learned almost nothing as an adult about handling myself.

I looked around me with bemused contempt at the antics and tantrums of the grown men I was playing against—the excuses they gave in advance about injuries or sicknesses or lack of sleep or being out of practice, excusing themselves in advance in case they lost; the cursing at themselves for missed shots they weren't really capable of making in the first place; the ways they cheated a little, or a lot, by "not remembering" the point score or the game score, or calling balls "out" that were on the line or even within it, or foot-faulting a few inches or an entire step on every serve; the way they suddenly cut short the match when they were losing badly; their volubility between games when they were winning and their silent pouting at changeovers when behind. I could go on with the list of their irritating little infractions; I was onto all their little devices for protecting their egos and soothing their bruised feelings. I understood because I was guilty of just about all of these things myself.

I could handle guys who just wanted to win by any means. That was superfamiliar. That *was* male competition as I'd known it from age five. What I couldn't take were the guys who wanted something from you off the court as well, men whose egos weren't satisfied simply with winning, who also needed to dominate in every exchange, no matter how trivial. These were adult males who needed to put you down in some other way besides beating you in tennis, say by giving you important advice you didn't ask for or, less subtly, by calling you names.

I couldn't help developing a new sympathy for women and gay men, as I got apparently unavoidable insight into what now seemed to me the absolutely hellish experience that must be involved in dating men. In taking up singles, it was like I'd gone undercover as a woman into the dating scene.

Take Marco. Marco was a very tall man from Italy, and every time I played with him he reminded me that he was older than me (four years older) and therefore deserved my elaborate respect. Of course, I always failed to show it to him. I needed lessons in showing him respect: a long, perhaps even endless, series. So naturally I didn't even try.

On arriving at the courts, if I didn't say hello to him properly, in the manner of a formal greeting, the way one might, say, at a diplomatic summit of heads of state, he would take me to task for it. Every time we played, he would find some reason to accuse me of thinking that he was stupid, of feeling superior to him because I was a professor: oh, how sorry I was that I told him I was a professor. At first I said, "Of course I don't think you're stupid." But after having gone through this routine with him several times, I didn't say this anymore because I'd actually changed my mind. He was right. I did think he was stupid.

He would keep on saying what he'd already said until I walked off. Our conversations ended only because I was fifty yards away and could no longer hear him. One December morning after walking the dogs, feeling more rattled than I usually did in the morning and wanting to get in a better mind frame for work, I thought, "Maybe a game of tennis is what I need." So I called Marco, even though I'd told him a number of times I didn't play in the morning, and I'd strenuously asserted that under no circumstances whatsoever could I play on a day I worked.

Then Marco regularly called me for months afterward and asked me to play first thing the next morning. Marco loved to play in the morning; it was, according to him, the only proper time to play. And nothing I could say would disabuse him of the belief that I could play in the morning if I just put my mind to it. How I regretted playing with him once in the morning.

Unless I didn't regret it at all, but the truth was that I'd played with him in the morning one time because it was sure to drive him absolutely crazy. There was nothing stopping me from playing in the morning except that I preferred not to.

I hated knowing I had to get up in the morning. Knowing I had to get up early made it almost impossible for me to sleep. In fact, my hatred of getting up in the morning was the single most consistent force in my life. More than anything else, more than my love of scholarship—which was also a hatred of scholarship—more than a love of literature—and I detested most literature, let's be honest—it was a hatred of getting up in the morning that had determined my choice of career and really the entire course of my life. It would not be inappropriate if someone put on my gravestone the words, "He liked to sleep in."

An imp had clearly seized me. I knew playing with him in the morning this one time, and on a day when I worked to boot, would confuse him forever; I knew that I could never explain, or rather that he would never understand, that this was a singular event, never to be repeated.

Marco's being older meant that he didn't have to show anyone else respect. In fact, he routinely referred to younger people as "babies," and did so to their faces. After hearing him use this word countless times—it was perhaps his favorite word—I understood that he used it cleverly, as a non-native speaker who couldn't be presumed to understand its pejorative connotation. When Marco, with his Italian accent, used the word "baby," it was clear that he meant a "young person," a slightly quaint usage a foreigner might just employ. But the cleverness came in because it was also clear, at least to me, that he also very much meant "a crybaby"— though he could never be accused of implying this figurative sense since he was a non-native speaker.

At first I felt bad for Marco because I saw that almost no one would play him in matches more than once, and I initially accepted his explanation that the "babies" didn't like to play someone they realized they couldn't beat. Though older, and not a hard hitter, Marco had a big reach and was almost inhumanly consistent.

He had nothing but contempt for men of any age who only wanted to rally—to him they were simply "superbabies" protecting their egos.

"Like that Asian guy over there," he said one day, pointing to another court a ways away. "Chong." He indicated a man, not particularly tall or big, with thick graying hair. "He looks like a great player, but only hits, and many times with weaker babies. It's disgraceful. I have asked him to play a match several times. Don't bother. He says no to everybody." Marco smacked his lips. "Superbaby."

I'd noticed this man before. It was pleasant to watch him move. He would be a 4.5 USTA player if his rallying translated to his game. Maybe it didn't. There was a huge difference between rallying and competing in matches, for the latter brought in tactics as well as what commentators called the "mental side" of the game. In professional tennis, it was to a large degree that side of things separating champions from other extremely talented players.

Marco was also clever in another way: with sixteen years of tennis experience, as he told me more than sixteen thousand times, he was onto the myriad devices that players used to gain a psychological advantage. But as I got to know him better, I saw not only that he was oblivious that he regularly used the very same tricks he accused the "babies" of indulging in, but also that the real reason they didn't want to play with him more than once was that he was disrespectful and insulting: for starters, he called them "babies."

Marco really got to me, even if I got to him too. One afternoon on the courts he told me I was like "Eminwhy"—because I didn't like to make plans (I was happy to, but not for the morning). It took a minute before I realized he was talking about Hemingway, whose social elusiveness I hadn't known about, and then I shuddered. Only Marco, trying for some insidious reason to compliment me by comparing me to "Eminwhy," could have thus irritated me: Hemingway was notorious for being competitive with everyone he knew, and of course I was familiar with his racism and anti-Semitism. I now remembered that in *Sun* Jake originally comes to know Robert as a "tennis friend" and that Hemingway played singles with his third wife, the great war correspondent Martha Gellhorn. Of their games, he told Lillian Ross: "You had to let her *almost* win for her to be happy," he said. "If you *let* her win, she became insufferable." I could imagine just how insufferable *he* would be if he lost. (He was probably a bad husband, as well as a bad friend and a bad person.) Though I wasn't remotely like Hemingway (I hoped), I could see him fitting right in with my unbearable opponents.

Why did *I* play with Marco? Half-consciously, I was actually seeking out assholes: because I'd become an asshole myself as a result of my father's wrongful death. Competitive singles was in part appealing for the ridiculously furious confrontations.

Most men in amateur tennis are jerks but less obvious about it than Marco. Often they are thus more poisonous to the spirit. Several players, some quite nice and some exasperating themselves, have wondered aloud to me why this is the case. This "mystery" may have a simple answer: singles players may be largely a self-selecting group of men who are highly competitive and very angry. And they don't want to mix it up physically and, say, box or do martial arts, and get their asses kicked.[1] I liked to believe I didn't fall into this category, though obviously to a large extent I did.

As one of these guys, named Ralph, keenly observed, "These guys are frustrated in their lives and can't get along with anyone. They look to tennis to be heroes in a reality that doesn't exist. Thus their phenomenal anger, their inability to accept it, when they lose." (And here I did part company with the biggest jerks.) By the way, Ralph's acuteness didn't keep him from being insufferable himself. He talked relentlessly about the beauty of the world, the magnificence of even a speck of dust, but in a domineering, overbearing fashion that made the world seem mundane and ugly as shit.

Switching from doubles to singles was really shocking. Though I'd anticipated some ugly competition, I often found myself in terrifically awkward, weirdly intimate encounters with other men—as I brushed up against their vulnerabilities as well as my own. Though male tantrums do occur in doubles, which involves four players, they occur much less than in singles because, when two of the men start squabbling on the doubles court, there are a couple of witnesses. Singles is just private enough so that men are willing to completely let themselves go behaviorally.

---

1. Unlike Hemingway, to be fair, who did box.

CHAPTER 11

Scholarly Detective Story IV

DISCOVERING PRIMARY-SOURCE HISTORICAL
EVIDENCE IN MY WIFE'S FILE CABINET

Suspicious that in rereading these famous modernist novels I'd stumbled on a secret history of officer selection in the World War I US Army, I thought about how it would be nice at this point—perhaps even intelligent—to dash off to the National Archives, where I pictured gray boxes of records stored behind long counters manned by silent clerks. There I might discover how a "nobody" like Gatsby might have been promoted to captain in the training camps, a bizarre inquiry important only to me.

If this were a movie, and I was researching something that intensely mattered, and my character were being played by someone along the lines of Tom Hanks in *The Da Vinci Code* (at the time, we shared the same middle-aged man's "I'm-still-a-hipster" haircut) or Nicolas Cage in *National Treasure* (who wears a wig and thus bypasses the whole problem), we would smash-cut to an airplane taking off and then watch the character enter, from above and behind, a stately neoclassical building in Washington, DC. But this wasn't a movie. The National Archives were no longer housed in a stately stone building on the Mall but had been moved out to a building of newish, not-exactly-stately but rather mall-like construction in the Maryland suburbs. And even if I was onto something, there was definitely no world-historical conspiracy to keep this mystery dark. The stakes involved in this search, though urgently high for Beth and me, were extremely low for nearly everyone in my profession.

To be sure, as Americans, our brains had been crammed with a load of shit about Hemingway, Fitzgerald, and Faulkner, starting in high school, and there might be some benefit to cleaning house. Oddly, the American on the street probably had more interest in my questions about Hemingway and Fitzgerald than my colleagues did these days. The vast majority of the academy would happily wait another eighty years, or eight hundred, to have the American Lost Generation writers properly assessed.

My personal timeline was rather more pressing. The urgency was unfortunately no joke. I knew I was very fortunate to have a job as a professor. But I also understood that my workplace frustration and especially my ongoing legal problems were wearing down my zest for life. Beth, though outwardly coping, had been subjected to this conflict too much as it was. She wasn't complaining—that wasn't her way—but I could see she was unhappy. I will not try to describe the distress you feel being even partly responsible for putting someone you love through repeated pain. (I was too old to blame others for my problems, and she had entered my life with neither of us understanding what we were in for.) We had to move away to someplace else. If I could get lucky with this research and write a killer book, I might be able to land a new job in my profession.

Then, oddly, as if in a dream, I remembered something, and this *was* suddenly exactly like a movie, as I walked across the room in my apartment, pulled open a filing cabinet drawer—and reached into the National Archives.

Still in a trance, I removed a couple of bulging file folders and began leafing through some old, brittle, yellowing sheets of paper that were strangely familiar. In a few minutes I had in front of me, in my hands, a typewritten copy of a document titled "Interpretation of Scores in Intelligence" that contained some aggregate IQ test results of World War I soldiers.

In the middle of the page there was the absolutely astonishing handwritten note—it was Xeroxed, and not in my handwriting—seemingly jumping now at my eyes: *Results at Camp Taylor.*

Gatsby's camp.

I looked more closely at this extraordinary document that was on my desk—it was in the classic Courier font native to old typewriters. In one table, various score ranges were correlated with different "Characterizations" that were sometimes army ranks: the highest scores indicated "Skilled thinker in abstract relations" or "Superior officer," together accounting for 6 percent of all test-takers; then came "Officer (type)," which was indicated for the next 12 percent, then "Private (type)," 57 percent, and finally, "Unskilled laborer," "dull laborer," and "Feebleminded or bordering on fm.," making up the bottom 25 percent. Another table gave "Medians by rank in Army" and showed that the higher the rank, the better the median score, in an arbitrary range from 0 to 414: privates averaged 164 and "Capts., Lieuts" 294.

Hardly breathing, I reached back into the filing cabinet and took out another old folder. In it was a letter from someone connected to the Military Sales Department with the almost ridiculously aristocratic name of E. I. du Pont de Nemours (the same name as the man who founded, in 1802, the DuPont explosives company, which during World War I was the largest producer of smokeless powder explosive). The letter stated that, among other things, the "tests [were] used in the qualification of army *Captains*."

I felt I had to sit down.

There was of course no supernatural portal or wormhole in our tiny apartment in Chicago's Humboldt Park. I looked over to the not-at-all mystical, though fairly high-quality, filing cabinet that Beth had brought away from her first marriage (one of the very few things she'd asked for, a restraint which drove her divorce lawyer crazy). I saw there were hundreds of pages of World War I military documents still in the drawer, thick, dusty files I'd been hauling around with me unopened for nearly a quarter of a century.

I kept digging in the files, and I found another letter, titled "The Training School at Vineland New Jersey." It asserted that the intelligence "tests [were] tried out . . . in the four cantonments at Camps Devens, Taylor, Dix, and Meade"—the word "Taylor" again leapt out at me. "Psychological examining began" at these camps "in the fall of 1917."

To my innocent questions—was anything new and unusual going on at the training camps in terms of selecting officers? and at Camp Taylor in particular?—I now seemed to have the answers.

Yes: Taylor, where Fitzgerald put Gatsby in the fall and winter of 1917, was one of the four camps that had pioneered the famous intelligence test, the great-granddaddy of all standardized tests to follow, the SATs, MCATs, and LSATs, which would torture future generations of students. (Later I'd understand that Taylor was the only one of these four camps at which Fitzgerald had been posted.) Therefore, Gatsby would have undergone the intelligence testing at Taylor in the fall or winter of 1917. Or to put it more precisely, because I don't mean to insinuate that Gatsby was a real person, the real-life experimental testing at Taylor existed during the period Fitzgerald imagines his title character is there.

And, yes again: there was something new going on regarding the selection of men for officer training. The tests themselves were part of it. They were used to identify potential officers and also "in the qualification of army Captains." Two more documents pulled from the drawer, these from the Committee on Classification of Personnel in the U.S. Army, indicated another innovative method of choosing officers: one sheet was titled "Individual Rating Sheet for Selecting [Officer] Candidates in Each Training Unit"; the other, "Rating Sheet for Selecting Captains." These indicated desired traits of officers in general and captains in particular and provided scoring systems. All of which seemed germane to Nick's cryptic remark about Gatsby's captaincy.

I jumped up.

The dogs thought we were going out for a walk and started barking.

"Not now," I said. I took the tiny tour of our living room.

They followed me.

I sat down again.

They did not.

This was an exciting moment, the primary one of discovery. In finding this documentation in the military papers, I knew I'd stumbled on something real about *Gatsby*. Such literary-historical discoveries, though, again, involving no obvious stakes in the larger world, are nonetheless exceedingly rare events. Fitzgerald's seemingly throwaway line about Gatsby making captain stateside apparently wasn't offhand after all.

I had my hands in the file cabinet again. I pushed Lazarus aside, who had her snout in there, curious about what I was doing and no doubt still hoping this was all some sort of new and elaborate preparation for a walk.

What I now knew was that Fitzgerald wasn't the only person ever to refer to the promotion of someone to captain before hitting the front. It was something US military leaders during World War I had given some real thought to—and put into practice. I didn't know what it all meant, but that wasn't the point. The point was that there was undeniably an "intertextual" connection, to use the lingo of my profession.

In a matter of minutes—due to the bizarre coincidence that I had a cache of military papers in our living room—I'd affirmed this mystery, and taken my first steps to cracking it.

Unless I was in the grip of new delusions. I stopped digging in the drawer. After all, the idea that somebody like German American Gatsby could have benefited from the intelligence tests went counter to everything I "knew" about them.

Everything I'd read about the intelligence tests had told me not only that they were biased against ethnic Americans and African Americans (so someone like Gatsby wouldn't have scored well) but that the military hadn't really made much use of them (so it wouldn't have promoted anybody even partly on their basis). All the commentators said they were a huge but fairly useless experiment for the army, coming to mean something only after the war, when the psychologists who managed the testing amassed the data and notoriously concluded that "Nordics" (northern Europeans) had more intelligence than members of other "races"—and white supremacists successfully argued that these "Others" should be kept out of the United States in order to safeguard the national intelligence. The result in 1921 was the first restriction of European immigration in the history of the country—the Chinese had been banned in 1882—and essentially the end of immigration from southern and eastern Europe until the 1960s. (The psychologists also concluded there were a lot more "feebleminded" or "idiots, imbeciles, and morons" in the population than anyone had imagined and, moreover, that the average mental age of American male adults was thirteen.)

But, I thought, pacing the small room again—and this was a potentially big "but"—if poor, ethnic Americans like Gatsby in some cases actually benefited from the tests, then I really had discovered something.

I almost tripped over Quilty. I decided to give the dogs treats to get them off my back. Anyway, it was a special moment, and they ought to participate in the happiness. I wouldn't tell Beth, who didn't want to encourage them to beg.

But I picked up my cell phone. I wanted to tell her immediately about my find. Here was the seed of something historically revisionary about the use of the intelligence tests in the selection of an officers' corps in World War I, most likely something important about *Gatsby*, and maybe something big about Lost Generation literature in general. I had something real.

PART III

FEAR AND DOUBTING

For several days he was as good as dead.... As a means of variation from a normal type, sickness in childhood ought ... not to be classed under any fitness or unfitness of natural selection.... The habit of doubt; of distrusting his own judgment and of totally rejecting the judgment of the world; the tendency to regard every question as open; the hesitation to act except as a choice of evils; the shirking of responsibility; the love of line, form, quality; the horror of ennui; the passion for companionship and the antipathy to society ... [these qualities] seemed to be stimulated by the fever, and Henry Adams could never make up his mind whether, on the whole, the change of character was morbid or healthy.... His brothers were the type; he was the variation.

—The Education of Henry Adams

CHAPTER 12

The Spleen of Tennis

I felt a ball whiz by my ear as I walked back from putting away a volley at net. The guy I was playing had slammed the fuzzy yellow thing just past my head. I spun back around.

"Sorry," he mumbled, but I was ticked off. I picked up the ball, which had rolled back to me after hitting the back curtain, and hit it back to his side.

He scooped it up and swatted it back to mine.

I did the same.

Again, it came back.

So we were driving the ball, back and forth, at each other, quite hard. It was surreal but oddly cathartic. I felt better. I smashed it right at him, and he had to jump out of the way.

Suddenly, my opponent threw down his racket and declared he was leaving. He strode toward the net, hurling words now, not balls. He said some unkind and jumbled things about me—

"You take too much time between games."

"You don't hold the third ball for me when I'm serving."

"Your hair is too long."

"You have a weird backhand."

Then he snatched up his bags and huffily started to walk out. "I don't know what your problem is," he said, blaming me entirely for the incident he'd certainly participated in and definitely started (at least I thought he did).

At which point I said, "I'm sorry." For what I wasn't sure.

So my partner didn't walk out, and our rivalry continued.

It was late January. My sabbatical had just started, and while my research was thankfully developing, my tennis game wasn't. At first it had seemed symbiotically linked to my research, but then it had stalled. And if it was going to develop further, if I was going to play USTA tournaments within the time frame I'd set, without humiliating myself, I had to find a way past what turned out to be a couple of stumbling blocks.

Theodore, who'd hit the ball at my head, was a supercompetitive and angry middle-aged man. I was drawn to him because I was at the moment another such man. I was runner-up to Theodore in that first tournament I entered, earning a trophy. Bigger than me and more experienced, he beat me in the finals in three sets. Thus our tennis acquaintance and rivalry was innocently—and ominously—formed. One thing I learned very quickly about adult men in amateur sports is that their ideal adversary is someone they can regularly win against, but not in a blowout. Guys in competitive sports want some competition, but most of all they want to win.

I was willing to put up with losing because I wanted to play someone who was better than me so I could improve. It's the only way.

Theodore was at the moment the perfect opponent for me in terms of his ability. As a person, he was irritating from the start, an awful partner, but, angry as I was, I was not only seeking out bad partners but was one myself, as Theodore sort of articulated after our mad volley.

Theodore was an irritatingly normal-minded person, despite his own interesting abnormalities. When we first arrived at the courts and during changeovers between games, especially when he was behind, he often had a mildly disparaging remark to make about my person or behavior, about anything the slightest bit out of the ordinary.

For instance, though his hair was quite a bit longer than mine, he often made cracks about the fact that I had long hair. When he was losing, Theodore would find all sorts of things in my behavior to mock: my diligence in removing stray balls from the court or the fact that I wore a glove. In the manner of a wounded animal fending for its life, he would pounce on any sign of weakness whatsoever. Like my having my back turned.

One of the reasons I had potential for improvement was that I started out so lousy in so many ways. Not only was I out of shape for singles, but my habits as a competitor were drastically self-defeating. The first mental block I faced was that no matter how freely I could hit away while practicing, as soon as I started playing a match, I froze up and played with all the caution of someone defusing an explosive device. The second was something I couldn't even recognize until I'd begun to make headway with the first.

Years of playing sports with the wrong attitude had handicapped me. When I started playing singles, this handicap was even more obvious than when I'd been playing doubles. In doubles, you can place a lot of blame on your partner for whatever goes wrong, which is one reason doubles is so much more pleasant. Even when you make bad shots in doubles, it's easy to feel that your partner is still partly, if not wholly, to blame. But in singles it's hard to blame your partner since you don't have one. You can blame your opponent, and I guess that's why opponents can easily become hostile when losing.

During match play, I was so afraid of making a mistake that I "pushed" the ball rather than struck it with force. If I could have, I'd have walked the ball over the net while holding its hand.

It was obvious what I needed to do. I told myself at the start of every match not to behave like a prissy little boy but instead to play with all the freedom of my tennis avatar, Serena. But I stubbornly refused. It was as if I was trying to pedal a bicycle while simultaneously squeezing the hand brakes as hard as I could.

Theodore being himself didn't help matters. He was the kind of guy who took an unmistakable glee in his opponent's mistakes. After a wild shot of mine, he might smile or giggle or even double over with laughter, fall to the ground, and scream with joy.

Though I wanted to blame Theodore for the entirety of my problem, I honestly couldn't. So I decided to blame my older brother.

I was, for most of my childhood, a small boy, and my brother was a big boy—not just relative to each other, but for our ages. Apparently, instead of keeping in mind that my brother could crush me at everything because he was older and bigger, I seemed to conclude that the best I could do in any game was to prolong the experience of defeat.

My perception of myself should have readjusted when I started playing organized sports with kids my own age. I should have been excited to make the Little League all-star team each year and to make captain of my suburb's Junior Davis Cup team for boys twelve and under. But I wasn't, and my sense of myself didn't recalibrate. The mere presence of my older brother had destroyed my psyche—and as older brothers went, he was pretty decent, maybe one of the best.

I considered these achievements in Little League and Junior Davis Cup to be unworthy of remembering. I concluded this because I had no memory of them, which sounds healthy—especially when you read, for example, Jack Kerouac's *Vanity of Duluoz*, written just before his death, and are appalled to see that he recalls the specifics of all his junior high football games from more than thirty years before, even the touchdown runs he made that were called back because of a penalty, and believes other people are walking around badmouthing his middle school sports performances half a lifetime later. But completely forgetting everything positive isn't particularly healthy either.

Around this time, I happened to run into a guy I was very close to in elementary school, who was brilliant but somewhat uncoordinated as a kid and had grown up to be a lawyer and an author. I was in my tennis gear. He started to reminisce about a time my Little League teammates had supposedly carried me on their shoulders after I pitched a shutout. I couldn't remember any such occurrence and figured he was making it up to mock my meager sports ability thirty-five years later—much, I realize, as Jack Kerouac in *Vanity of Duluoz*.

He insisted it really happened. I told him to give it a rest. But he wouldn't let it go, then he started describing particulars of the event.

Even if it had happened, how would he know all these details? He wouldn't have been there because he wasn't in my league. What was wrong with this guy? I wondered. I started to get irritated. "Listen, you successful lawyer/author," I was on the verge of saying, "I may not have been any good, but you could barely throw—"

But just as I was about to savage him, I started to remember being carried on the shoulders of my teammates after pitching a shutout.

This admirable fellow knew all the details because, as my friend, he'd come to watch my game—something else I'd had no recollection of and more understandably couldn't remember. But was it natural to completely forget what he called a "Hollywood moment" in my own sports past—no matter how small I was and how short all the other players were, compared to my brother? I'd forgotten about it so completely it was like I'd repressed it. As if at the time I'd considered it embarrassing to be celebrating a puny achievement in such an overblown manner.

Evidently because of my older brother—whose primariness I was beginning to believe had blighted my experience with sports—I hadn't had much confidence in my athletic abilities as a kid. And since I'd stopped playing sports back then, I'd taken that lack of confidence fully preserved into adulthood.

My parents had never told me I was good at sports. Actually, my mother did once say that she thought I was "a natural" at every game I took up and more talented athletically than my brother, but for some reason she didn't mention it until I'd graduated high school and finished with competitive sports.

Plenty of psychologists now know that middle children like me are screwed, as "family-systems theory" predicts. Shakespeare, who compulsively wrote about sibling rivalry, and whose plays are full of evil bastard half brothers and evil legitimate full brothers and sisters, could have provided any number of apt names for such a complex: the Claudius Complex (Claudius who murders his brother, Hamlet's father), the Edmund Complex (the crazy, homicidal bastard brother in *King Lear*), the Regan and Goneril Complex (*Lear* again), the Don John Complex (*Much Ado about Nothing*), or the Macbeth Complex (he doesn't kill his brother, because he doesn't seem to have one, but he kills his best friend and every other actual and potential rival he can identify and get his hands on).

I realized now that when I almost died from illness at eight, though it wasn't exactly to have something my brother didn't, including some much-needed parental attention in a private setting of quarantine, it was because he was one of the things making my life not worth living. Thanks to my encounter with my kind childhood friend who once saw me lifted into the air by my teammates, I also now remembered what had made me vulnerable to the Hong Kong flu—and how my brother and the rest of my family nearly drove me into an early grave.

CHAPTER 13

Early-Life Crisis, 1968, Age Eight

At the beginning of third grade, I came home from school and said to my mother, "I have to prove myself all over again. I see how it's going to be. Each year I'm going to have to start over with a new teacher who doesn't know anything about me, except that I'm Neil's younger brother."

My mother nodded, smiled weakly, and went on with whatever she was doing.

A few weeks later, this drabness, wastefulness, and "secondariness" inherent in my world, and my apparent powerlessness to do anything about them, were the least of my problems. School was far away, as was my brother. I was hospitalized with one of the first cases of a new Asian flu that local doctors hadn't seen before and didn't know how to treat.[1]

Or so I gathered through the haze of my profound sickness, as I was given test after invasive test, seen by physician after gray-haired physician, prodded with stethoscopes and needles, and treated with this and that medicine to no effect. I even underwent a spinal tap, during which a burly nurse held me with an iron, suffocating grip since any movement on my part was dangerous. All this was new to me, and very unpleasant. I would have the odd cold or headache, but I'd rarely missed a day of school and had never stayed overnight in a hospital. Now I'd taken up permanent residence.

---

1. This pandemic of 1968–69 originated in Hong Kong in July 1968; it reached the United States in September, which is when I got it. It didn't become widespread in the United States until December 1968. A vaccine was developed a month after that.

So had my mother, essentially. I didn't have my own room, but rather a cubicle separated from the other "cases" by green vinyl curtains. They allowed my mother to bring a rocking chair into the space, where she slept the night. While they kept me under observation, they housed me in the pediatric wing, seemingly among kids with chronic or incurable conditions.

I had a high fever. I was so dizzy I couldn't even sit up. I had to be helped to the bathroom because my equilibrium was gone. I threw up a lot. I tried to learn how to swallow pills, which was also new to me, and I mostly gagged and vomited some more.

Since I wasn't getting better over days and then weeks, despite the near constant medical attention, I concluded I was going to die. Oddly enough, this didn't bother me much. I was inexplicably stoical.

And I felt I needed to keep my mother in the dark. Though she was often by my bedside in the room at night, I didn't share my knowledge of my impending death with her because I figured it would bother her tremendously.

I wasn't too far wrong about the mortal danger I was in,[2] though I was about protecting her. Years later, at my high school graduation, when she confided in me that I was good at sports, she also told me she'd indeed been terrified I was going to die.

I wasn't a particularly tough kid at age eight. My mother's being around in my hospital cubicle probably gave me confidence—and maybe even a budding sense of personal worth I wasn't sure I had. But something more was at work.

The only possible explanation for my strangely detached attitude was that I was depressed. I was undergoing my first severe episode at the age of eight. I don't mean I was depressed over my perhaps mortal sickness. I mean I was sick to begin with, as well as indifferent to death, because of depression. The flu was an effect of my depression. Okay, the virus came from Asia, brought by troops returning via California from Vietnam, which turned out to be as close as I would get to the war both

---

2. The flu killed one to four million people worldwide and over thirty-three thousand children in the United States, about one out of every two hundred who came down with it.

fought and despised by men barely older than me. But I had caught the flu because my depression had managed to perilously lower my immune system—that's why my brother and sister didn't get it.

No one thought so at the time, least of all me. It was 1968, and traditional Western medicine, which treated the body as a machine and was untroubled by thoughts of a mind-body connection, was at its apogee. No doctor would have thought to ask my mother if a traumatic event had happened at home just before I became ill. A divorce, a death in the family, a parent losing a job? And if there hadn't been a traumatic spike in our family, was there instead a smooth, ongoing decline: a depressed parent, perhaps?

There would have been pay dirt there—as there continues to be now, quite literally, in a psychobabble industry that has exploited these realities. My mother was five years into a decade-long clinical depression, which caused her to treat almost everything fatalistically and hopelessly, and which would only let up a bit five more years down the line with the three of us kids getting less helpless, as well as her divorce from our father, and her remarriage. But her depression and anxiety would never really go away. It was a lifelong inheritance, which had profound roots in our family's recent Jewish-immigrant past and the long history of the subjugation of women.

She and I were close, too close—that, too, was an aspect of our dysfunctional family. It was a couple decades later, then experiencing my second major illness, that a practitioner of "combat" therapy would tell me that my mother had imposed an "emotional incest" on me. A phrase meant to shock me into some much-needed self-understanding, it did its work. Distant from my father, who was rarely home, working long hours to hold on to a job he disliked but didn't have the will to leave, my mother relied emotionally on her children, perhaps especially me because at the age of eight I already said things that mimicked her state of mind. I'd definitely picked up her fatalistic sensibility, and I was all prepared to slip into listlessness, sickness, and death when I glimpsed the nature of grade school segmentation.

But maybe my decline had really started during the previous summer, which saw riots at the Democratic Convention in Chicago. My parents had sent me to an inexpensive sleepaway camp. Day one, when I was out of the cabin, a bigger kid requisitioned the upper bunk I'd staked out. I told the counselors, but they didn't care.

When I later read *The Lord of the Flies*, I found it clichéd. I already knew it all. Sure, in our neighborhood streets, might made right among the boys, but a crucial rule was that you didn't mess with someone smaller than you. If you did, you'd better get ready to be confronted by that kid's big brother, or cousin, or friend, who would inform you, as part of the required protocol before he kicked the shit out of you, "Pick on someone your own size." I had my brother looking out for me, as well as kids named Billy, Don, and Sergio, all three years older. Billy and Don were strong; Sergio, though smaller, was truly terrifying, and I called him the Tasmanian devil, though not to his face. Here I was on my own.

I cried for maybe six hours straight. Though I didn't have the words to explain why, I wrote my parents trying to ask them to take me out of this horrible place. They wrongly concluded I was homesick so didn't.

Then I dried my eyes and adapted. Even in this wilderness, sports mattered. During an elaborate capture the flag game, our counselor gave me the honor of being the one to swim across a leech-infested swamp in a daring backdoor assault. Then a very bad thing happened. One day I smashed a kid's full dinner tray into his chest. I didn't know why. Maybe I did it to prove I was tough. Maybe it was just because his weakness enraged me. When my parents came to pick me up at the end of camp, I didn't even look up from the card game I was in. After a week or so in this dump, I was ready to stay on.

I never told anyone about what I'd done. It hadn't upset me at the time, but, home now, it was too ugly and shameful. I'd bullied a defenseless boy knowing there would be no consequences. Maybe entering third grade and understanding I had to prove myself again and life would go on like this, without meaning, and with the occasional violent act perpetrated by me: it evidently triggered something deep and horrible in my psyche.

Perhaps if my mother had been able to sense my precocious despair on the first day of third grade and had taken a few minutes to talk to me, I never would have gotten so ill to begin with. I could then have settled on a mild cold or a short-lived rash. Maybe all she needed to do was laugh and say to me, "Listen, buster, nice observation, but let's keep things in perspective here, shall we? Sure, it's a drag to have to prove yourself again each new school year, but I'll lay odds you'll manage that seemingly herculean task in about a week. Look, grade school may seem endless now, but it's over soon enough. In high school, you'll start to build a permanent record. Then you'll go off to college, and the sky's the limit. No one will know or care that you're someone's younger brother. Now, thanks for telling me, give mommy a hug, eat some candy, go out and play, and don't worry so much, you little devil."

But my mother was no more capable of such an empathetic, upbeat, confident exchange than she was of turning lead into gold. She didn't believe the things I've just imagined her saying because they bore no relation to her own experience or my father's. Though my brother and I got straight As every year in elementary school, our parents never complimented us on it, let alone rewarded each good grade with small sums of cash, as happened with some kids we knew. "We expect nothing less" is what our mother would say when she saw our perfect report cards, but she never told me what excelling could mean in the long run for me. She didn't talk to me about my "limitless" future because she didn't believe I had one.

That was probably because she didn't see any future for herself outside of exactly what she was doing then. It would always be for her the same city and the same job—it always had been. When she was little, she'd gotten excellent grades as well. But it hadn't meant much—though she'd wanted to be a doctor, as she later told me—because it had been the 1930s, and she was a girl. In the late 1940s, when she graduated high school, on top of the fact that she was female and "you didn't send girls to medical school," there were Jewish quotas at medical schools. (First contemplated during World War I by academic guardians of Anglo privilege—I was learning about them in my research—the quotas were instituted in the 1920s and weren't done away with until the 1950s.)

My mother probably wasn't aware that a meritocratic revolution had recently taken place at American colleges, universities, and medical schools because she'd been busy working as a teacher and raising us. My father drove a delivery truck for the Home Juice Company.

It may have been 1968—free love, rising feminism, and insurrection in the streets—but my parents were still living in the spooked 1930s and

1940s, when they had been children and sometimes gone hungry, anti-Semitism swelled to a crescendo, and our relatives told my mom's father he was stupidly wasting his money sending her to college.

A generation earlier, in the waning era of the Wild West, my mother's mother's mother, "a pretty Jewess," as the local paper referred to her on the occasion of her murder, had been raped and strangled one dark night in the family store in Trinidad, Colorado, in 1910. The killer got away with it, and my grandmother's father died a few months later of tuberculosis and a broken heart, leaving four female children who would grow up in the only Jewish orphanage in the country at the time that would take them, in Cleveland, Ohio.

My mother's mother, the grandmother I loved—a lifelong manic-depressive who would mysteriously disappear from our lives from time to time to get hospitalization and shock treatments—believed she carried the "shameful secret" of her mother's murder to her grave in 1993 at the age of ninety, but my mother had actually learned about it some forty years before from one of her aunts, who later committed suicide, and she herself had been keeping it secret ever since. In the end, two of the four orphaned girls had killed themselves.

When I was young, the family was no longer poor; it was lower middle class, but it was spiritually defeated and, thanks to the Protestant-Enlightenment roots of the country at large and thus the taboo on psychological understanding, intellectually impoverished. My brother put it to me succinctly and rather out of the blue one day when we were adults: "Our parents couldn't extend themselves to us very much," he said. "They barely kept it together moment to moment and needed all their limited resources simply to get through the day."

I was released from the hospital uncured and unable to return to school. There was some medicine I could take that actually allowed me to keep my head up for a little while. The doctors had more or less thrown up their hands, but I was apparently no longer contagious. I wouldn't infect my siblings. I might as well be at home where I could be more comfortable and maybe die in familiar surroundings.

Also, my mother needed a good night's sleep after so many nights in a rocking chair. We had the doctor's number and were to report in. I had the green light to return to school if I ever again felt up to it.

I came home in my mother's arms, like a broken toy, temporarily paralyzed due to a botched exit spinal tap, where the nurse had been too gentle. When that wore off, my intense nausea meant I still couldn't take the stairs on my own. So the room I shared with my brother, on the second floor, was now out of reach. No doubt my brother was relieved. Contagious or not, I had the smell of quarantine on me, and I obviously wasn't better. He didn't need a roommate who was going to moan and groan throughout the night, would maybe throw up on him, and might be a corpse in the morning.

I took up residence on the convertible couch, which was in the living room. My grandmother, who generally stayed over one night on the weekend, was the only one who ever slept on it. She called it a "davenport," a word I'd never heard spoken by another human being. But then she had a lot of strange words in her vocabulary. It was from her that I learned the word "gentile"—as in, "He's a nice gentile boy, but in general gentiles aren't nice and can't be trusted." It was one of the weekly pleasures of our little household for us children to join our grandmother in the davenport bed on a Sunday morning and get a hug (when she wasn't in the mental hospital). That first day back my brother stared at me with overlarge eyes and kept a superstitious distance. Perhaps he was also surprised to see me still alive.

My mother's presence in the hospital and the validation it implied had probably kept me from dying outright. And maybe it was also good for me that I wasn't rooming with my brother for the moment. But if I was ever to get up and regain my equilibrium so I could walk again, I needed somehow to break the debilitating spell that his primariness and my mother's listlessness had cast over me by having colonized and discolored every inch of the known world before I could get to it.

Only I couldn't for the life of me remember how that spell was lifted and I'd recovered.

CHAPTER 14

Scholarship Lessons, 1983

WEDNESDAYS WITH MICHEL (FOUCAULT)

These military papers were the documents I'd collected at the National Archives back in the late spring of 1984, just before Foucault died. Why I'd held on to them deserves an explanation.

For had I not stubbornly kept these papers for two decades, packing them up and carrying them with me each time I'd moved house—and I'd moved plenty, at least a dozen times, and each time I'd moved, especially in the last dozen years, I asked myself if it wasn't time to throw this useless shit away—I might have let this line of inquiry go.

I'd like to imagine that I doggedly held on to these papers because I understood their special value: that they documented a story not available in any published book. But I didn't know that because I basically knew nothing about the recorded history of the US military. The papers also seemed to me trivial and uninteresting. Who the hell could care what personnel devices the US Army developed to identify captains in the training camps during World War I?

No, I'd held on to these papers through the years simply because I held on to just about everything: I was merely lucky in this case that I was a pack rat. I also held on to threadbare socks and old tennis shoes with no tread. You never knew when you might need a ragged pair of shoes, for some really dirty job—like house painting, laying sod, washing windows, hanging drywall, putting up wallpaper, pouring concrete, breaking up pavement with a sledge hammer, building a wall out of rocks, moving boxes, or cleaning out an office—the kind of tasks I now, as a middle-aged adult, tried to avoid at all costs, having done them as a kid and young adult.

In early February, Beth quite reasonably demanded that I throw away some half dozen pairs of crappy tennis shoes I no longer wore, which were cluttering up the front hall—one of the minor but more expensive side effects of taking up tennis was that I went through shoes at an alarming rate.

I'd probably developed this habit as a kid growing up in a family where I didn't have a lot of possessions and started working as a paper boy at age seven to augment the meager set I had. Naturally, I was still in possession of—and was able to show Beth one wintry day when UIC shut down and the blizzard also meant I couldn't drive to the indoor courts—my favorite stuffed animal from childhood: a cat, which my grandmother, who'd been handy with a needle and thread, mended for me several times and once "overhauled" by enveloping, with the help of huge safety pins, the whole radically decaying object in a striped athletic sock of my father's. When I showed it to Beth, who couldn't help laughing, I was kind of appalled. It was so grievously battered and also so grievously repaired that it gave the impression I'd lived through some horrific conflict or grown up in the nineteenth century.

My being a pack rat couldn't have grown simply out of my having been raised in modest circumstances. My older brother grew up in the same household and was the opposite of a pack rat. He was so eager to get rid of things, presumably for the sake of order, that when my mother finally sold the house we grew up in, he threw or gave away our best toys from childhood, which I'd otherwise still have: All-Star Baseball and Hot Wheels.

There is another factor in my pack-rattery; it is philosophic, or perhaps neurotic. To put it philosophically, how could one know what was valuable and what was not until much later? Neurotically speaking, I often couldn't distinguish between what was valuable and what was not, just as I often couldn't tell the difference between what I should and shouldn't do, and what I liked and didn't like to do.

I contend that being a pack rat is actually a somewhat unpleasant manifestation of a fundamental openness to personal and intellectual discovery and change. And I submit, even though I don't quite believe it, that only closed, static, or dogmatic people can be super tidy. That may not be a fair characterization, but I'd like to hold on to it.

When Michel Foucault, back in 1984, had invited me—along with two other Berkeley students—to write a book with him, it seemed hard to believe. But it had become a little bit easier to understand now that I was closer to Foucault's age at that time (around fifty-six) than to my own age at that time (twenty-three)—once you took into account that he was gay and liked to be around young men whether he was sleeping with them or not.

How I met Foucault and came to be a member of his circle in California wasn't at all dramatic—though the academic scene in Berkeley at that moment was pretty hepped up, which is important to understand for putting this encounter in context. When I was about to graduate from college and was accepted to Berkeley for grad school, I received a call from Stephen Greenblatt encouraging me to enroll there. This, too, is hard to believe. But the late 1970s and early 1980s were a different time, economically and academically (though not a minority student, I'd been able to attend an elite undergraduate college as a scholarship kid), and Greenblatt was not yet really famous within academia, though he was a rising force in a profession that was undergoing a sea change. The baby boomers were coming into power and reimagining the humanities with all the confidence of a generation that had successfully stood up to the government with the antiwar movement.

One of Greenblatt's enticements to me for coming to Berkeley was that Foucault was going to be there. That convinced me to go, along with the university's reputation, a scholarship offer, and probably most of all, the climate. (I'd grown up in Cleveland and gone to college in New England, which I came to consider a naive person's mistake, on meteorological grounds.)

The sense of headiness at that time within humanities departments at Berkeley is hard to recreate. A mere shadow of the sixties movement, the "poststructuralist" academic revolution of the early eighties was still a powerful aftershock of the Vietnam-era quake. Arriving in Berkeley in 1982 from little Amherst College in western Massachusetts, I felt like I'd gone through a time warp, into a brave new future I could barely understand.

I explained Foucault's importance to my father by saying he was kind of like an Einstein for the humanities. A sort of Copernican figure, he'd said that power, which we were used to thinking of as basically prohibitory—as saying "no" to specific acts, like murder and theft and coveting your neighbor's wife, but otherwise leaving us alone—actually worked mostly by positive means and nowadays almost never left us alone, even when it came to the most private issues. According to Foucault, power encouraged us, through norms, to observe certain mores and even to think of ourselves in our most intimate moments in particular ways. Say to identify ourselves in terms of our gender, our race, our religion, our sexuality, our health, our aptitudes, and so on.

The poststructuralist "discovery" was that everything in the world—*everything*—was "socially constructed," to use the parlance of the day. Which is to say, everything finally had a social cause and there was in reality no other kind of causality. There was (perhaps, who knew?) no reality either because "reality" itself was something constructed by culture, by society, by the things people routinely said and wrote—in short, by "discourse," at that moment the most important word ever invented.

That sounds rather abstract, and no doubt the abstraction was a big part of what was so thrilling. It's easy to understand why such a theory, which had its origins in the contemporary French philosophy of Foucault and also Roland Barthes, Jacques Derrida, Jacques Lacan, and Gilles Deleuze, would appeal to the baby boomers who'd already had so much success in transforming the social reality they grew up in.

The giddiness of this intellectual moment was probably best brought home to me at a memorial service for one of the professors in the English department, a young, brilliant Shakespeare scholar named Joel Fineman, whom I really liked and who suddenly died a few years into my studies.

This was like no other memorial service I'd ever attended or been to since. How can I put this? As one English professor after another got up to eulogize Fineman, in the dazzling rhetoric of the poststructuralist revolution, I began to wonder, on the basis of their bold and fascinating remarks I couldn't entirely comprehend, whether he was *really* dead—

whether, in fact, there was such a thing as death. I knew he'd died of throat cancer[1] and was buried in the ground, and I was very sad about that, but what issued from the throats of the living that day at the podium seemed to make out that what had happened to him—that is, his dying—was fundamentally rhetorical or discursive in nature. It seemed altogether possible, and a small part of me was almost hoping, that on the way out of the auditorium Fineman—the physical Fineman—was going to thank me for coming and shake my hand.

This intellectual excitement bordering on hysteria was the backdrop for my encounter with Foucault. When he was scheduled to give his inaugural talk on campus, I went to Zellerbach Auditorium, which was overflowing. After the standing-room-only lecture, and despite the fact that there were two thousand people in the audience, I was determined to introduce myself immediately, seeing as how, along with the weather, he was one of the main reasons I'd come out to Berkeley. I couldn't balk here—even if I had to hang around for an hour. I made my way down the stairs, against the flow of the mass.

It turned out that only three of us stayed to talk to him after the throng filed out and disappeared. I waited my turn, until it was just the two of us in this gigantic auditorium. I told him, calling up to the stage from below, that I had some questions I'd like to ask him at some point about his work if he had time. He had a shaved head, no hair at all. I had no idea what he would say.

The following Wednesday I was outside his office at two o'clock sharp. There was no line of students at the door, as I'd been expecting. I had a ruled page of questions in my notebook. In my hand. Yes, I was ready. The other hand was free but was not acting as planned.

"Okay, come on," I told myself.

I knocked. He opened the door. No one was meeting with him. It seemed unbelievable. Here was Michel Foucault, for my money the greatest living thinker. But there he was, this intellectual colossus, in Dwinelle Hall on the Berkeley campus, alone, like the Maytag repairman.

---

1. The *New York Times* obituary reported the cause of death as colon cancer. So either the throat cancer was a polite lie, or more likely the *Times* writer got it wrong because s/he didn't know Fineman personally and got information secondhand.

"Come in," he said. He was dressed in exactly the same clothes he'd worn for the lecture, a light-colored striped polo shirt and a shiny, sky blue polyester suit jacket. We sat down across from each other, and I opened my notebook.

"I have some questions," I said awkwardly.

"I see that," he said, looking down at the page in my hands, and smiling. "Go ahead."

So I did.

After that first day, I continued to go with a carefully written-out set of questions every week for the entire semester. One Wednesday I asked, "*Discipline and Punish* ends up off the subject of discipline. You write instead about the creation of a criminal underclass. Why?" He continued to wear the same outfit. His answer to my question was something like this:

> Everyone would agree the prison has failed to produce the reformed inmate who has internalized the aim of the institution, become disciplined and self-monitoring, and prepared to re-enter the work world. And, meanwhile, the punishment continues after the prisoner has served his time; he finds himself branded as an ex-convict and unable to get any but the most menial job. So why does the prison system persist? Because in practice it still functions in a way that is socially useful: to create a permanent class of criminals who are excluded from the mainstream—subject to police and parole surveillance and often a return to prison.
>
> We know what we say we are going to do; we know what we do in fact, · but we rarely are aware of what our doing does. And that unintended strategy is the ultimate stake of the analysis.

Occasionally, another student would show up. But Foucault was patient with me and answered my very specific queries about his work, and his intellectual method, in great detail—as if he weren't pressed for time.

What I was discovering, to my fascination, was that in spite of his being a "poststructuralist," one of the founders of the movement at that, I could understand Foucault, follow him better than I did some of my regular Berkeley professors. Despite his genius and his thick accent, he was much more down to earth, grounded in history, and logical and rigorous in his thinking. I came also to understand that there were different camps of poststructuralism: Foucault was not a "deconstructionist" like Derrida or Stanley Fish, who thought (or pretended to think) everything was rhetorically or socially constructed. For Foucault, there *were* "prediscursive" realities—for example, the physical world described by physics, the hard sciences—but you had to be more circumspect with the assertions of the "soft" or "human sciences" like medicine and psychology, because here could enter cultural biases and thus supposed truths that weren't the result of the scientific method. For example, psychiatry's longtime claim that homosexuality was a sickness. As someone trained in physics and math, I expected this grounding. I was back on planet earth.

Moreover, Foucault wasn't the deductive thinker he'd been cracked up to be—supposedly important for his surprising characterizations of Western culture as a whole as "a disciplinary society," which increasingly subjected people to normalizing surveillance. Rather, he was an inductive thinker who rejected all deductive approaches, including the new deconstruction and the older Marxism.

Coming from science, which since the Scientific Revolution of the sixteenth century has proceeded by induction, I had serious problems with deductive thinking, which was in my view literally medieval. Literary study seemed to me to proceed much like the Scholasticism of Thomas Aquinas back in the 1200s: you applied unproven theories; you cited ordained authorities, and you made connections based on metaphorical similarities between literary devices and operations in the real world. It was like magical thinking to me: Hogwarts with only theoretical courses—no wands.

After two quarters at Berkeley, I was feeling alternatively bored and baffled by the stuff. I'd wondered if I should drop out. Foucault's inductive approach was a big breath of fresh air.

It was amazing, surreal really, talking to Foucault once a week: a repeating version of the classic scene from *Annie Hall* where the cocksure intellectual guy is spouting off in a movie-ticket line about Marshall McLuhan, and Woody Allen's character gets irritated then finally fed up and turns and says, "Well, I happen to have Mr. McLuhan right here," and then he drags the famous media theorist into the camera shot, who says to the man, "You know nothing of my work."

In this instance, I was both the Woody character and the blowhard rolled into one. Not because I was a blowhard (not yet, anyway) but because I'd already internalized, in the course of spending two terms in the hermetic intellectual atmosphere of poststructuralist Berkeley, the more or less full collection of "received ideas" that were circulating about his work. But now, well, I happened to have Mr. Foucault right there. The Woody character concludes the scene by saying, "If life were only like this!" For me, at that moment, it sort of was.

The more I talked to Foucault, the more I realized that no one had really used his later, induction-based work to devise a method of literary study.[2] And I thought, "Hey, maybe I can do this. Maybe I can achieve a true marriage of the literature and history disciplines in my own work."

---

2. This included the literature professors who called themselves New Historicists. Foucault presented an alternative to the New Historicism that Greenblatt was credited with inventing. It was sweeping through the Berkeley English Department like a brush fire. New Historicism was "new" because the previously dominant generation of critics, the New Critics (who had been, confusingly, once "new" as well) claimed to interpret literary texts in isolation, without recourse to historical context. (In practice, as far as I was concerned, this meant the New Critics could unwittingly, or purposefully, project their own concerns onto a text without any limitations, which would be imposed by knowing the historical context.) New Historicism put history back into literary study, which was needed, but it did so in the new style of poststructuralism. That was also needed, but New Historicism was often unconvincing to me because it too tended to work by deduction. So New Historicists, for example, argued that middle-class "hegemony" or disciplinary "society" or the "master discourse" of nativism resulted in such and such a literature. It was still a top-down, deductive analysis.

New Historicism as generally practiced was also, not incidentally as far as I was concerned, unconvincing to professors and students of history (whom I was getting to know at Berkeley thanks to Foucault's presence)—to them, it was deeply flawed in its methodology, unrecognizable really as history. Just to be clear, New Historicism was entirely a phenomenon of literature departments and didn't imply, by any means, an interdisciplinary cooperation between the literary and historical fields.

By the time I met him, Foucault, refreshingly, eschewed general terms like "society," "culture," and "master discourse" even though earlier in his career he hadn't. (And, to get rather specific, New Historicism, as far as I understood it, derived from an earlier work of his, *The Order of Things*, which he came to dislike—sensibly I thought, as I found it bewildering—and even asked his publisher to stop printing. The most important of his later work were the books *Discipline and Punish* and *The History of Sexuality, Volume I: An Introduction*.) There were, according to him in 1983, various discourses, institutions, and social agents that acted on one another. This was the kind of inductive analysis that I, as a kid trained in science, could embrace.

Meanwhile, Foucault needed students to come to him, since he wasn't teaching. Also, he didn't really know anyone in California very well: he was spending most of his time in the university library doing research (as he told me) or in the all-male bathhouses and clubs in San Francisco (something I put together later when I learned he'd died of AIDS). He found things wonderfully strange here. One day I ran into him coming out of the library with a big smile on his face. "It's amazing," he said. "They let you take the book out for the entire weekend." Having one-on-one discussions with students was appealing to him because it was also different: at his French university, his lectures were open to the public and always crowded. He didn't have seminars or office hours there. I was, simply, the first student to show up.

I was also young and boyish-looking. On the day of that blizzard that shut down the city, I showed Beth a picture of me and a bunch of other grad students in my dining room with Foucault wearing an American cowboy hat we'd given him, which made its way into one of his biographies. "Jesus," she said, "you look like you're fifteen."

The book idea Foucault proposed was to write about "the New Man of the 1920s" (I took "man" here to mean something like "human"). He also referred to it as a book about "new arts of government in the postwar era in France, the USSR, Italy, and the US." Foucault would take France; the other Berkeley grad students studied the early Soviet Union and fascist Italy, and I, as an American literature student, was presumed, quite wrongly, to be familiar with post–World War I American history.

The New Man of the 1920s (and "woman," I added, mentally): this was tremendously exciting, fascinating stuff. Except I had no idea what it meant. Yes, it was easy to see that there was a "new man and woman" in the USSR because the Soviets talked about the new "communist man and woman." I figured it was more or less analogous for the Italian fascists. As for what this might mean in the United States, I had no clue.

I was hesitant to ask Foucault what he had in mind. Presumably he'd been interested in working with me partly because he thought I knew what we were talking about. I still could have asked him, in some clever way that didn't reveal the full weight of my ignorance—I guessed maybe he had a sense of the rise of the welfare state (social security, workers' compensation, managing the economy, and so on) and industrial organization (personnel management, industrial psychology, time-motion studies). But not only did these not exactly imply to me a new man; they also were quite boring. I didn't want to hear that he had *this* in mind, so I didn't ask. I preferred to walk around saying to myself, "the new man, the new man, the new man"—a thrilling but completely empty phrase. He may as well have sent me after the Holy Grail.

But, if I didn't know what Foucault was thinking, I knew how he worked and—after talking to him at least once a week for a semester—a bit about how he thought. I knew that, for starters, what he did was to go to archives and more or less take up residence in them.

All of which meant that, in anticipation of Foucault returning to Berkeley the following academic year, I was, if I could get a little funding, going to imitate him and go spend some serious time in the National Archives in order to look at the World War I military papers there. The US Army archive was my own idea; Foucault didn't tell me to study the wartime moment, and it was technically outside the purview of the book he'd suggested on the 1920s. But I figured the unprecedented and monumental task of mobilizing and "governing" a huge army had to be pretty revealing about "new arts of government" of the time, and was a good place to start, even if my dating was a little off. Yes, it was a gamble, but it seemed like a safe one.

My intention was to look at the less dramatic and little-or-not-at-all-known military records that had almost nothing to do with waging war but instead concerned organizing the army. It also meant that when I got to the Archives in Washington, I had only a broad idea of what I was looking for.

So I collected eclectically, anything and everything, especially to do with topics that had promising names, in terms of "a new man" or a new way of thinking about "men" (this was the army, so by "men" here I meant "men"): "personnel," "human resources," the "scientific utilization" of "manpower," that sort of bureaucratic thinking and speech that might have some relation, however oblique and uninteresting, to a new man.

All these years later, I'd discover that Hemingway had a passage in *Sun* parodying this military bureaucrat-speak, which—though I hated to find I agreed with Hemingway—I'd felt back then at twenty-three like mocking, too. When Jake and his pal Bill encounter another vet named Harris while on their fishing trip, they start talking about "utilizing" things not usually considered for their "utility," like the wine. The joke inheres in the mixture of religious and bureaucratic language. "Let us rejoice in our blessings," says Bill. "Let us utilize the fowls of the air. Let us utilize the product of the vine. Will you utilize a little, brother?"

My wild, almost indiscriminate, collecting of documents on the period of 1917–1919—I spent whole days really at the copy machine—made me a little nervous. I wondered what the hell I was doing. Would it really help to have a letter from Mr. Du Pont, stating that the army "tests [were] used in the qualification of army Captains"? I couldn't see how, but I copied it anyway. My research slogan at the time was "When in doubt, make a copy." And not quite knowing what I was looking for, I was always in doubt. My other slogan was "When almost certain the document is worthless, why not make a copy anyway?"

I had one clear aim for this research project. That was to spend all the money I'd been granted by the university. And even though I hadn't been given much, $800 went a longer way in 1984, especially as my lodging and meals, except lunch, were taken care of by an uncle living in DC. After transportation costs and money for a hot dog vendor on the Mall, I still had hundreds of dollars left for copies. Not paying for room and board also meant I was able to spend an unheard of amount of time in the Archives: around thirty days.

Back then in 1984, at age twenty-three, I had no life, or almost none. Certainly nothing that couldn't be suspended for a full month, or even years, with hardly anyone noticing or caring.

The upshot of all the tedious, time-consuming, spirit-draining, and nearly indiscriminate copying of documents, followed by many subsequent years of mindlessly hoarding, or perhaps open-mindedly holding on to, just about everything I acquired, no matter how many times I relocated and how little use I made of anything I came to possess, meant that more than twenty years later, Beth's filing cabinet was absolutely flush with military papers from the war. After the Archives itself, which had the original carbons, the largest collection of copies of personnel-related documents of the US Army during World War I was no doubt in our apartment.

In a weird, storybook way, it was as if I'd teamed up with a younger version of myself, having magically—retroactively, as if through time travel—assigned to that younger, novice, bright-eyed, "intern" self the

long mind-numbing days of grunt work I could in no way afford or toler-
ate doing now. It was as if I'd exploited this graduate student peon who'd
been myself. It may not be the case that we have our best ideas in our
twenties and thirties—and I'd definitely had some pretty bad ones then
much as I still do—but we certainly have in our young adulthood an
energy and blind enthusiasm almost completely untempered by knowledge of the world that we naturally lose as we get older. We are willing
to undertake titanic tasks because we have no idea how little will come
out of them.

Even if I was able as a forty-five-year-old to hide out in the Archives
for an ungodly stretch, I wouldn't have the patience or ignorant hope
necessary to sift through the reams of documents that I'd pored over
more than two decades before.

But there it all was, in front of me.

CHAPTER 15

Professional Blunder, Berkeley, 1986

It's a wonder I didn't throw away these military documents back in the mid-1980s when they caused me to almost flunk out of the PhD program, and helped sour my initially enthusiastic relationship to scholarship and my chosen career.

I didn't come to use the papers in the way I intended, in the project with Foucault. As a result of his dying so soon after my trip to the Archives, I never really found out what he imagined for the book. And I didn't even have the chance to embarrass myself by asking him if any of the hundreds of papers I'd collected were even relevant.

A year later, I went to Paris to do some research on him—again I had a little grant and a place to stay. Also, flights were cheap: demand was low because of recent terrorist bombings in France. You were met in Charles de Gaulle airport by military guards with machine guns.

I was going to learn details about Foucault's political involvements because I wanted to see if they bore out my sense of his thinking. I also thought maybe, just possibly, I might discover what he'd had in mind for the book. Though unlikely, perhaps there would be something in his apartment I could read. His longtime partner, Daniel Defert, had, upon meeting me on a visit to Berkeley and recognizing my name, suggested Foucault might have left something for me. He couldn't remember.

This research trip was a way to pay Foucault back for what he'd given me. (The article I was going to write, I understood, couldn't do much for my academic future. It was definitely irrelevant to my PhD in American literature.) I wanted to set the record straight, as he was often caricatured and dismissed. Ideally, I could use the facts of his political engagements to undergird my very different understanding of his intellectual work. I couldn't just claim by way of evidence, "Hey, no kidding, he told me this in Dwinelle Hall on the Berkeley campus on a Wednesday in March 1983."

Some people accused Foucault of being a nihilist because they took his message to be that we're always in the grips of "power," so there's nothing we can do. This struck me as nonsensical and childish: just because there was no utopian state of total freedom from all relations of power didn't mean that they were all equally bad. The point was to make things better and always be aware of dangers. There was also the fact of Foucault's plentiful activism. Why be politically involved if it's pointless? To humor his Marxist friends?

One of the "stars" to be interviewed on this trip, not only for my own research but for a newsletter some of us Berkeley students had founded to carry on Foucault's project, was the political figure Bani-Sadr. (It was newsletter money that was funding for my trip, and Foucault's French cronies were setting up the interviews.) The first president of the Islamic Republic of Iran, he'd served between 1980 and 1981, before he was impeached and Ayatollah Khomeini ordered him arrested on charges of conspiracy and treason, which was tantamount to a death sentence. He'd eventually fled the country and took refuge in France, where he was granted political asylum.

The interview was considered important to our newsletter because Foucault, who'd gone to Iran to document the developing revolution there, as well as met with Khomeini while he was still in exile in France, had been harshly criticized, as naive politically or worse, for the awe he'd expressed in the late 1970s for the Ayatollah's Islamist movement—before Iran rapidly devolved into a nightmare state. I found this confounding too.

I remember the day I discovered that Foucault, though a genius, wasn't infallible. We were talking about AIDS as we strolled through the streets of Berkeley back to the campus after having lunch at a Chinese restaurant on Shattuck Avenue. He told me he thought AIDS was a social construction: yes, people were getting sick, but, he explained, it wasn't all from the same cause: a variety of illnesses were being collected together under the rubric of a supposedly mysterious virus. He thought America, in its usual puritanical manner, had found a new, pseudoscientific way to strike out against gays, drug users, and Blacks. (At the beginning of the epidemic, only members of these groups were getting ill.) I thought, as we walked, that he was wrong on this one, which was a discomfiting experience for me.

For starters, French doctors, not just American ones, were making the discoveries about AIDS and what came to be called HIV. I told him I wasn't convinced: "But this is doctors, not psychiatrists, here." Physicians did lab work, used microscopes, looked at cells. To use his language, there seemed to be a "prediscursive" virus that researchers were trying to isolate, though, admittedly, they weren't sure they'd found it at this point.

In response, Foucault smiled his knowing smile: this was the guy who'd written a poststructuralist study called *The Birth of the Clinic*—about the social history of medical practice.

We dropped the subject. (I had yet to develop my own deep suspicion of doctors.)

But I could understand how Foucault was poised to be mistaken on this one. Fatally mistaken, as it horribly turned out. The issue was deeply personal to him as a gay man, and touched a nerve. Not only did he not want it to be true, but he'd already suffered growing up gay in a world that had long tended to "medicalize" same-sex preference as a mental disorder.

Foucault's enthusiasm for Khomeini's Islamist movement was less comprehensible to me. Christ, Foucault of all people might have seen the crackdown by the clergy in Iran coming or at least have been wary of the possibility. He often talked about the need to be endlessly vigilant. He was also well aware that most revolutions turned into terror, like the French one. What had happened here with Foucault? Perhaps Bani-Sadr could shed some light.

Before I left for France, I read something like six books on the Iranian Revolution to bring me up to speed; it perhaps goes without saying by now that I should have instead been reading American literary criticism or even American literature. I didn't know anything about Bani-Sadr's current personal situation until I got to France—though I probably should have.

Before the Bani-Sadr meeting, I had an appointment with another star, the philosopher Gilles Deleuze. A few minutes into the interview in the living room in his richly furnished Paris apartment, and without explanation, this sixty-year-old slid down from a couch to the floor. I followed suit. I looked over to the American professor, fluent in French, who was running the interview. He too dropped from his chair.

There was something else quite peculiar about Deleuze: his finger-nails were the longest I'd ever seen on a human being, so long that they rolled up at the end three or four times, sort of like a window shade. Later on it was hard to describe what I'd seen, partly because it was, at the time, hard to believe what I was seeing.

I was learning from Deleuze about Foucault's activism on behalf of prisoners, which was to be the centerpiece of my article. Or rather, the tape recorder was—and I would, after someone transcribed and trans-lated the recording. My French listening ability was too poor to follow Deleuze after, say, his first three words. All I could do by way of commu-nication was to ask the questions. And mirror his body language.

Deleuze may have slid down to the carpet out of respect for Foucault, and I followed him partly for that reason. Perhaps my whole trip was a way for me to mourn.

Deleuze's fingernails were maybe even more mysterious. How long would they be if he unfurled them? Three inches? More? Could he do that without breaking them? Did he clean them? How did he handle sim-ple tools? Wouldn't the nails hit unintended keys when typing? What if he had an itch that needed scratching? (I had a lot of time to think about this issue because I didn't understand anything he was saying.) When had he stopped clipping his nails—how long did it take to grow nails like that? Was he in a bad mental place?[1]

A few days later a number of us sat in a brasserie, the type of infor-mal bar and restaurant, with both indoor and outdoor seating, that was apparently on every street corner in Paris. Things with Bani-Sadr were set, or rather weren't quite.

I didn't understand.

---

1. Much later I learned that he apparently claimed that he left his fingernails untrimmed because he lacked the usual whorls on his fingers, which made them ultrasensitive and in need of protection.

Bani-Sadr was still in hiding in Paris, something like four years after fleeing Iran.

"Oh," I said.

The plan was for Bani-Sadr to meet us, in a few days, at some undisclosed location in the city—which we would learn about the day of.

Maybe an out-of-the-way brasserie?

No one knew.

He would be coming in an armored car, for his own protection, as he was still being hunted by the Iranian regime.

"Oof," I thought. I was aghast upon hearing this plan.

Yes, I'd devoted a good deal of time reading half a dozen books I otherwise would not have. And, more to the point, maybe what we were doing was important to Foucault's reputation. But, in my view, it was hardly worth Bani-Sadr coming out of hiding and risking his life for, not to mention the lives of others definitely or potentially involved, like the driver's for starters—and incidentally our own, which we were by contrast entitled to jeopardize.

In the pursuit of my intellectual work with Foucault—even if I was a bit hazy on what that was—I was willing to take some professional risks. I was willing to alienate some of my Berkeley professors, who thought I was getting woefully sidetracked from the pursuit of my degree. I was even ready to mess up my career some, but I was unprepared to accept casualties.

In fact, I realized at that moment in the brasserie that, no matter how intuitive or messy my approach was, I had two basic rules about research.

The first, which I'd learned from Foucault, was that you had to look at the "primary sources"—the archival material—with your own eyes. Or, in this case, meet with people who had relevant personal experience and ask them your own questions. You couldn't rely on other scholars' summaries or presentations—even if they included part of the documentary evidence, for example, quotations. You had to see for yourself because you might notice things that they ignored or left out, which they considered unimportant because they'd gone looking with a set of questions or a hypothesis different from your own.

The second was: no one must die.

The second trumped the first.

Here I was a twenty-five-year-old having rather strong objections to a plan being laid out for me by a bunch of full-fledged adults in their forties and fifties. It seemed things really ought to have been reversed. Theirs was just the sort of scheme a bunch of wide-eyed graduate students, with a youthful overestimation of the stakes of their intellectual project, might have come up with (while high). But it was of course something a group of PhD candidates wouldn't be able to begin to arrange. Here, right now, in this French eatery, things were in motion.

It was astounding to me how seriously people were treating this tiny newsletter that had a subscription list of a few dozen intellectuals in the United States, Europe, and South America—and was run by a bunch of grad students with no intellectual or political credentials. In any case, I not only didn't want to participate in Bani-Sadr's armored-car visit to us in a secret location to be announced the day of; I felt I had to nix this plan somehow. But how would I do it? I was the lone person who objected, and the rather junior member of the group.

"This just has to be canceled," I started.

But that was all it took.

Luckily, just as everything else seemed to be reversed in this topsy-turvy world I'd stepped into in Paris, so was the veto power, which fell to me—I guess as the only editor of that minuscule newsletter who was present.

The next day Daniel Defert kindly took me to Foucault's apartment in the rue de Vaugirard, where, on the desk, was the cowboy hat we'd given him. There was also an envelope addressed to me, in his by then familiar handwriting. I felt a rush of adrenaline.

This was the moment I'd been waiting for—maybe crossed the ocean for. I couldn't help imagining it contained a letter that finally explained what he'd meant by "the new man." And if the letter didn't really address that—after all, Foucault probably had no idea how little idea I had of what he meant—it was wonderful to be getting it nonetheless. I was honored that he'd thought of me and left me a final communication. I wanted to read whatever it was he'd wanted to tell me. I'd treasure it.

I approached the desk and picked up the envelope. It didn't seem to be well sealed. I opened it. Inside, there was—and life was more often like *this*—nothing.

So now I had all these military documents, but I was left wondering what relevance they had to me, as a doctoral student in literature. I had yet to teach the 1920s novels of Hemingway, Fitzgerald, and Faulkner and had only a passing acquaintance with them.

Moreover—and here was where the trouble started—my oral exams by rule involved a field outside of lit, and I chose US history. Here the documents were relevant, and here the subject of personnel began to be mildly interesting. In anticipation of my orals, I constructed a simple schema, in which I identified different periods in what you might call the American history of "the changing conception of the human person," no doubt inspired by Foucault's phrase, "the new man."

First, I described two earlier periods, arguing that the kind of litera-ture you got in each followed from the current conception:

1. Late eighteenth through mid-nineteenth century. Human beings possessed of reason, will, and passions: literature of Romanticism/ sentimentalism/moralism. For example, *The Federalist Papers*, *The Scarlet Letter*.
2. Late nineteenth century. Human beings possessed of a psychology: self-esteem, sexuality, etc.: literature of realism/ naturalism. For example, Henry James, Stephen Crane, Edith Wharton, Kate Chopin.

This was kinda neat though it wasn't entirely new. But then came the centerpiece, which was. It issued out of my reading of the military papers.

3. Early twentieth century. Human beings possessed of aptitudes: IQ, physical abilities and disabilities, talents, and personal qualities: literature of modernism. For example, ???

I had no examples. But this was just my orals, and I figured it was okay to present a yet untested hypothesis that my dissertation could explore. I imagined I was like a theoretical physicist, predicting that certain subatomic particles would be found that hadn't yet been observed.

And I nearly flunked as a result. When my examiners asked me questions about post–World War I fiction, I gave derivative answers that offered no evidence for my theory, despite that I'd just made an enormous insinuation, namely that modernist literature needed to be totally rethought.

And the room was full of modernist scholars who perhaps didn't want to hear that their literary period should be completely overhauled without at least some explanation of how that might proceed. It didn't help that I was also implying, in particular, that the Great War mobilization was crucial to American modernism—again, without offering any explanation of how—since my questioners were part of the new generation of critics who considered the war to be unimportant here. And I was a little hazy on this significant trend in the field, though for the exam I should have been acutely aware of it. I might have spared myself this fiasco had I bothered to meet with any of my advisers even once in preparation for this exam.

Understandably, the questions coming to me were getting more and more irritated. It got so bad that one of my examiners, the aforementioned Walter, called for a "time out" and took me into the hall. He was probably mortified at the moment to be connected to me as a mentor, so didn't want to see me totally go down in flames.

He said, "So far you're flunking, so you better start making some sense."

"Okay."

I'm forever indebted to him for that unorthodox maneuver. When I got back in the examination room, I didn't suddenly, miraculously, have any relevant examples of modernist literature to offer. And I thought it would probably just generate more hostility to clarify that I'd merely formulated a fairly reasonable postulation based on data from previous periods.

Instead, I explained that, despite the connections I'd made regarding the two earlier eras and the comparable ones in the third era I'd unwittingly implied, I didn't mean to conclude that there was definitely a connection between the military developments I'd identified and the modernist literature that everyone else in the room was deeply invested in and I had, at that point, barely thought about. I said clearly that I had nothing earthshaking to say. And thus, feeling cowed, embarrassed, and stupid, I passed the exam.

Later, when I set out to write a dissertation, I didn't want to revisit the same blasted territory. I simply put aside my archival research and wrote about a different subject and period.

The subject of poverty and the slums I turned to was as much an emotional choice as an intellectual one. One of the unspoken secrets of scholarly work is that many intellectuals choose their subjects for personal reasons. This should hardly be surprising—if it's in fact true—given the investment necessary to carry off a multiyear research and writing project. Foucault, who wrote about the "mad," the sexually "perverse," and the imprisoned, was without doubt this kind of intellectual. His being gay led to his feeling ostracized and misunderstood as a child and young man. (And, by the way, his outsider interest in outsiders explains why I was attracted to his work.)

After the disgrace of my orals, I felt like a failure. On top of that, I was still smarting from Foucault's death, which had no doubt played into my striking unpreparedness for the event in the first place. Whereas other students met regularly with their mentors in preparation for the orals, I'd decided—in a quite unorthodox maneuver—to study for them alone on the other side of the country and arrive back in Berkeley the day before the exam.

As a result of this sense of abjection and abandonment, I gravitated unconsciously to the subject of the urban poor: the socially abandoned and humiliated. My ancestors' roots in the immigrant ghetto and an orphanage along with my own family's modest-to-shaky economic status during my childhood no doubt also drew me to the subject. I felt in some weird way like I was going home—where I really belonged, despite my having provisionally, "fraudulently," as a scholarship kid, taken up residence at an elite college and now a top graduate university.

Much like Stephen Crane himself, who ended up spending lots of time in zones of poverty, I carried around a secret shame and isolation

that propelled me to associate with the poor—or mostly with the writ-
ings of middle-class writers who had associated with the poor. I did my
own tour through contemporary bohemian New York and San Francisco
that Crane and Jack Kerouac might have appreciated: hanging out in
bars, becoming best friends with an ex-con jailed for being "drunk and
disorderly," getting pretty good at pool, and trying to write a publishable
work of fiction.

The academic life I'd loved I now rejected as prissy and emasculating.
I decided I was relieved to be bombing out as a scholar. Though I'd been
preparing to be an academic—putting years and years into the enter-
prise—I suddenly found I had a big problem with that identity.

Meanwhile, I was still teaching during the day and, from time to
time—when I wasn't working on the novel, talking shit with my tough
buddy, finding myself on a misguided sexual adventure or in the resulting emotional shell shock, or nursing a black eye and a busted nose from
a fight—writing my dissertation and then revising it into a marketable
academic book so I could maybe land the tenure-track position I wasn't
sure I wanted.

Later, I figured out what I'd been up to. The poet Robert Bly has a very
apt chapter about this, called "Road of Ashes, Descent, and Grief," in his
Iron John: A Book about Men, a text that academics lambasted and I, too,
made fun of, until I later came across it on my mom's shelves and read it
with absolute self-recognition.

After my oral exam, I forgot all about the documents I'd amassed that
almost caused me to flunk it—until that late January day some twenty
years later, when it became obvious I'd never really forgotten about them
at all.

CHAPTER 16

Paralysis on the Court

How was I ever going to do this project in the course of a semester? It was too big; there was too much to figure out. Valentine's Day was next week.

I got up from the desk and went to the bedroom.

"You're a great partner," I said.

"I'm not so sure about that," Beth said, hitting the pause button on the remote.

She'd reached her limit this weekend with my ongoing legal problems, as she sometimes did. Having retreated to our bedroom, she'd been watching a violent horror movie, *Ginger Snaps*. A dose of cinema horror was how she attempted to recover before she went to sleep—horror movies evidently externalized and thus exorcised the demons left over from her rough childhood. It was something we realized she badly needed after the night a few weeks ago when she'd done some unprecedented, and quite aggressive, sleepwalking.

Dreaming she had to find a new way out of our tiny room because a gangbanger had broken into our place, she'd climbed out of bed and pulled the huge old TV, which required two people to carry and was in the closet on the dresser, onto the floor. Miraculously, she wasn't hurt, and even the TV was unharmed.

"You're giving up your time," I said, "time you might otherwise devote to premed."

She shrugged. "I can't think about it that way. All other life can't just stop. I'm putting in everything I can. But if it's not enough, if I don't get into medical school, I don't get in."

It was a remarkable attitude. I knew it was one thing to think about failing and another to go through the experience. But I also knew that, though she would suffer if she didn't make it, she wouldn't regret the way she'd done things. She stood by her choices. I could almost hear her thinking, like a modern-day Marcus Aurelius: "One person prays, 'How I may not fail to get into medical school.' But one should pray, 'I mustn't be afraid to fail to get into medical school or be devastated by that failure. It doesn't finally matter whether one has success or failure, but how one approaches these things.'"

"Really, you're doing a great job with everything," I said.

"Well, thanks. Now get out of here and leave me in peace."

As I closed the door, I heard a terrified scream from the TV that reminded me of noises I'd heard in the hospital at the age of eight.

If I froze up in tennis matches, I couldn't blame it entirely on my brother. There were others in my boyhood past to blame.

At the beginning of eighth grade, I'd come home from school and said to my mother, "I see how it is. It doesn't matter what you're really like. There's a set of slots already set up and everybody falls into one of them."

I didn't like the one I'd been assigned.

I thought I understood why, but I didn't, not really. I chalked it up to the fact that I hadn't grown and most kids around me had. My catcher from Little League was now five feet nine and had a five-o'clock shadow. I literally didn't recognize him, and maybe he didn't care to recognize me because I still looked pretty much like the fourth grader I'd been then.

What I didn't realize was that all of my new junior-high classmates were from the wealthy, entirely white part of town in which the school was situated, whereas I lived in the poorer, integrated part of town, bordering on a Black ghetto. Nor did I consider that my elementary school classmates and I were bused to this junior high while there was one closer to us, in walking distance.

By chance, my seventh-grade junior-high class had included my then best friend, Stefan, from my neighborhood, who was African American. He gave off a feeling of danger because he had older cousins across the border who were violent men—so I had clout by association, and no one was going to fuck with me. But now Stefan was in another classroom.

The pants of the boy who sat in front of me in homeroom were too long, and bunched up at the bottom. But I knew somehow they weren't hand-me-downs. That kid's pants legs *meant* something. What I was suddenly aware of in eighth grade was fashion—and the unfashionableness of my secondhand clothing. Just about the only thing that mattered in my little neighborhood was how good you were at sports. The only material thing of importance was your bicycle, and, though it pained me that my parents couldn't afford to buy me the banana seat that had cachet, it didn't affect my reputation.

Though I didn't understand why not, I now saw that my neighborhood wasn't the norm. And everything in American culture that enforced "de facto" segregation had pushed Stefan and me apart too, including the junior-high administration, which apparently had little consciousness that for integration to be meaningful it needed to extend to all classrooms.

I was blotted out as a physical being. In the social system of junior high, I'd fallen into the slot of the "brain." My still childlike body was the target of insults and jokes. I didn't fight back because I was isolated and felt newly doubtful about my physical self. Since I was so small that no one was in my weight class for wrestling, it was assumed by the gym teachers that I was no good in sports in general, and, soon enough, I no longer believed I was either. I started to fail on the playing field—where I'd always excelled.

It was then that I began to write fiction.

My failure to grow didn't really explain things. I'd always been small and sometimes isolated, yet that had never stopped me before. In fifth grade, as safety patrol captain, I hadn't been afraid to write up much bigger sixth-grade jaywalkers, who threatened to beat me up if I did. I didn't give a crap about jaywalking per se; I did it all the time away from school, but little kids had already started to copy the big ones, and in the end some first grader was going to trip and get hurt, maybe even get hit by a car. More importantly, perhaps, as safety patrol captain I couldn't let the authority of my sacred office be undermined.

Now, for the first time in my life at age thirteen, for reasons I didn't understand, I was afraid. By the time I finally grew six inches in the summer before junior year of high school, and became taller than my brother, I'd lost my sense of myself as an athlete, and I was stranded somewhere on the wide spectrum between Jimmy Connors and Gilles Deleuze.

If I was going to excel at tennis, I needed a shift in mentality. A South African friend, Reuel, suggested I look at a book called *Zen in the Art of Archery*.

If I'd been sure that during my sabbatical I wouldn't become obsessed with a sport, it was because I thought I'd overcome these lingering demons from childhood. But I was still haunted.

I'd been certain my masculinity didn't need any bolstering by proofs of extreme athletic accomplishment and physical victories over other men because in my thirties I'd found a very Jack Kerouac way of healing psychic wounds: my bohemian stint involving inadvisable relationships, bar fights, and similar misadventures.

Actually, there was only one fight, and it wasn't in a bar but in the building where I was crashing on a friend's couch for a semester after a bad breakup. However, as one of my old graduate school friends who quit grad school put it, one fight can go a long way. I'd managed to get over a fear of getting my ass kicked by provoking a fight with three guys; the one who kicked me in the face happened to be an expert in karate. Lacking a normal caution in that period, I then proceeded to extort half the cost of my medical bill from the black belt, by intimating a possible escalation in violence. My old friend, maybe trying to make me feel better about this ugly and stupid event, noted, "There are essentially two types of guys: those who have had the shit beaten out of them and those who haven't."

Meanwhile, I'd palled around with that hard-drinking, sometimes belligerent, ex-con. And as a result, in my midthirties, a full fifteen years after high school ended, I'd finally stopped having recurring nightmares about my poor athletic showing during that time. I was cured.

But compensatory as my Kerouacian phase might have been, it wasn't the same as conquering my failures in sports. One of the rules of the human psyche seems to be that it's always more nuanced than you think. You always need more therapy. My mild humiliation by school bullies and my craven failure to fight back and face getting my ass kicked was one thing. But my failure to realize my athletic potential because I'd lost faith in it: well, that was apparently something else.

I'd thought after my midthirties bohemian exploits I was entirely fine because I was like Kerouac. But I didn't know that Kerouac had tried and failed to be a starter on the Columbia football team and so had quit football and, in fact, college—and that even Kerouac's Kerouackian phase hadn't assuaged his frustrated dreams of playing college ball. I was more like Kerouac than I knew—too much like Kerouac, although I couldn't know that because I knew almost as little about myself as I knew about Kerouac.

Zen in the Art of Archery is a book by a German in Japan who trains for years with a bow and arrow under a Zen master. In the lessons, the master dispenses with aiming, even with releasing the arrow, and instructs his pupils to let the arrow fly on its own when it is ready. The message is: "You don't shoot the arrow; *it* does."

I found it incomprehensible and pretentious. It reminded me vaguely of Heidegger, the German philosopher who wrote the thick, impenetrable tome called *Being and Time*, but this slim volume wasn't about the nature of existence. It was about archery lessons. After a couple of chapters, I put it aside (though I felt like ripping it to shreds).

While perhaps I really could have used one, I wasn't likely to find a Zen tennis master in the Chicago area. A trip to the Far East was certainly out of the question. I didn't even know if Zen masters any longer even existed in Japan; *Archery* came out in English in the 1950s, and the author's training had taken place in the twenties. This wasn't entirely a joke. Based on my own experience, I believed that inspirational mentors were indispensable.

At the start of my postcollegiate academic training, I'd found Foucault. Spending time with him wasn't fundamentally about the juice you got from hanging out with someone famous. Without the experience of asking him questions and getting answers, I wouldn't have become the scholar I no longer was (but was trying to become again). I may even have simply dropped out of grad school.

Not that it mattered in comparison to everything else hanging in the balance, but my tennis game was stuck.

PART IV

THE LOST-OUT GENERATION

We thought of John Wayne as a draft dodger.

—World War II vet in conversation

CHAPTER 17

Scholarly Detective Story V

HYPOTHESIZING HISTORICAL REVISION
AND SEARCHING FOR PROOF

"Damn it, Quilty," I said.

"What in the world are all these for?" Beth said to me one day after she watched the dog accidentally knock over a pile of books.

I was seated on the floor, skimming through the back pages of one after another.

She was of course aware of my project, but the sheer number of hard-bound library volumes was kind of shocking. I had dozens scattered around our place in makeshift pillars. I was trying to keep them low and ideally against the walls, given the canine traffic, but it was impossible with the space limitations.

"The research," I said, getting up and reassembling the stack Quilty had toppled.

"Can't you return some? You're taking over our space."

"Not yet. Sorry. I've got to go through all their bibliographies."

She looked at me. "Maybe I could help. What are you looking for?"

She had enough to do. I shook my head. "That's a little problem. I don't really know. A needle in a haystack." And if I don't find it, and soon, I thought, this whole thing is screwed.

"Well," she said. "If we gotta have all these books around, you gotta throw away some more pairs of old tennis shoes. And socks. You don't use them anyway."

◎

What the military papers in my apartment seemed to imply was that these famous 1920s novels of Hemingway, Fitzgerald, and Faulkner, featuring military-connected outsiders who bedded the extremely desirable Anglo "girls," obliquely registered a lost history. It was possibly a forgotten story of how, as the US military tried to develop meritocratic devices for evaluating and utilizing men's aptitudes during World War I, social outsiders—working-class and ethnic American men (excluding African Americans)—were welcomed into the army and given unprecedented, basically equal, opportunities there. And those outsiders who were designated combat soldiers, and especially officers, were socially elevated.

When it came to the question of how Gatsby, "Mr. Nobody from Nowhere," made it into the officer class and thus through Daisy's front door and eventually into her arms, the answer maybe wasn't that he'd somehow tricked his way in. It wasn't the result of a fabricated heritage that he laid on the narrator. Rather, it was on the basis of new meritocratic personnel procedures that the army applied to all recruits except Black ones. Perhaps.

On the other hand, there was the widespread ethnic prejudice of the era—that historians, and critics on the left, said was rampant in the early twentieth century, a prejudice you could find just about everywhere, including, hardly incidentally, in these very novels. Wouldn't such prejudice have stood in the way of the extension of equal opportunity to ethnic Americans that I thought I was glimpsing in these military documents and connecting to Gatsby's rise in the ranks stateside? Maybe, for example, the use of these meritocratic devices, such as the intelligence test, was limited to Anglo recruits—and only opened the door of opportunity to lower-class Anglos.

And after all, it was well known that the World War I army was vicious to African Americans: segregating them, mostly keeping them out of combat, consigning the majority to labor battalions and allowing only a small, essentially token number to become officers. Wasn't it the same for ethnic Americans? Maybe Gatsby *had* managed to fool the army into believing he was from an elite Anglo family—and maybe all I was seeing were small hitches in a traditional system of privilege.

But then I came across another document that threw doubt on that idea that Gatsby, though a master of fraud, could have tricked the army into promoting him: one of the benefits of the tests pioneered at Camp Taylor was to eradicate, as the Committee on Psychology put it, "the danger of charletans [*sic*]." The army didn't have to care who you said you were but only how you performed.

So—presuming for the moment that I myself wasn't a charlatan—if Fitzgerald put his poor, apparently German American protagonist at Camp Taylor (rather than Sheridan, where he'd met Zelda), then something special must have been going on there. And if one of the special aspects of Taylor was the experiment with the tests (later, I'd find out that another special thing there was a large population of German American troops), then two things must have been happening:

1. Essentially equal opportunities were open to someone like Gatsby to become an officer, despite a working-class and an ethnic, probably German American, background.
2. For someone like Gatsby to become an officer, he must have done well enough on the intelligence tests to indicate potential.

But each of these conclusions flew in the face of what I knew—or what I thought I knew, what I'd been told—about the ubiquitous prejudice of the period and the bias of the tests against ethnic Americans.

Then I got a hint from the pages of *Sun*, actually pages 1 and 2, and I tried, as it were, to triangulate Hemingway, Fitzgerald, and army policy to solve the problem. Describing the background of his character Cohn, Hemingway wrote: "At the military school where he prepped for Princeton . . . no one had made him race conscious. No one had ever made him feel he was a Jew, and hence any different from anybody else . . . until he went to Princeton." According to *Sun*, top universities were hotbeds of ethnic prejudice, but not military schools.

So there it was, or at least maybe there it was, if Hemingway's novel was historically accurate. Military schools weren't part of the US military, of course, but then, as now, I figured (and confirmed by research), they tried to copy the ethos of the armed forces. Maybe the military, in an era of almost universal prejudice, was exceptional in its treatment of ethnic Americans.

There was nothing in my cache of documents to settle the question, which wasn't surprising, because back in 1984, I hadn't tried to collect items concerning the subject. And I reasoned, "If ethnic Americans were given a fair shake in the World War I army, there's got to be something in the library by now: it's been almost twenty-five years since I visited the Archives."

If there wasn't, it would be a big problem for me: my perhaps unreasonable plan was to research and draft this book during the semester sabbatical and if necessary the following summer. The military archives, I knew from my previous visit, were vast. I would have to comb through them, which could in no way be quickly accomplished, even if the relevant documentation I hoped existed really did. Not only would I fail to get the project done during the sabbatical; it might be slowed down by years. A book took about eighteen months from submission to publication. Then, after the book came out, I'd have to find a new position. That would take a minimum of two academic years, if I got really lucky: the pickings in the job market at anything but the lowest level were slim. Best-case scenario—a finished draft by the end of the term—Beth and I were looking at four more years here. I didn't know if either of us could endure my ongoing legal problems for another four years without breaking down. Anything more was unthinkable. Of course, having a finished book out would change the calculus, as it would stoke our morale.

I went back to the library once more. Though I was ostensibly looking for a new book, I was open to examining obscure old ones. And I was particularly open to investigating a forgotten text by a "minister." My attention to books by clergy was not a matter of superstition. As scholarship about the nineteenth century had taught me, ministers have historically been quite literate people who like to address the issues of the day. Their observations are sometimes the sole documentation of social conditions that would otherwise go unreported.

The little volume I stumbled upon was *A Jewish Chaplain in France*, by Rabbi Lee J. Levinger, published in 1921. I pulled it off the shelf because the title was promising: a Jewish chaplain would presumably have written about Jewish soldiers. And maybe, just maybe, there would be something about how the army treated Jews.

The book was filled with anecdote and polemic: anecdotes about brave Jewish soldiers who served America in the war and polemic against anti-Semitism, given that brave service. And yet I sensed that this book might contain, somewhere, almost by accident from the author's point of view, the sort of crucial statistics I hadn't come across anywhere else.

Indeed, some minutes later, tucked away on pages 121 and 123, I found them. The chaplain wrote that there were perhaps as many as two hundred thousand "American Jews in service during the war," and the "army, Navy and Marine Corps altogether had nearly 10,000 Jews as commissioned officers," including "more than a hundred colonels and lieutenant colonels."

"Fuck, yes," I exclaimed. Though this statistical information may seem dry, it was for me electric. I looked around the stately DePaul University library. Fortunately, the place was fairly empty, and no one was around to overhear my profanity—apart perhaps from the ghost of Rabbi Levinger.

This was a major discovery. I knew by then the proportion of US commissioned officers to soldiers in World War I: around 200,000 to 4.1 million, or around 1 to 20. And I could quickly calculate that the proportion of *Jewish* officers to soldiers was much the same.

In short, Jewish Americans in the US armed services in World War I had as good a chance of making officer as your average recruit. And this during a period of intense anti-Semitism. In 1917, while brave Jewish soldiers were dying for America in France, Ivy League college presidents and deans were getting together back home to figure out how to solve the "Jewish Problem" of "too many" Jews getting on campus due to their scholastic success, and soon enough they came up with the solution of "Jewish quotas." This was the sort of thing that Levinger's book was written to repudiate.

If I believed the standard historical line on the subject, it made no sense. Apparently, the books that claimed that nativist xenophobia was essentially universal among Anglo-Americans during the World War I era had to be wrong. There was one glaring exception to the undeniably widespread prejudice. The military brass.

This was an irreplaceable book: Levinger's seems to be the only source in existence that contains figures on ethnic Americans in the World War I officers' corps.

But this wasn't the book I'd been hoping existed, the one I was pretty sure now could exist, the one that would save me another trip to the Archives: one by a contemporary historian. I didn't yet know for certain that other ethnic Americans, besides Jews, were getting a fair shake. I also didn't know exactly how the army had moved out of step with the rest of the nation and rapidly generated its officer corps of two hundred thousand almost from scratch—there were only nine thousand such commissioned officers before the war—in a manner that welcomed working-class and ethnic American men.

The military papers suggested a combination of personnel methods, including the intelligence tests, but all the books that took up the subject claimed the tests weren't used much by the army. And anyway, they also made clear that the tests were biased against non-Anglos, so it seemed their use couldn't have resulted in an ethnically diverse officer corps even if all these books were wrong and they had been used. So I kept looking for that book.

Then—a few days after I painfully parted with two more pairs of tennis shoes—in the bibliography of one of the books cluttering up our living room, I came across a reference to a volume called *Americans All! Foreign-Born Soldiers in World War I*, by Nancy Gentile Ford.

I went in search of the book. It was an arctic February morning—I was so excited I went first thing after walking the dogs—and I had to trudge through a foot of snow. Thick flakes were falling. The book was housed in the concrete monstrosity of the UIC library. I was dripping in the dim stacks, as I thawed out. My glasses kept fogging up. Finally, I laid my wet hands on the book, pulled it off the shelf, and opened it rapaciously to get a quick idea of whether it was really *the* book.

My hands were literally shaking. I pulled off my now useless glasses. At the book's beginning, there was a quotation from a French soldier, shocked at the makeup of the US Army and officer corps, especially for a country fighting Germany: "You could not imagine a more extraordinary gathering than this american [*sic*] army, there is a bit of everything, Greeks, Italians, Turks, Indians, Spanish, also a sizable number of boches [Germans]. Truthfully, almost half of the officers have German origins."

I'd found the book I'd hypothesized.

It would contain the information that all the clues in Fitzgerald and Hemingway's novels pointed to. I wanted to raise a glass to Nancy Gentile Ford; I could have hugged this woman, but instead I swore I'd raise a statue to her right there inside the UIC library. There was a weirdly empty spot across from the circulation desk. Maybe, I thought giddily, I could fit a second statue of the rabbi, next to the Gentile.

CHAPTER 18

"Hitter's Block"

So there I was, at nine o'clock on a Sunday night in mid-February, slapping balls in a crosscourt drill with a bunch of guys in their twenties and thirties. It was a month into my sabbatical.

What the hell was I doing? I wondered. Why wasn't I instead at home, like a normal adult male in his midforties, with my wife, or the television, or my work (which was actually rather pressing).

It had become clear to me that in order to overcome my "hitter's block," I was going to have to think a little. That didn't sit well. If there was one thing I didn't want to do during my research sabbatical, it was waste mental energy thinking about things other than my research.

But the answer didn't seem like it was going to come to me thoughtlessly, readymade in a book, secondhand from a coach, or wholesale by joining a ritzy club and playing tennis in super nice conditions. I nonetheless tried all these things. My dedication to easy answers and mental laziness was no mean thing.

A few days before, in a state of disbelief, I'd joined Chicago's elite Midtown Tennis Club. I told myself this was a "serious gesture of commitment to my game," a phrase that made things seem even more unreal.

I'd agonized over this decision for some months. I'd never belonged to such an institution in my life. I wasn't from that sort of family. But I'd entered a second tournament at the public courts at the highest level available, only to beat my first opponent way too easily. So I pulled out and got my money back. My aim was to improve, and I wasn't going to pay $175 for a set of effortless matches and another little trophy. Instead,

120

I was going to shell out hundreds more for membership at a veritable cathedral of tennis, where I could in addition pay for instruction with teaching pros and generally begin to wonder if I'd lost touch with reality.

I guess I figured if I was going to waste huge amounts of time on tennis, I might as well be squandering large sums of money as well. I couldn't afford lessons—or, rather, though I couldn't afford any of this, I reassured myself that I wasn't quite deranged enough yet to blow even more cash on individual instruction, so I joined one of the club teams, which, less expensive but still financially unwise, also involved guidance from pros.

That first night of practice, I was feeling green. On trial. As I was smacking crosscourt balls, the nearly bald-headed coach, who was around my age, came up and watched.

"So, what's your background? Did you play college tennis?" he asked. "Where?"

No, not only did I not play college tennis, but college had ended decades ago. What would it mean if I *had* played college tennis at the remove of a quarter century?

Though I didn't stop rallying, I was in a secret hysterical rage. Shouldn't I be judged on the basis of my play and not a résumé? Christ, in the adult, professional world, it was always about your degrees, your record! Wasn't that what made tennis so precious? None of the stuff of résumés mattered in tennis; you weren't judged by editors or personnel committees; there was nothing subjective in the outcome; all that mattered was what you could do on the court in the course of a match. This was something almost, well, sacred. My imagined rant nearly brought tears to my eyes.

I snapped at the coach, "I can't remember what the hell happened in college. It was too damn long ago."

I was evidently a bit uncomfortable that initial evening.

Later, back at home at midnight, when I'd calmed down a little, I realized I'd failed to see that his question was perhaps a compliment and not an attempt to murder all that was holy: I looked like I'd maybe played college tennis, though I hadn't even played in high school.

The same question soon came up again. But this time I was a little less self-conscious about doing drills on a Sunday night that included men a generation younger. When another coach, the head one this time, asked me (that first coach pretty much steered clear of me after my bizarre, openly hostile response), a very different answer popped out of my panting mouth.

I told him I'd played tournaments as a kid, but, because of problems at home, I quit tennis after elementary school, and now I'd taken it up again, having missed my chance to play growing up.

He looked at me—he, too, was about my age, with a shaved head—nodded and walked off. (We forty-somethings were all losing our hair.)

I stumbled off too, contemplating what I'd said.

It was when I was thirteen that my mother had gotten remarried, to a large man who bullied me, and I'd not only quit tennis but become for the first time studious and withdrawn. Before then, I'd never read a book outside of school, aside from *Strange but True Baseball Stories*. I also started writing stories of my own, likewise "for fun"—but more accurately out of pain and dislocation. It became my dream to be a writer.

Ah: it was then I'd lost my physical confidence. That was partly why, in junior high school, I was for the first time afraid of bigger kids.

I'd never made the connection before: huh. For what it was worth, I now understood what had happened to me back in 1973.

The first practice was exhilarating because we team members played doubles against the coaching pros. There were two in particular who were "the real thing"—not on the professional circuit but just the next step or two down. Trying to cope with their shots was thrilling. It was like I was suddenly transported into the rarefied world inside the television set where the tour players lived. It's one thing to watch a professional-speed serve on TV, from a remove and an angle that allows you to see both players; it's another to step through the looking glass and have that 120 mph ball coming right at you.

Other serves had so much English they jumped a full three or four feet sideways upon hitting the ground, as if they'd exploded (this is something else you can't quite perceive on TV). Trying to return the first of these "kick" serves, I ended up whiffing—and feeling more than a little foolish. I had the shocking visual impression that the ball had disappeared into thin air. These guys were like magicians with that little yellow projectile. But I soon got the hang of this superspin, and I noticed to my delight I was quick enough to return the flat high-speed serves. Maybe it was worth all the time and money.

Playing with the pros, however, turned out to be a one-time deal, not to be repeated. The second week I wondered if my plan to join a club team was perhaps misguided. I was hardly ever playing singles, given the limited courts available. Moreover, since everyone else there avoided the weakest players, I ended up in the doubles game with them. I'd been relegated, as a newcomer, to the "kids' table."

It only took me a few minutes to figure out what was going on, but it was already too late. I wanted to get away from this little group as well, but it wasn't easy. I looked over longingly at the other courts, which were all filled.

One of the players in my foursome, Bill, a small guy in his thirties, came over and cornered me.

"I know we're not good enough for you," he said.

"No, it's not—"

"This must be a real drag for you; I'm sorry we're no good."

"I . . ."

"Where are you going?"

"Uh—the restroom . . ."

"You're not trying to sneak away from us, too, are you?"

Despite the head coach's promises to keep me flush with challenging singles matches, he had a number of other, unfathomable duties at these practices, which kept him mostly out of sight. The reality with the practice sessions was that I was putting as much energy into the personal diplomacy necessary to get myself on the right court as I was actually playing. I found myself most of the time impressed into doubles drills with Bill and his crew: I tried to make the best of it, to not think about the money *and time* I was wasting—I was on sabbatical, and my career and well-being hung in the balance, I couldn't help remembering occasionally. But these distracting social interactions with volubly self-deprecating Bill and the mysteriously busy coach, who was perhaps not entirely straight with me, were the kind of thing I needed to get away from so I could focus on tennis and experiment, and at least occasionally play singles.

The last night, in a sitcom finish to the whole season, the lying son-of-a-bitch head coach showed up long enough to pair Bill and me in singles, and I easily beat poor old Bill. But, since he played so poorly, I was able to do so playing at a level beneath the one I'd been at when I joined the club. Bill was perversely satisfied: I hadn't escaped him. It was as if he were part of an elaborate conspiracy to keep me from improving. Immediately after the match, I went to find the head coach, to give him a piece of my mind, and to tell him flatly that I was quitting the team—only he was nowhere to be found.

Though this experience with coaches had set me back weeks in my tennis development, I'd also learned something. I hadn't always been debilitatingly overshadowed by my brother as a kid. If I'd lost my confidence at thirteen, then I must have had it previously. It only remained— for some reason I was convinced this personal archaeology was important to my progress on the court—to remember where my confidence had come from.

And then, one morning, on a dawn walk with the dogs, so exhausted I was in some kind of altered state between sleep and consciousness, too groggy to worry about lawyers, crazy relatives, military history, tennis, or anything else, I watched Lazarus fall into a ditch. Before I could react, Quilty started pulling her out by biting down on her leash and backing up. That sprang the memory.

CHAPTER 19

Why I Didn't Die at Age Eight

Everything changed when, with no further medical treatment, I was "miraculously" cured of the Hong Kong flu. Not dying, when a lot of people, including myself, thought I would, was itself a big step. It was the next summer that I joined Little League and Junior Davis Cup and had organized sports experiences I hardly remembered but was pretty sure I'd loved.

My mother dated my recovery from the day that Billy Weber came over to visit me.

Friendship between boys can be a powerful force, and it is strongest before girls, or sexual relationships, are on the table. Billy Weber was no ordinary kid, not to me anyway. To my grandmother, he was a "nice gentile boy." I didn't care about his religion—though his being a gentile was maybe in a way crucial to my recovery—and the basis of his exceptionalness was something incomprehensibly grander.

He was not my peer: he was three years older (so older even than my brother), and three years to a third grader is like a generation. He was in sixth grade, then the senior grade in elementary school. He was the leader of our neighborhood gang of some half dozen kids; he was also the elected president of our large elementary school, in which nearly all four hundred children, from first grade through sixth, voted (kindergarteners were considered too immature to be trusted with suffrage). Given the nature of elementary school elections and neighborhood gang leadership, it can be said without question that Billy Weber possessed a great deal of charisma.

125

Children are pagans and conflate the good with the beautiful and graceful. Meanwhile, they have to have the abstract ethics of the Judeo-Christian tradition painstakingly drummed or beaten into them. Billy Weber was physically striking and also athletically gifted; he was great at everything he attempted and was almost always on the winning side. He never lost in tetherball or one-on-one basketball. He had a hot temper, but he could also keep his cool in the heat of a sporting event, when a mustache of sweat would form on his upper lip. He was in possession of that indecipherable X factor that no kid could articulate but everyone could recognize.

It is hard, and maybe slightly embarrassing, to remember as adults the absolute adulation with which we, as little kids, looked up to the leaders of our elementary school. I still remember the names of the school presidents, all gifted athletes, whom I stood in awe of as a first and second grader. Michael Higginbotham, Chris Green, Ernie Emory: these three boys, this triumvirate of grade school heroes—all African American by the way, in what was one of the first integrated elementary school districts in the country—were to me the equivalent of Greek gods or the Founding Fathers.

Ernie could hit the school building on a fly in a kickball game, maybe fifty yards distant. I believed Michael and Chris—the latter was the son of a professional football player with the Cleveland Browns—to be bound for the major leagues.

Billy Weber walked among these titans of Lomond Elementary School. I loved him with an enthusiasm usually reserved for deities. Perhaps therefore it is no surprise that when it came to me, he had the power to heal. His visit caused me "to perk up for the first time," as my mother put it.

His coming over and spending some time with me while I sat propped up against the pillows on the davenport was not just an act of condescension. It is probable that it was prompted by the intervention of my mother, who, aware of my feelings for Billy, if not their lunatic intensity, called his mother to report that I was back from the hospital and, though noncontagious, still ill and liable to die. And thus in rather desperate need of cheering up. Billy was, after all, very familiar to me, though not quite accessible, not really my friend; we played together all the time, with other members of the gang, whatever major American sport was in season. But interaction had previously been mediated by the group, and in particular by my brother. Here it was just him and me. I felt special. I felt that I had an individual existence.

Billy Weber represented nothing less than my possible future, someone to emulate who was fearless, undaunted by the football field, the segmentation of elementary school into separate grades, or anything else. And though I didn't know it, he was daring and unbowed partly on account of his gentile roots, or more precisely his Anglo-German Protestant family background. His father had a successful career as a university dean. Billy wordlessly brought all that with him when he visited me that day. And, suffocated as I was between a fatalistic home life, where I lived under the shadow of my brother, and a bureaucratic system at school in which I excelled but that seemed to me to lead nowhere, it was exactly what I needed. It was an exit from my own extremely limited, warped, and actually outdated viewpoint, which led out into a brave, new, uncharted world of possibility—and risk-taking.

Billy Weber's three hours with me in the living room, with just me, playing board games and trading baseball cards, communicated to me that I was worth more than I'd figured. It told me I had a destiny. I couldn't imagine that sixth graders who were dominant athletes and school presidents often went around visiting third graders on sick calls. And even if they did, they didn't stay for hours, laugh, and enjoy themselves. Unless that third grader was himself a potential athlete possessed of some personal charisma. Billy Weber may as well have anointed me with oil or tapped me on the shoulder with a sword.

And a few weeks later, all my intimations of that day of his visit were confirmed and more: Billy Weber took me aside on a street corner after a pickup football game at the school field and told me my future. He said, "You'll be president of the school when your time comes."

This was a huge statement, with magical implications. Presidents of our elementary school, whether boys or girls, were basically worshipped by the first and second graders; they were athletic, talented, and beautiful; they received "love notes" from younger kids of the opposite sex and had girlfriends or boyfriends. How he could know that I'd be president I wasn't sure. The way he saw me fitting into and succeeding in the system was something I definitely hadn't yet seen for myself, and nobody else, certainly no one in my family, had noticed or bothered to comment on it. But I believed him. At age eight, I trusted his judgment above my own. He was the president and an athlete; he ought to know. The important thing was that I believed there was a future for me, as an individual, in the real world.

I also realized that I could share this prediction with no one. Talking about it might even change the future—because it would provoke mockery or disbelief. I didn't need my brother laughing at me or, worse, my mother hearing it and saying, "I expect nothing less." In the basically communal world of childhood, I instinctively guarded my secret, the new private friendship and understanding of the world I shared with Billy Weber, which began the day he visited me when I was deathly ill.

After he left that first afternoon of his visit, I rose up from the davenport sickbed like one reborn. I was completely cured.

Then, like prophetic kings who rule during a golden era, indicate a successor to take over in some future time, and then retire to a mythic land in the West, Billy moved with his family to Phoenix. Actually, what happened is that his father got offered a more prestigious deanship at the University of Arizona.

But I was now equipped to carry on without Billy. And a few years later, I was indeed elected president of the elementary school, as he'd somehow foreseen. That magnetic older boy had cured me of the Hong Kong flu and given me the confidence I needed to pursue tennis on my own at the age of nine.

CHAPTER 20

Scholarly Detective Story VI

EXAMINING THE HISTORICAL REVISION BY
ANALYZING DISCREPANCIES BETWEEN ACCEPTED
HISTORIES AND NEW EVIDENCE

I sat down at my desk with a large cup of black coffee. It was time to
think things through. There were still a couple of big questions looming—
whose apparent answers confounded me because they didn't jibe with
the classic histories on the subject.

I knew from Ford that immigrants and children of immigrants had
been treated well in the World War I army. And by this point, I had
another book that concurred with hers—which was much better known
but not for briefly addressing this issue, focused as it was on a combat
story, Richard Slotkin's *Lost Battalions*.[1]

I also learned from Ford that in terms of ethnic Americans' promotion
to the officer corps, the army actually went looking for qualified bilin-

---

1. Slotkin, a famous literary critic, publishing his book a few years after Ford's, declared
   that the military promised ethnic American recruits they "would not be subject to
   discrimination or unfair treatment in the assignment of tasks or the making of pro-
   motions." It went on: of "all the major institutions that shaped the life of the nation—
   schools and universities, government, corporations—the wartime army may have
   been the one most willing to acknowledge and accept ethnic difference as an inescapable element of national identity." Even the Chinese "were integrated with White
   soldiers," which was "quite remarkable and flies in the face of the passions and legal
   proscriptions that isolated Asian-Americans."

gual speakers who could lead companies of immigrants in their native tongues. Hemingway seemed to know about this policy; it's alluded to in *A Farewell to Arms*. There, the narrator's nemesis, this time a boring and conceited Italian American war hero (as opposed to the boring and conceited Jewish American military school graduate in *Sun*), a man about to be promoted to captain in the Italian army and thus to outrank the narrator, talks about how he might go into the US Army and how he'd be more highly ranked than the narrator there as well, explaining, "I can command a company in Italian. I could learn it in English easy."

But Ford's book didn't reveal *how* there ended up being so many ethnic American officers in the US Army: for example, ten thousand Jewish commissioned officers, according to Levinger. There was no way the army had anything approaching ten thousand Jewish immigrant companies that needed Yiddish-speaking leaders. Back in 1983 I'd been bored to tears by the subject of military personnel management. Now I had to understand precisely how the military's openness to ethnic American promotion was translated into practice.

Apparently, even most military historians were still bored by the subject, which was understandable. Ford didn't talk about the intelligence tests or the rating sheets for identifying potential officers. And the consensus among historians who bothered to mention military management at all seemed to be that the army didn't make much use of either of these meritocratic devices. The most important recent book on the war asserted that the personnel committees moved too slowly, in compiling their test results and the qualification cards, for the pressing need to assign recruits in the first few days of service. There was no mention of the rating sheets, which meant either that they were even less important or that no one else knew about them. And, as I kept intermittently remembering then and keep intermittently repeating now, I knew that ethnic Americans, including Jews, had done badly on the tests, so they evidently couldn't have had much to do with the way these ten thousand Jewish guys made commissioned officer.

Maybe most of these Jewish officers were college students or graduates, and, as such, eligible, like Fitzgerald, to take an entrance exam that could qualify them for officer training. But why would they do well on these exams and poorly on the intelligence tests, which were similar?

Also, and I kept coming back to this as well, since it was the point for me: what about an ethnic American like Gatsby? He had a high school diploma but only a couple of weeks of college, which he'd dropped out of years before the war. Someone like Gatsby would not have been eligible to take the entrance exam for college grads.

Gatsby (or rather someone like him) must have been the beneficiary of the newfangled personnel programs in the camps, but was he, as such, an anomaly, one of the very few working-class ethnic guys who benefited from them? But if an anomaly, why was Fitzgerald so interested in him?

It sounds like I'm talking about Gatsby as if he were a real person, but I don't mean to. I'm trying to talk about Gatsby as if he's a fictional character whom Fitzgerald has promoted on the basis of a real army practice that he (Fitzgerald) doesn't identify (for some reason). It often happens in "realistic fiction" that imagined characters resemble real people at the time and are depicted experiencing real events. And based on information in Ford's book, I knew Fitzgerald would have encountered plenty of German American soldiers at Camp Taylor. What was unusual here was that Fitzgerald was cryptic about the "real events."

I decided to go back to the drawing board since I couldn't think of what else to do: Would Gatsby, as a German American, have done well on the intelligence tests? I had the data, compiled by psychologists after the war, and, well, German Americans from northern Germany (back then considered "Nordic") did better than German Americans from southern Germany (classified as of the "Alpine race"), and I didn't know where Gatsby's ancestors were from.[2]

Then I almost fell out of my chair. Quilty started barking. I'd seen something breathtaking that should have been obvious to me weeks earlier.

When it came to the postwar numeric compilations by the psychologists, all we had were aggregate results by national origin. They didn't

---

2. For that matter, I wasn't entirely certain the family name Gatz was German. If it wasn't German, it was eastern European. (But Gatsby's not Jewish and almost certainly German; Fitzgerald has him go to a Lutheran college and also indicates his ethnicity by the rumors circulating that he was a German spy during the war and nephew to the kaiser.) Overall, German Americans did less well than Anglo-Americans but better than, say, Russian and Polish Americans (who were considered racially "Slavic").

tell you anything about how an individual of a particular nationality had done. The compilers, being racist, had created categories based on race, but, as everyone now knew, race didn't matter in the performance on the tests, and other things did, most of all education and familiarity with American culture. So these racial categories were absurd—and all the low aggregate test results by men with southern and eastern European backgrounds really told you was that most of them were immigrants without much education or familiarity with American culture.

So Jewish Americans who were born and educated in the United States were going to score much higher than immigrant Jews who'd received a third-grade education in Poland. And the reason Jews did poorly, in the aggregate, was simply that there were, in the army, many more Jewish immigrants than American Jews born in the United States. Something along these lines could be said for German Americans as a collective and an individual like Gatsby.[3]

Born in America, educated in the North (North Dakota), where schools were better than in the South, and with a high school diploma at a time when the average US recruit had a seventh-grade education, someone like Gatsby was poised to ace the tests, no matter how German Americans as a whole did.[4]

The strong correlation between education and test score was why the psychologists thought they'd discovered that the average mental age of American men was thirteen. What the psychologists had in fact "discovered" was something that was already known by other means and was basically a tautology: namely, the average recruit had a seventh-grade education, or had left school at thirteen.

---

3. Soldiers of German ancestry did better overall than Russians and Poles precisely because German immigration to the United States was older, and thus a larger proportion of German American test takers would have been American-born, as compared to those of Russian or Polish descent.

4. In fact, given the percentage of American-born white recruits who had any high school education then—about 18 percent—along with the strong correlation between amount of schooling and test score, someone like Gatsby, who finished high school, was very likely to score at the officer level, which was exactly the top 18 percent according to the scores recorded at Camp Taylor, on that first sheet I'd found in my file cabinet.

I calmed Quilty, who was still barking. Then I decided I'd better read in depth about the test results in Stephen Jay Gould's *The Mismeasure of Man.* I pulled it out from one of my makeshift pillars.

Apparently, the test takers basically fell into two different groups: the first group tended to score okay or well; the second one tended to score not just poorly but zero. On most parts of the alpha tests (for those who could read English), there was not a "normal distribution" to the graph that showed the test results, as one would anticipate, but a "bimodal" curve (that is, with two summits); in addition, the mode, or the most common score, was zero. On many of the parts of the beta tests (for non-English speakers and American illiterates), zero was the second most common score. As Gould deduces about both tests, "The common-sense interpretation of this bimodality holds that recruits had two different responses to the tests. Some understood what they were supposed to do, and performed in various ways. Others, for whatever reasons, could not fathom the instructions and scored zero." It wasn't much of a leap to conclude that the educated were used to taking tests and the men with not much schooling weren't.

Jesus, was I an idiot. If the army had made use of the tests, then individual ethnic Americans born in the United States—Jewish, German, whatever—who had some high school education or more would have benefited from them. That I hadn't noticed this about the IQ tests indicated I had very little intelligence, or marginal capability of using the smarts I supposedly had according to the standardized tests I'd taken.

No one else had bothered to notice this either—but that was because everyone else knew the army didn't make much use of the tests, and thus no one else wondered about how individual recruits did on them. Everyone else was focused on the postwar use of the test results by racists, not the wartime moment. In addition, most everyone else who'd written about the tests hadn't been math majors as I had.

Since it was well known that the tests were culturally biased against African Americans and men with eastern and southern European backgrounds and that these groups consequently did poorly, I'd figured, like everyone else, there was nothing else to say about them. But there was more. The first thing was that what we all said about them wasn't even quite true. They weren't entirely culturally biased against African and

Jewish and Italian Americans. They were biased against Black men and Jews and Italians, and all other sorts of men, including Anglo-Americans, who had poor educations or little experience of American culture. If they were biased against most eastern Europeans, that was because in 1917 and 1918 most eastern Europeans in America were immigrants. And if they were biased against most African Americans, that was because most of them were poorly educated. But not all.

In the aggregate, African Americans and men with eastern and southern European backgrounds did poorly, but some groups of Black men excelled, and some groups of men of eastern or southern European heritage did also. Despite what everyone thought they knew about the prejudice of the tests, Black men from the North scored better than white men from the South (I saw, paging through another book, which I noticed was slightly nibbled at the corner). And I inferred that US-born Jewish, Polish, and Italian Americans who finished high school outscored Anglos who'd dropped out before eighth grade.[5]

---

5. Though no figures were available there, I did find some pretty strong circumstantial evidence to back up my inference. After the war (as I soon learned from another book), WASP racists, interested in preserving their prerogatives, or reasserting them after the egalitarian wartime moment, were excited about the aggregate wartime tests. Of course they misread the results and did so similarly to the way most everybody has, namely concluding that an aggregate nationality result says something about how (educated) individuals of that nationality performed.

Racist university officials tried to use standardized tests to keep Jews and other "undesirable" minorities off campus. Naturally, this wasn't going to work in practice because the Jews seeking admission to medical programs weren't in the main immigrants who didn't finish grade school but mostly American-born and all college educated.

Jews were turning out to perform very well on Medical Aptitude Tests (MAT) of the 1930s. Med school deans became very upset with this early version of the MCAT, angry that it wasn't working the way the army tests seemed to have worked—when most Jewish test takers were uneducated immigrants. In reaction to this surprising reality (which should've been expected), these deans had a sudden, violent change of heart about using standardized testing in selecting students. Some med schools, for example George Washington University, simply dropped the MAT.

I'd have felt quite proud of myself if I didn't also feel stupid (almost as dumb as racist Anglo East Coast medical school deans of the 1930s, who went so far as to institute their nefarious admissions policies based on this numbskull reasoning).

But wasn't all this about the test results moot? If the army didn't make much use of them, it didn't really matter that educated ethnic Americans did well. Just as it hadn't mattered much that African Americans from the North did well—because the army wasn't giving Black men equal opportunity.

So I now I flopped down on the couch next to Lazarus (were those her teeth marks or Quilty's?) and buckled down to read about the army's not making much of the tests.

And the more I read about the army's not making much use of the tests, the more I was convinced that the army used them quite a bit—in fact, quite a bit in the area I was concerned with, the promotion of officers. It all depended, evidently, on what you meant by "much use." Gould, whose otherwise cogent book has had the most impact on establishing the common wisdom on the subject, had declared, "I do not think the army ever made much use of the tests." But he also asserted—somewhat oddly given the aforementioned statement—that the tests had "a strong impact in some areas, particularly in screening men for officer training," which he thought extended, in some fashion, to about two-thirds of the 200,000 officers chosen by the army by war's end. To me, a "strong impact" on around 130,000 men seemed like a lot of use. But that might just be me.

Clearly, Gould has in mind a pretty high bar when he uses the phrase "much use." And the weirdest part of his measure here seems to be that it has no relation to the army's oft-stated intentions for the tests, which was the mobilization of an effective army and qualified officer corps. The illogic of Gould's assertion that the "army never made much use of the tests" is that the army used them fairly extensively and precisely as it set out to. It was akin to saying that your neighbor doesn't get much use out of his lawnmower: he only uses it to mow his lawn.

After puzzling it out, the only way I could understand Gould's strange measure was that he didn't have in mind the army's aims for the tests but rather the Psychology Committee's. These were indeed grandiose, as the psychologists, led by program head Robert Yerkes, compiled the test data by nationality and made intelligence evaluations of "racial" groups as a whole. This was something the army never did, since it was exclusively interested, as was said repeatedly in intramilitary correspondence, in assigning individuals to appropriate roles and ranks. I had to guess that Gould didn't have in mind the army's aims for the tests because he didn't know about them.

Gould notes that "some army officials became suspicious of Yerkes's intent and launched three independent investigations of the testing program," one of which "concluded that it should be controlled so that 'no theorist may . . . ride it as a hobby for the purpose of obtaining data for research work and the future benefit of the human race.'" Gould's book gives the impression that the psychologists set the goals for the testing program—and the army didn't have any particular aims for it at all. It's like Gould thinks the army was just kind of hosting the psychologists, humoring them, giving them a chance to do whatever the heck they wanted, within reason, so they could, well, feel they were contributing to the national cause or something. "Here's some extra cash, guys; we're trying to fight a world war, but go knock yourselves out with some irrelevant research."[6]

Actually, the historian David Kennedy, whose important book *Over Here* came out the year before Gould's and was the other influential book in establishing the "received idea" on the testing program, may be responsible for kicking off this odd interpretation. In introducing the subject of the program, Kennedy wrote, "The army cooperated less eagerly with another social experiment in 1917–1918," thus giving the weird impression that the military wasn't attempting to use the tests for its own purposes but rather tolerated the psychologists and their divergent agenda for some extraneous reason, maybe some sort of political pressure—like maybe Yerkes was President Wilson's in-law or something. It made no sense to imagine, as Kennedy's comment otherwise seems to imply, that Yerkes and company somehow had the institutional clout to impose themselves on the military since neither the public nor people in high places generally at the time cared about some wonky psychologists.

Then it struck me why perhaps Kennedy and Gould had this bizarre impression. Neither of them had consulted the military papers in the National Archives. They'd both relied on the same secondary source: a

---

6. Gould also ignores what was to me a key fact, namely that when the program was investigated, it wasn't abandoned: the army decided to continue it, with revisions.

journal article that basically told the story from the psychologists' point of view. But I had the primary-source materials in my filing cabinet. (Actually, most were, like the books, on the floor; what a mess; it was good Beth was out of the apartment for class at the moment, and the dogs could only bite, and not talk and tattle.) These papers laid out the army's aims over and over again. As the army's surgeon general wrote, recommending the "continuance of psychological work" in December 1917:

The purpose of these tests . . . is as follows:

(a) To aid in segregating and eliminating the mentally incompetent;
(b) To classify men according to their mental capacity;
(c) To assist in selecting competent men for responsible positions.

What Gould doesn't explain—because he doesn't seem to know it—is that the army didn't want to manage the testing program simply to prevent the psychologists from pursuing some crazy racist agenda for the supposed "benefit of the human race"; it wanted to prevent the psychologists from following their own aims because any other agenda impeded the military's. Since I had the military papers, I had the sentence in full that Gould actually quotes only in part (because the secondary source Gould used quoted it only in part): the sentence that cautions about a "theorist" potentially riding it as a hobby horse goes on and sums up, "and this at the expense of present military training."

But before I could assert that the military made widespread use of the tests despite what everyone claimed, one final problem remained. What about the claim in the most important recent book on the war (I moved Quilty aside and grabbed it up again) that the personnel committees moved too slowly, in compiling their test results and qualification cards, for the pressing need to assign recruits in the first few days of service?

Well, that turned out to evaporate rather quickly with a little examination. As this historian knew, but had maybe temporarily forgotten (and I knew how easy it was to temporarily forget things), the recruits were quarantined for two weeks when they first went into the service, so there was time enough.

In the military papers I found this precise issue addressed: when the program was investigated and then overhauled, one of the revisions was to give the tests in the first couple weeks of muster, or else forgo them.

At the war's end, the army had given the tests to 1.7 million recruits; well over a million had been given to soldiers after the program was revised. And it had given personnel interviews to approximately 3.5 million (resulting in that number of qualification cards). In retrospect, I guess I'd always found it a bit hard to believe that the military would have wasted so much time and energy on something it was making only "lackadaisical" use of. I'd found it especially hard to believe the army would have wasted time and energy evaluating, revising, and then continuing with something it wasn't doing much with.

I myself was perfectly capable of wasting incredible amounts of time and energy on things I never made much use of. I'd written thousands of pages of novels that had never seen the light of day. The things I'd done in my life that weren't a waste of time but succeeded were rare exceptions.

Maybe *I* was capable of administering almost two million stray tests. But was the US military in a time of war?

I didn't think so. Not that many in World War I anyway. In the "interoffice" mail I had from the army, they were always going on about efficiency, utilizing things, making use of resources, "the necessity of utilizing to the last degree every available bit of human material," as the Classification of Personnel committee put it, not exactly poetically.

It wasn't that the army didn't waste things (and lives) along the way: after reading a lot of this interoffice mail, I could definitely imagine the army experimentally administering a few hundred thousand tests over the course of several months without consistently using the results in the assignment of men. Things were happening fast and on a mass scale. But once some older senior officers started criticizing the testing and asking for its termination, and once the army decided instead to keep the program and revise it, partly because younger senior officers liked it, well, then I couldn't see them administering a million more to no real purpose.

The army's devotion to avoiding waste was also central to the racier story of the forgotten mobilization, which was for me, as a budding Lost Generation scholar, another crucial part of this "secret" mobilization. The main reason the military ended up giving immigrants and ethnic Americans a fair shake in the assignment of roles and ranks wasn't that it was socially just, but that it was wasteful not to.

Here's what had happened, as I learned from Ford: At first, after drafting foreign-speaking immigrants along with everyone else, the army had dismissively—and wastefully—tossed them into "development battalions" where, counter to official policy, they were indiscriminately mixed in with soldiers who had venereal disease or who'd been declared physically or mentally unfit. Not exactly smart and certainly not nice, but perhaps understandable: the army brass had a lot to contend with, including the language problem and the ethnic prejudice of many of its officers. The scale of war prep was new and shocking, and the military was working things out on the fly.

Anyway, these development companies often had no common language, so recruits couldn't communicate with each other or their officers. And the bulk of these foreign-speaking soldiers were given nothing to do or else assigned unskilled jobs including kitchen patrol, or KP, duty. This went on for a while.

But then, as a report stated, "The War Department finally came to the conclusion that having about 100,000 [non-English-speaking] men in the army for six months, clothing them and feeding them, with no benefit, no result in any form is pretty serious." Another report calculated that by July's end in 1918 each such unused man had wasted about $1,000 in "pay, clothing, food and time expended upon them in training." These are the words of one Lt. Stanislaw Gutowski, a multilingual, Polish-immigrant officer whom the military command tapped to figure out how to solve this problem of waste and sell it to senior officers.

The solution of Gutowski and the task force called the Foreign-Speaking Soldier Subsection of the Military Morale Section was to treat immigrants well, put them in "ethnic-specific companies" that had a common language, and then select, promote, and train bilingual immigrant and ethnic American officers to lead these companies. As with recruits in general, the selection of officers was to be done after "the men of the Development Battalions . . . were classified physically and mentally." What came to be called the Camp Gordon Plan was dramatically successful. Initially, "All of the foreign-speaking soldiers had refused to go overseas. However, after the 'Camp Gordon Plan' was implemented, 85 percent expressed their willingness 'in no uncertain terms' to fight in Europe. Later, this number increased to 92 percent."

I was really getting somewhere—though I knew my research and thinking weren't quite done (never mind the writing). It was late February. Starting to face the possibility that my plan to produce a book draft during the sabbatical might be another one of my fantastical ideas, I decided after all to apply for a grant from the National Endowment for the Humanities to continue this project.

An unfriendly reviewer (who sank my chances of getting the grant) was dubious that the mobilization of the US Army and its officer corps could be relevant to our famous modernist literature. After all, eighty years had gone by and no one had noticed its relevance. By this logic, of course, science would never advance. For example, the influence of the moon is not germane to the tides of the oceans: nobody spotted it for a very long time, so it must be unrelated.

And, looking back on my whole process of discovery—if it can be called a process—it's easy to see why knowledge, especially knowledge about something that doesn't really matter, advances so slowly. If I hadn't gone to the Archives a quarter century before as a tireless twenty-three-year-old on a vaguely related grant that *was* funded, hadn't had an uncle in Washington whom I could freeload on for a month, hadn't been a hoarder and held onto seemingly useless papers for more than two decades, hadn't been assigned to teach the Lost Generation novels for years on end, hadn't had Beth in my life to give me confidence, hadn't stumbled across Rabbi Levinger's slim volume, and hadn't majored in math; if Nancy Ford and Nancy Bristow hadn't written their books about immigrant soldiers and charity girls, and Foucault hadn't in the first place found me boyish: if all of these things hadn't fallen into place, or most of them, this discovery would never have happened.

I suspected there was one other crucial, less obvious factor: my socioeconomic background. Most literary critics of the last eighty years had come from families that were either WASP or well-off (often enough both); I brought a fairly unusual perspective to the field by virtue of my lower-middle-class, non-Anglo perspective. As mentioned, most working-class Jewish American kids who were beneficiaries of meritocratic opportunities for elite higher education did not squander them and disappoint their parents by becoming lit professors. (And such individuals who went into the humanities tended to be politically motivated, and gravitated to the fields of history and sociology.) To summarize the problem of critical point-of-view concisely and perhaps unfairly, literary commentators from privileged backgrounds, though able to notice the racism and anti-Semitism of Hemingway and company, were unlikely to entertain the idea that these privileged WASP literary giants might have had a reason to be jealous and resentful of the status of poor or ethnic American men in the United States in 1917 and 1918.[7]

I looked over at my massive orange, black, and white Head racket bag that was cluttering up the hall. As I contemplated the growing time crunch, I wondered if I should put tennis on hold, or at least pull back from it.

---

7. For similar reasons, the subject of my first scholarly book was one that had previously been mostly ignored by my discipline. My monograph on literature and photography of poverty was one of only three such book-length studies by English professors in the previous 30 years. This is largely because the poor are not represented in the professoriate; while women and minorities were under-represented therein into the 1980s, and minorities still without question are, they have a voice, while there were and continue to be almost no tenured professors who are living in poverty. Yes, instructors are an exploited group, and a significant percentage qualify as poor, but they are not producing monographs: because they are generally being overworked for little pay and don't have the time.

CHAPTER 21

Is Zen for Real, or a Con?

"Will you turn out the light?" Beth said, groggy. "For Christ sake."

"Sure, sorry." I closed the book I was reading.

"I really enjoyed that stuff tonight," she said, having listened to some of my material (described in the previous chapter).

"Thanks."

"But you have to take a break. You said you had another real breakthrough," she added.

"I did." I sighed. "But I'm still pressed for time." I nodded at the book I'd just jammed between the mattress and the wall. "This one's about tennis," I admitted.

Having reaffirmed my lack of faith in coaches, I turned to my lack of faith in self-help books. Though I decided I couldn't get the answer from reading, I did a bit looking for an answer. I read Timothy Gallwey's *The Inner Game of Tennis*, which could have been titled "Zen in the Art of Tennis"—but was promisingly, it seemed, not written by a German in Japan just after World War II. I read John McPhee's *Levels of the Game* (which is by no means intended to be a self-help book; it's a highly literary work of journalism). I read Brad Gilbert's *Winning Ugly*. I actually purchased and read these books in their entirety. Buying and reading how-to books was slightly embarrassing; I'd never under any circumstances done it before. I needed help, no question. But I was a firm believer in the necessity of firsthand experience in helping yourself: you had to construct for yourself the nature of the problem to be solved. It was a testament to my desperation at this point that I was willing to take a step I so little believed in.

The self-help books didn't help me much. I could understand what they advised. I needed to relax, yes—I had a thousand voices yelling at me to relax—but I had no idea how to do so in the context of a match. Gallwey talked a lot about "being in the zone." It was where you felt like you couldn't miss; the basketball hoop appeared as big as a whale's mouth; the opponent's side of the court seemed longer than an airport runway.

The zone sounded great—kind of like "You don't shoot, the arrow does" did—but most of all it just sounded like an idea. I wanted to believe in Zen, in "the zone"—in a Zen zone. But wanting to believe in it didn't mean I did, and it surely had nothing in common with experiencing it.

In his book, former player and coach Brad Gilbert suggested humming to calm yourself: that kind of worked, except sometimes I was so nervous I couldn't remember how the tune went. And when I could, it made me only slightly less edgy. If the zone was real, I didn't know how to gain entrance.

I also heard about the Zen-tennis connection from players. Maybe this intimate secondhand contact would be more fruitful. One of the few things I did understand in the almost entirely incomprehensible *Archery* was that the master insisted the art couldn't be learned from reading about it. It could be learned only from a teacher.

There was a compact forty-year-old named Raj who talked about "oneness" and becoming "one" with one's environment, and who I came to think of as "One-ball." He was a strong rallier; he hardly ever missed. And he never lost his cool or spoke much above a whisper. Often it was hard to hear him. His pursuit of spirituality was so serious he was about to move to Nepal or Sri Lanka or his father's ancestors' homeland, India. This was particularly impressive because his dad's family had been in the United States for generations and was thoroughly Americanized; seeing or hearing him, you would never suspect his background was anything other than blueblood WASP; his mother was from North Carolina, and he only spoke English; he knew no one in Asia and had never been there. He'd already given up his apartment and was temporarily staying with a friend.

Everyone at the UIC outdoor courts on the Near South Side knew him and respected his almost otherworldly consistency. Of course, obnoxious Marco would have mocked him because he only rallied and never competed in sets, but Marco didn't play at UIC. If I was going to learn to relax on the tennis court, as all the books counseled, I'd perhaps have to choose partners who were not angry assholes but instead spiritual nice-guy types.

One day, after a few sessions of just rallying with One-ball, which were indeed somewhat meditative (though also a little tedious), he suggested we play a special sort of competition.

I'd never known him to do anything but rally, and I thought, "Ah, now perhaps my real initiation into the mystery begins."

What he proposed was a lot like a single game of tennis, but it was longer—the first to ten points won—meanwhile, there was no serve. The point commenced by rallying: once the ball had gone over and back, within reach and not too fast, it was a live ball, and the competition began.

I accepted the challenge. One-ball didn't explain why he preferred this game to actual tennis, but I remembered that in *Archery* the master occasionally has the initiate undertake somewhat bizarre activities with the bow that fall short of archery itself—without any explanation.

A cynical voice in my head had a different reaction. It couldn't help observing that this "special" game played to One-ball's strengths—all he ever did was rally from the baseline. He never served or returned serve. This voice wondered if he preferred to whittle tennis down to his strong suit. But I told this voice to pipe down; to learn anything, I needed to be open-minded.

However, if One-ball chose this game out of a desire to dominate— the voice wouldn't quite shut up—he'd failed to take something into account, which became evident from the first point. Once the ball was live, I was no longer hitting groundstrokes, nor allowing him simply to hit rally-type balls from his comfort zone: not only was I heading to the net, taking time away from his usual rhythm, but I was making him move off the baseline by hitting short balls. He was much less adept at coming forward, hitting approach shots or volleying the ball on a fly, since he never did these things.

I took the first game by a couple of points. We met at the net.

"Let's do another one," he snapped. I'd never heard his voice so clearly.

"Okay," I said.

It seemed possible from his not exactly composed reaction that he thought the result of the first game was a fluke.

I quickly went ahead in the second game, and was a point away from another victory. Then suddenly One-ball was screaming at me.

Maybe he'd been stung by a bee. I once again couldn't hear what he was saying. But this was because he was yelling from the baseline, where he apparently always remained unless driven off it. I could hazard a guess as to why his face was contorted in a snarl, but I really had no idea what he could actually be saying.

"What's wrong?" I called.

He kept yelling, but didn't move forward.

So I did.

"You're only using *one* ball," he was shouting.

"What?" I said.

"All the balls are on your side, and you keep picking up the same ball to start a new point."

I turned around and looked toward my backcourt. There *were* two other balls back there. "You're right," I said. "So what?"

"Why are you using only one ball?"

Did he think the one I was using was somehow "loaded"? A trick ball? "I only need one," I said. Because there was no serve or second serve.

"Why aren't you picking up the other balls? They're sometimes closer."

Was this guy for real? "You want the other balls?" I barked. "Okay." I went to retrieve them.

By the time I turned around, One-ball—as I, at that moment, and forever after, thought of him—was packing up his gear.

"I'm not playing anymore," he squawked.

I stood at the net. I didn't even bother saying it: was the problem really my use of only one ball, or was he angry about losing—and finding a way to stop the thing, and save face, before I won again? After all, he was sure he was the better player and could beat me, and he wasn't going to let a little thing like the fact that I was winning the idiosyncratic game he'd devised stop him from believing this.

A player named Trip gave me fresh hope about the reality of Zen. He was a kind of legend around the Waveland courts, and I'd heard a lot about his skills—and aura—before I saw him in the flesh. Coincidentally, as I'd learned, he'd gone to the same college as I had though I didn't know him: he was a few years older and a trust-fund kid.

The day I met him, a few of the regulars and I watched him approach from across the green. It was like something out of a movie. He was on the short side but muscular, a South American guy with long bleached dreadlocks, a dark beard, and dark glasses, decked out in skintight athletic wear and a thermal vest and beads and a woolly hat, and on his feet were not tennis shoes but some sort of state-of-the-art slippers, the sort of thing I imagined one wore for yoga or rock climbing maybe, when one wanted, for reasons of safety or spirituality, to feel very fully the earth beneath one's soles—as long as it wasn't raining. How could he play in those, and with no socks (let alone two pair), without tearing up his feet? His stride was long and slow; he sauntered like he was not and never would be in a hurry, as though he was utterly unencumbered by things.

He certainly wasn't weighed down by the usual supplies players brought to the courts. He carried no tennis bag or backpack; he also had no towel or water bottle. He looked like he was ready to scale a wall, or trek in the outback, or stalk a deer, compactly equipped for a thousand-mile hike under aerodynamic conditions, though he lived a few minutes' walk away, in one of the iconic apartment buildings that lined Lakeshore Drive. And wait, the oddest thing of all now struck me. Inexplicably, he carried no racket! No water bottle—that was impressive—but no racket; that made no sense. Was he somehow going to play tennis with his bare hands, or his mind?

It was only when Trip was upon us that I realized he had his racket tucked into the back of his shirt, under his clothes, and thus hidden from view.

"Ciao, gentlemen," he said.

One of the other guys introduced me and suggested that Trip and I should hit sometime. We bumped fists.

"That'd be cool," Trip said. "I'm up here most afternoons. Just come on by."

I said I preferred to make a plan for a specific day and time if that was all right—since it took me half an hour to drive there.

I soon learned that he always arrived late because he was unconcerned with time. I started to come late to coincide with his arrival because I was *very* concerned with time at this juncture, and it irritated me to waste it waiting for him. I always brought the balls when we played because Trip would have been satisfied picking up old, worn-out ones on the far side of the fence; he couldn't be bothered with buying them, and, anyway, he wouldn't carry anything that couldn't be slipped into his clothing without bulging.

Every time Trip got on the court, he went through the same involved, idiosyncratic sequence. The first time we played, he didn't mention that he had a routine; he just launched into it.

It turned out that he indeed began without a racket. He initially warmed up near the net, playing "small ball" with his hands. (I used my racket.) Then, when he moved on from handball to tennis, we rallied for an irregular amount of time, and for part of it he attached weights to his ankles. (Where he carried these on his person I didn't know.) At some point, he announced he was ready to include the serve. Then we would take turns serving and returning serve. In this phase, we played out points but didn't tally them.

At the very end of this intricate preparation, if and when he was ready, we would finally play a single seven-point tiebreaker. Very occasionally, there was not even this brief competition, as he would instead suddenly announce that he'd had enough for the day. Was it a question of whether he'd made it into the zone?

I had some truly memorable afternoons on the court with Trip because of his unusual attitude. One day we played in the pouring rain for nearly an hour, sliding around on the courts until the balls became so heavy with water that they were more like rocks and we had to stop.

I wasn't sure what I thought about Trip. Though in certain ways a free spirit, he was very particular about what we did on the court and when—and asserted control over it quietly but with an iron hand. I was convinced he was following an elaborate ritual that had meditative value to him. So maybe it was Zen.

His absolute control over what we did, and when, was so silent and complete that things could get weird. Once, at the end of warm-ups, when I thought we were about to turn to the tiebreak, he said to me, "Good set. Well done."

"Huh?" I said.

"You lost 6–3, but well played."

"What?"

Apparently, during what was usually the practice serving phase, and because he carefully regulated how much each of us served, we'd played not only games but an entire set without his mentioning it to me or ever citing any score. It was a bizarre experience, playing and losing a set without even being aware that I'd been in one.

If and when we finally got to the tiebreaker, which he did announce, he invariably won. He was very strong and quite athletic—he'd played soccer on a Division I team and tennis at two other colleges (he'd gone to half a dozen schools in the United States and South America). His strokes were stronger and more consistent than mine. He had a monster first serve and a wickedly kicking second serve that bounced above head height; both gave me trouble.

Nonetheless—notwithstanding his total dominance, and based on no evidence—I had the sense that I ought to be able to beat him: that I was for some reason hamstrung in the tiebreaks, never quite playing up to my potential. It was a strange conviction and seemingly unfounded. But it lingered—and bugged me.

I still found the zone hard to believe in. It sounded again, oddly, ominously, a bit like Heidegger. (Was he in the zone when he joined the Nazi Party?)

Which made me wonder: Was the zone somehow related to "being" after all? Yes, this was only tennis, but weren't the Buddhists, or like-minded folks, Kerouac and the Beats, always saying that you could take any path, ride any activity, to enlightenment? The Samurai sword, the tea service, archery, motorcycle maintenance?

It didn't matter though. These questions, though very deep, were rather moot since the zone seemed to me a complete fiction, just like nirvana, enlightenment, satori, and so on seemed utter fantasies.

But for some reason, I didn't give up on it.

I was asking myself these "deep" questions and continuing, on the court, to pursue the elusive zone I thought I didn't give credence to precisely because I'd come to believe in it at some level. And I'd done so because—though unaware of it—I was, after decades of academic research and writing, hitting a kind of "scholarly zone."

For the first time in my academic life, the writing itself was coming easily, without the self-doubt, sense of fraudulence, and drive for self-torture that had made me so ambivalent about scholarship for almost my whole career. It suddenly seemed altogether possible that I *would* manage to write an entire draft of the monograph during the sabbatical, as planned.

No doubt my relationship with Beth was the most fundamental ingredient behind all this change. She was a model of bravery. And balance.

The intellectual transformation she'd gone through was startling. But even more striking was her attitude about an undertaking that had no guarantees. She was pushing herself hard, but she knew what her limits were and wasn't willing to go beyond them. Some people would say she was being naive and reckless. Wasn't she just setting herself up for failure, given that medical schools would want to see evidence of a person who was devoting all of her waking time to premed preparation?

But was failure the worst thing that could happen? Beth was interested in being a doctor for reasons other than money. Maybe, in a deeper sense, she was being just the opposite of reckless.

Meanwhile, with her support I was fighting pitched battles everywhere in my life, conflicts I might have slunk away from as a younger person. And I too might fail where it mattered intensely to me, no matter how well I did. All this scholarship might not result in publication with a top press, and, even if it did, I might not be able to parlay it into a better job in some other part of the country. Then what would Beth and I do? She and I had talked about it. We'd agreed that moving was definite and nonnegotiable. Was I willing to leave academia if necessary? Give up tenure and try to start over in another line of work? If I wasn't willing to, would she leave me? She might, and who could blame her? I didn't even want to think about any of that.

CHAPTER 22

Smashing through the Looking Glass

I shut the door behind me and dropped my tennis bag on the floor. It was spring.

The dogs jumped on me. They needed a walk. I needed a shower. But all that could wait a minute.

"Enough is enough," I mumbled. I'd just returned from another tie-break defeat against Trip.

I stood in our half living room in my sweaty clothes with the dogs barking and proceeded to take a private vow. Yes, an oath about tennis. I pledged to myself, "I will start playing at the limits of my ability in competitions—and damn the score. I resolve to grade myself on the basis of my level of play: shot speed, risk taking, and . . . that sort of thing."

I could adopt a new measure, like the army.

Hitting the ball out would now be all right, no longer an error, as long as I hit it hard. And hitting the ball in, if I hit it in tentatively, would henceforth be considered worthless.

It all sounded simple, childish even, but I couldn't remember the last time I'd taken any kind of private vow—besides I guess the one I took in eighth grade to avenge myself on my enemies even if it took decades. There is a weird power in this kind of pact with oneself, I thought. And, at least in my life, which had no history of religious conversion or attempts to quit smoking, it was exotic—if also absurd.

Then I got back on the court and found out that this weird power was not very strong. A private vow is easy to break. The first time out I found myself violating it. Maybe not in the first two games; the third was borderline, but by the fourth I had definitely reverted to being tentative and caring about the score.

I was on this supposedly special day playing my weekly game against my original nemesis Theodore. I'd taken a vow, but years of bad habits quickly overrode it.

However, I was also aware that I was violating my not-exactly-but-kinda-sacred vow. And if Theodore was going to mock me for wild shots, I was ready to ridicule myself for taking safe ones. My vow meant I was apparently going to be shamed no matter what I did.

With the score tied, I reminded myself of my new measure. "What the fuck will it take?" I said under my breath.

Then Theodore made a dubious call. From the next point on, I was hitting away with furious abandon. I swung with such recklessness that just about every ball off my racket smacked the back curtain on a fly—and would have been out by a dozen feet or more. (We were playing inside because it was winter again in Chicago even though it was spring.) What I was doing seemed pointless, unsportsmanlike, and surprising even to me. I wanted to laugh.

I rapidly dropped the next few games. But I didn't care.

Rather, I was oddly elated—while still quite angry. I'd hit on something. My mental promise was not enough. I needed a physical device to break me out of my emotional trap. And suddenly, accidentally almost, I'd discovered the mechanical antidote to being tight.

I'd happened on something else: to hit away with *angry* abandon. Hitting hard shook out the nerves; anger dissolved them. I didn't realize I was infuriated because I was also happy.

Theodore was just irate. On the changeover, he accused me of throwing the last three games. "What in the hell are you doing? Are you mad about that 'out' call back a few games ago?"

"What call? No, I'm not," I assured him cheerfully, angrily, definitely lying, but to a degree unaware of it because I felt so liberated to be exercising my freedom to fuck up entirely in a match. And now my pleasure was increased by knowing that he knew he'd made a bad call.

"You're throwing the set?" he continued.

"No." Was I? Who cared?

He kept at it. "You think I cheated?"

"Not at all," I lied again, this time totally aware of it. The whole exchange was making me giddy. I was barely able to keep a straight face. The great thing was that Theodore was no longer smugly mocking me; he was instead petulantly confronting me. Had Theodore's bad call—as much as my vow—provoked me to hit away and lose a dozen points in a row? What unexpected joy. I wanted to thank him, but I couldn't because part of the gift was his present huffiness.

I didn't know what finally did it. But in the next game, abruptly, for seemingly no reason, I was playing the best I'd ever played. I was hitting just as hard as I had been when the balls were twenty feet long, but now they were landing within the lines of the court.

I was loose. I was relaxed. I was pissed off. I was on fire.

This may sound paradoxical, but here, I'd realize later, was a true Zen paradox. Then something else bizarre happened.

There was a shot I'd never been able to figure out. I didn't know how to crack a high forehand—off a shoulder-high ball. I'd seen pros do it on TV, and the best amateurs knew how to too. I'd tried different grips, various swings. One day after a doubles game with Bobby Lewis, exasperated, I'd cornered a teaching pro and got him to show me. I came away with a sore arm from making squid-like movements that were okay for an invertebrate but inadvisable for the human skeleton.

In the last game of this set with Theodore, along came a high ball to my forehand side, and I did it. I hammered the ball for a firecracker of a winner. I made the moves without my mind planning it out or even cognizant of how my body did it.[1]

I'd somehow relaxed without knowing how to do so. Here entered the aspect of sports that, if not exactly spiritual, was weird: you needed to relinquish your mental control. But you couldn't control that relinquishment.

I'd won a bunch of games in a row and the set.

My device of throwing some games to loosen myself up—what turned out in retrospect to be a gambit; at the time I had no strategy at all—had

---

1. It required holding the racket with an extreme western grip and hitting the forehand with a fully extended arm; meanwhile, the motion took my feet off the ground: I finished the shot airborne.

been the way. Naturally, Theodore, upset before because he thought I was throwing the set, was enraged that I wasn't but had actually taken it.

He sulkily collected his belongings and left without a word. That, too, was highly satisfactory.

I'd learned a valuable lesson thanks to him: sometimes you have to lose a few games to be able to win a bunch more. Sometimes it's really great to irritate your opponent. The answer to my problem of hitting tentatively was to get mad, or in my case to trigger my dormant anger (which was always nearby because of my father's murder by medical error, my unending legal case, my workplace, etc.).

And a world of difference from getting mad at yourself for hitting gingerly was to get enraged at your opponent for being an angry middle-aged man—who felt justified in cheating now and then because he was mad that the world was hard on him. The only problem with this strategy was that he might not always give you a reason. In my case, the opponents I was choosing gave you reason often enough: they were angry pricks who were a lot like me.

The fact was, I'd been "in the zone": the zone I didn't believe in until that moment. Yes, I'd stopped overthinking, which in the case of tennis is more or less the same as thinking. The anger shut off the mental noise— and let my body do its thing.

Maybe the weirdest thing of all was the moment of transition, when I went from smacking the back curtain to hitting within the court. The change corresponded to something foreign and inexplicable happening in my head. I didn't fully observe this moment the first time it happened, and only became familiar with it from repeated experience. It didn't have a smooth psychological transition. No, there was a discontinuity, an interruption: to use a concept from physics and math, a singularity.

Instead of a gradual change, the transition was like a switch had suddenly been thrown inside of me. I was instantly flushed with confidence. And I felt sure that I could make the shots I'd been missing.

It was a strange sensation, difficult to put into words. It was as if something were playing through me, the me who generally played pretty mediocre tennis. I felt different in my own skin. The experience made me think of ancient poets talking about being inhabited by the Muse. The Greeks had had several Muses for the several arts, didn't they? Clio was the one for historical study—scholarship—and I guess I'd recently felt like I'd met her too. They had Terpsichore, which meant "delight in dancing." That was close. Maybe they'd have had one specifically for tennis if they'd had tennis.

Later, I'd come to court this magical moment of transfiguration and wait for it.

If being in the zone was Zen, then Zen didn't mean mental quiet in the sense of serene peacefulness—the hippies' and Kerouac's idea of Zen, which I'd never bought. It meant mental quiet in the sense of joyful warlike pissed-off-ness.

I'd stumbled into this entrance to the zone by accident. A key to getting there had been selecting obnoxious, almost unbearable men as partners. I'd hardly have been comfortable getting furious with a completely courteous tennis opponent.

CHAPTER 23

Scholarly Detective Story VI, Continued

THE ARMY'S "INCONSISTENT" POLICY ON MINORITIES

"I am leery of the claim that 'meritocratic methods'... were used to evaluate [ethnic Americans] during World War I. I put that up against the history of a segregated armed forces and the refusal to allow blacks in combat during that war."

This was the judgment of another senior humanities scholar, on another review panel, in downgrading another grant proposal I submitted.

What was the logic of this comment? Was armed-forces policy required to be consistent in its bias? This scholar expected discriminatory coherence from the army, and actually the army too had initially wanted a policy of "no racial discrimination." However, the army was not entirely autonomous. Moreover, the issue here for this accomplished professor was that of prejudice, while for the army it was winning the war. Student papers have to be consistent in their argumentation, but is this the way things work in the real world of practical policies made by institutions (e.g., the military) ultimately under the dictates of other institutions (e.g., the federal government)?

No question, Black men were horribly discriminated against by the army (though it is simply false that the army refused to allow Black men in combat). But what if social justice or injustice had little to do with the army's decision-making, and instead it was motivated only by expediency?

What I learned from research was this: the military leadership initially hadn't proposed the horrible racial policy that it ended up adopting, namely that African American men were segregated, mostly kept out of combat, and shunted off to do manual labor, with only a token percentage allowed to be officers. But powerful civilian leaders in the South wanted the national government to segregate Black men in the army and exclude them from combat and positions of authority.

As social-military historian Jennifer Keene revealed in 2005, the army's initial plans for Black men in 1917 had reflected its policy of "no racial discrimination in the National army." The original plan had acknowledged white racial anxieties in merely one particular: African Americans would be allotted to the army bases such that there remained an "overwhelming white majority in each camp." When southern civilian officials committed to Jim Crow heard about this plan, especially the part about training hundreds of thousands of Black men in the use of arms, they went ballistic, and the White House was besieged with complaints.

But there was no such state-governmental "interest group" agitating for a like discrimination against ethnic Americans. The army wanted to use the men at its disposal in order to win the war; it didn't want to waste them—unless it was overruled by the commander-in-chief.

Relevant to my research story, the army probably did all it could to minimize the civilian opposition to its policy of extending equal opportunities to ethnic Americans and immigrants by doing so *on the down low*. The army, I surmised, didn't splash this egalitarian program across headlines because it didn't want to stir up public reaction in the wartime moment of public xenophobia, and its relative stealth here was precisely why this piece of American military history was long forgotten or "secret" and had to be "rediscovered" in the archives by Nancy Ford, who published her book in 2001. There was no public record of it in congressional acts or in newspapers; the only evidence of it was in the army's papers—and some of the most famous American novels ever written.

The military, like a few other institutions in our society, the prison system being another prime example, is given remarkable leeway in how it "gets the job done." Because these extremely autonomous select institutions operate in large part out of the public view, they tend to be able to develop practices radically out of step with the rest of the society to which they belong. Thus the generally barbaric conditions of prison life in our own time and the standout egalitarianism of the army in 1917–1918.

In the intramilitary discussion of the policy on ethnic Americans—when Lieutenant Gutowski pitched senior officers—he put forth the argument that if the army could get immigrants into battle, fewer "American boys" would die. Not exactly a "social justice" rationale.

If these two issues—the treatment of African Americans and that of immigrants—were related for the army, it wasn't a matter of having a consistent prejudicial policy on minorities. It was the fact that, having had to bow to civilian pressure to adopt a policy that alienated African Americans (13 percent of the troops), the army brass really couldn't afford to lose the cooperation of immigrants and second-generation ethnic Americans as well, another 33 percent of the force. They wouldn't have a functional army, and winning the war was considered pretty important. In reality, a consistent policy on discrimination—which the NEH reviewer expected presumably because of his or her expertise in literary, not military, studies—was exactly what the army could *not* afford to implement.

And that was why, even when it came to Black men, as vicious as the segregation and discrimination was, the army didn't entirely cave to southern demands. It still trained some Black men in arms and put some of them into combat: about 11 percent, or forty-five thousand men, which is a lot more than zero Black men in combat, the figure that white southern leaders wanted. (To contextualize the percentage of Black men in combat, overall only about 40 percent of non-Black American soldiers were designated for combat; the rest were assigned to support of one kind or another.) It still stationed Black men at army training camps located in the South. It still commissioned twelve hundred Black officers or 0.32 percent of Black doughboys (again to contextualize, the overall ratio of officers to servicemen was 4.9 percent, so this was definitely tokenism). It still sent about two hundred thousand African American men to France, a country not governed by Jim Crow. Many white southern officials considered these practices of the army plum dangerous, irresponsible, and outrageous.

The grant reviewer was "leery," and that was understandable, as I'd initially been plenty suspicious myself. But there was the option of checking the relevant sources I was required to provide rather than just go with an academic "hunch."

This wasn't much different from one of my graduate students who, knowing what "he knew" about William Burroughs, doubted that the counterculture writer would have tried five times to get into officer training during World War II.

"But he did," I'd replied to him in class at the end of the previous semester. "It's in the biographies. And he says so here in *Junky*, which is autobiographical. The line we just read . . ."

"Well, he wasn't *really* trying to get in," the student countered.

"In one of these attempts, he spent eight months learning to fly a plane," I pointed out. "On his own dime."

"Well, I don't think he was *really* trying to get in," he repeated, apparently by way of argument. "He was just screwing with the government."

"How do you know that?" I said. "I understand," I added gently, in a teacherly manner, "your view is based on the sense of Burroughs you have coming into class here—but you should research this a bit further before you make up your mind."

I guess I'm not surprised by anyone's tendency for ideological thinking, and I certainly understand the capacity for delusion. Reality is often complex and unpleasant. It puts a damper on our worldviews and self-images. But, as scholars, maybe even as people, we should try to get the facts and face them, not ignore them or explain them away.

I suppose I've learned this the hard way: while your delusions may make your life more enjoyable for the time being, you may have to pay for them—plus interest—down the line. I'd messed myself up for a good few years believing I could be a popular writer: sure, I wrote a pretty damned good novel, but it wasn't the kind of thing publishers and marketing people thought any normal, "well adjusted" person wanted to read. I'd seen more than one colleague do a number on himself by pinning his career hopes on a plan of action that most everyone around him saw as pure wishful thinking.

CHAPTER 24

Zen, Then Not Zen

"It's fucking mind-blowing," I said.

I'd called up my friend Reuel and was sharing my transcendent experience on the court. I thought he'd once gotten similarly intense about golf. I was wrong.

"Are you sure you're okay?" he said. (More recently he's told me that I came across to him then as someone "absolutely obsessed" and "in the throes of an addiction.")

Up until my first moment in the zone, my attraction to tennis had been mysterious. I couldn't say why I'd gotten so serious about a mere game, and stuck with it. But now I thought I understood. And if I still didn't entirely understand—and I didn't, not the deeper stakes—it didn't matter to the intensity of my feelings at this point. I'd been there. I'd experienced that sensation. And, for someone with almost no history of drug use, that high was mind-blowing.

It was more than that. I could see it was obviously better than drug use, and fundamentally different. Cocaine made you feel powerful, gave you delusions of grandeur. But there was nothing artificial or illusory about being in the zone. You *were* powerful; your performance *was* grand. You not only felt different; you were different. The evidence was incontrovertible: other people could see it; it was registered in the game score.

The only problem I could see was that it wasn't so easy to get back to the zone, and very difficult to stay there for any length of time. Even thinking, "Hey, I'm in the zone!" could knock you right out of it.

And because of my warped high-school perspective, I had trouble, strange as it sounds, believing what was happening.

"Wow, you hit a couple of professional-grade shots out there," a guy who used to beat me said to me one day as we packed up our tennis bags.

"I don't know about that," I said. It was unusual to hear guys offer praise; I was used to blustering and contempt.

"Maybe this isn't the sort of player I should be comparing myself to," I thought. "He's embarrassed, and it probably makes him feel better to exaggerate my level. Maybe I was a lousy player when he skunked me, and now I'm merely all right."

These niggling questions were debilitating. The human capacity for self-doubt—mine anyway—is something astounding. I couldn't simply deny the evidence of my eyes: here I was playing, now and then, at a level that I'd thought impossible for me. But I could definitely at the same time doubt that I could ever do it again.

"Maybe it was a fluke," I'd think. I'd sometimes say to opponents, after hitting a winner, "Oh, that was just a lucky shot." And when I had that knee-jerk reaction of doubt—each time I looked with awe, almost shock, at a hard winner I'd just hit—I backed up in my play a bit. And, just like that, I was bumped out of the zone.

If I doubted what was undeniably happening, I wasn't the only one. My feeling was quietly and bluntly put into words, one day during a doubles match by an opponent named Oscar, a seventy-year-old retired doctor, but perhaps one of the best septuagenarian club players in existence: he drove all around the country playing USTA tournaments. Abnormally quick for anyone of any age, he returned serve from just behind the service line, and would sometimes jump the net just for fun. (People like Oscar, by the way—and I played with other guys in their seventies in great shape—give the lie to our American sense of the diminishment that necessarily comes at this and that age.)

His partner, a white man named Max in his midfifties, was an accountant and played the unfriendliest game of anyone I knew. He would routinely aim for your head when you were at net, willing to lose points if you managed to duck in time.

My partner, Tim, was generally even-keeled and, at six feet three, didn't often feel threatened, but would have hostile exchanges with Max every time we played. Max pissed me off as well, which was crucial to the situation. Oscar and Max had won the vast majority of sets we played. Oscar was thus familiar with my game.

During the wintry spring day in question at the indoor McFetridge public courts, there was no unfriendly banter because Max was silent. I was taking dramatic cuts at the ball, and I couldn't miss. Tim's game was also on, though not supernatural. We took the set 6–0. Nobody'd muttered much of anything until Oscar said to me, on the changeover between sets, in a flat tone that belied its sage, paradoxical quality: "You're playing beyond your ability."

Our senses of ourselves run very deep and affect everything we do. I had to learn how to compete in sports all over again, to return to a way of playing I hadn't had since age twelve.

Andy Roddick, the American tennis player who won his only Grand Slam title as a young man and thus ought to know, commented, in a moment of philosophical conciseness, "Experience is overrated; confidence is underrated." Experience ideally makes us tougher, wiser, and more effective: as many people like to say, echoing Nietzsche, "What doesn't kill me makes me stronger."

But the problem with difficult experiences is that they can, instead, in a vicious cycle of self-fulfilling prophecy, create, confirm, and deepen a diminished sense of possibility, since we bring our limiting beliefs to almost every situation. Not to mention that horrific experiences tend to leave us post-traumatic and vulnerable to retrograde emotional states. What doesn't kill us often makes us weaker.

During my teens, I never approached a sports competition with the same sense of confidence with which I entered the classroom as a college senior to take the GRE. I remembered that Saturday morning in 1982 quite well. There I was in line at the door clutching my two sharpened no. 2 pencils, and I couldn't wait to get into the testing room—I didn't even care that it was at the ungodly hour of 8:00 a.m. I was boisterous, drunk with anticipation, joking and laughing loudly. I could hardly shut up when the test began.

At a certain juncture, I moved forward in the room because my 20/20 vision had just started to disintegrate—all the reading in college—and I was having trouble seeing the instructions on the blackboard. The proctor asked me why I was changing seats, and I shot back, so inappropriately that I still remembered it, "I can't see the board from back there cuz I'm going *fucking* blind." I walked out of that room having missed only one question on the whole three-hour exam.

I was going to have to recover my childhood physical confidence if I was going to hold my own in USTA tournaments or beat Trip in a tie-break. One final mental block still stood in my way.

CHAPTER 25

Scholarly Detective Story VII

THE NEW LITERARY-HISTORICAL SYNTHESIS

Once I'd gone through the military papers and done all the necessary intellectual collating, I was on my way to understanding these Lost Generation novels in a new way. I knew why they all featured ethnic American, working-class, or outsider characters with military ties who got the desirable Anglo women.

And soon I mostly understood why Fitzgerald, Hemingway, and Faulkner would all care so much about this: because I started looking at some biographical study, which was abundant.

They were the right age to be in World War I as young men. All three had wanted to be in combat and to be officers, specifically pilots, the stars of the war. And none of them were.

Both Faulkner and Fitzgerald were stymied in their bids to get into the war: neither made it over. Fitzgerald spent the war in various American training camps, often mocked by fellow officers, but what can you expect when you spend most of the time in your tent writing a novel? When Faulkner was told by the American air corps that he was too small to be a pilot, he put on weight and even attempted to stretch himself, but he remained, not surprisingly, too short. He ended up in a Canadian Royal Air Force camp where they didn't have such standards, but the war ended before he completed his training.

Their war ambitions were frustrated. They were understandably jealous of and intimidated by guys who managed to see combat, and they felt more than a little humiliated by the whole ordeal. Fitzgerald expressed, more than a decade later, his regret at not making it overseas to fight. Faulkner found a different way to deal with his similar disappointment. He came back to the States with a cane and a faked limp, telling a story about how his aircraft had been shot down in France.

Everything seemed to be falling neatly into place, except Hemingway. He'd made it over to Europe, and though he hadn't become a US pilot, he'd witnessed action as a Red Cross ambulance driver. It turned out he was the very first American injured on the Italian front, and as such, he was awarded medals, and his hometown newspaper reported the wounding as well as his own account of his heroics. According to the article, he'd somehow, miraculously, carried a guy to safety after being hit by shrapnel and shot in the knee with a machine gun.

But on reading a little further I noticed something that all Hemingway's recent biographers were aware of but that none of them, oddly, had bothered to consider too much when analyzing his novels of the period. Namely, he'd felt some shame about his noncombatant role ("a very sort of minor camp follower," he later called himself), the front he'd been on (he called the Italian a "joke front" in *Sun* and a "silly front" in *A Farewell to Arms*), and the actual details of his wounding. It turned out he'd fabricated the story about his heroism that made it into the paper.

Hemingway had indeed been hit by shell fragments on a Red Cross errand, delivering cigarettes, chocolate, and postcards to Italian soldiers. But he dropped on the spot, was immobilized, and had himself been carried to safety by stretcher-bearers. The event of his injury, then, didn't involve heroic action on his part. No big deal. But that the mundane nature of his activity in the trenches and his wounding troubled him can be gleaned from his having invented a miraculous version.

Hemingway had a bad eye and knew he'd fail the vision test for the air corps, so he didn't even try to get in. Too young (like Faulkner) to be drafted during the initial call-up in 1917 (when the draft age was twenty-one) but old enough to fight, he'd decided not to enlist and maybe end up on the front lines. He'd settled on driving an ambulance.

But he wasn't quite comfortable with that—at least not by the war's end. Like Faulkner, Hemingway altered his uniform after the war and attempted to pass himself off as a military veteran: he removed the Red

Cross insignia. He led his publisher to believe that he'd also been in the Italian infantry; I got hold of a 1970s copy of *Sun*, with the falsehood that first appeared in 1926 still on the back. This fabrication and the tall tale about his wounding weren't exposed until the 1980s.

Who could blame him for lying? By the war's end, masculinity was equated with being a combat soldier, and ambulance driving was considered women's work or, maybe worse, boys'. None other than Teddy Roosevelt—masculine arbiter extraordinaire—had publicly said so.

But no scholars had compared Hemingway's military embarrassments and frustrations to Fitzgerald and Faulkner's. Apparently, the Hemingway masculine mystique was just too strong and overrode what they knew factually about his experience and discomfort with it.

Not many critics had even wondered why Hemingway was so obsessed with masculinity. Since high school English, he'd always been presented to me more or less as a very manly guy, naturally occupied with supremely masculine things.

The point isn't that Hemingway was secretly unmanly but that the oppressive climate or hysteria concerning masculinity that descended on wartime America—in which service as anything less than a combatant was relegated to some form of unmanliness—had left all these authors feeling emasculated, even Hemingway, who got seriously wounded, for goodness' sake. They did all sorts of things to try to feel better about themselves, including writing the things they wrote for the next decade.

These artistically talented noncombatants had some pretty deep emotional scars. I called them "mobilization wounds." These writers might be more accurately dubbed the "Lost-Out Generation."

I'd come up with the thesis of my book. It was kind of surprising and would make good copy for a book jacket in the small and hermetic world of American literary scholarship:

> Ernest Hemingway, F. Scott Fitzgerald, and William Faulkner stand as the American voice of the Great War. But was it warfare that drove them to write? In truth, the authors' famous postwar novels were motivated not by their experiences of the horrors of war but by their failure to have those experiences . . .

What struck me most, after all this research and thinking, was that I'd come up with more than the beginning of an answer to Foucault's last question. He'd essentially asked: what were the new techniques of social organization of the World War I and postwar era, and who was the new type of individual shaped and controlled by these techniques? Now I understood that these famous American novels, which I'd been in awe of in high school, were reactionary—against a rising era that was characterized by a new meritocratic "art of government"[1] and favored a "New Man" with useful aptitudes, to use Foucault's terms.

These books of Hemingway and company were anguished cries, not about the horrors of war, but rather loss of the traditional privilege enjoyed by Anglo males from "good" (read: "well-off") families, and the consequent shameful loss of status before Anglo female peers, a privilege and status these writers had been brought up to expect. The army had abruptly changed the rules on them.

The "shock" of meritocracy and equal treatment to which the army was suddenly subjecting privileged Anglo men is repellently but concisely summed up in a paragraph in Fitzgerald's meandering and almost unreadable *The Beautiful and Damned* (published three years before *Gatsby*). The whiny Anglo upper-class protagonist detests the military for its failure to promote him in a manner consistent with his social status: in training camp, he finds himself "for the first time in his life . . . in constant personal contact with the waiters to whom he had given tips, the chauffeurs who had touched their hats to him, the carpenters, plumbers, barbers, and farmers who had previously been remarkable only in the subservience of their professional genuflections."

What had Fitzgerald and company been expecting? Compare the experience of the English social elite: when Robert Graves had wanted to get into the war, he essentially picked up the phone and called his high school guidance counselor, who got him a commission in something like

---

1. For Foucault, the word "government" did not imply federal, state, or municipal power, but meant social control generally.

half an hour, as he recounts in his autobiographical *Good-Bye to All That* (1929). Days later it seems he was commanding men at the front lines in France. Siegfried Sassoon recounts something similar in his *Memoirs of a Fox-Hunting Man* (1928).

Though the sudden change in America lasted only as long as the war, it shaped the American authors' coming of age, World War I being the central event in their generation's experience. The unprecedented US mobilization policy, consciously crafted as an alternative to Britain's "mistaken" one, meant in the end that none of them made the grade of combat officer. And it's easy to see why these American writers had different responses to the war than their European counterparts. Fitzgerald, Hemingway, and Faulkner, along with John Dos Passos (who served in an ambulance unit and also in the army's Services of Supply), were all preoccupied in their works with this problem of marginal status and emasculation. The famous British writers who became combat soldiers likewise wanted to prove themselves to their peers, but they were at the same time quite occupied with the more familiar and heavier wartime concerns of avoiding injury, maiming, and death; seeing comrades blown to pieces; and killing others.

The "big three" Anglo-American authors were subject to the limited meritocratic experiment that gave men they saw as their social and ethnic inferiors positions they themselves were rejected from. And that's why their novels, which reflected their anger at this unintended social justice, were truly part of the American literature of "the modern era of human aptitudes" that I'd ignorantly hypothesized and hazarded twenty years earlier at my disastrous orals, long before I came to understand what this phrase implied.

These authors belonged to this era precisely because they'd been lacking the "aptitudes" the army was suddenly requiring for combat officer and air corps status—and because their books were a backlash against this unprecedented meritocratic period. It was weird to think about, but you could say Gatsby, the lower-class, ethnic American man who qualified, in Fitzgerald's fiction, to be an officer in the country's new army, was a sort of poster boy for Foucault's New Man in the United States. No wonder Fitzgerald has him end up defeated and murdered.

What this meant in terms of the history of war and masculinity was that, as far as American postwar literature went, the United States largely missed out on that first shocked recoil from modern technological warfare that Europe profoundly experienced. There were American books comparable to the European ones by Graves, Sassoon, and others, by lesser-known authors who were never canonized. But because all the Lost Generation authors basically sat out the "Big Game," what they created in prose—and transmitted to future generations of Americans—was an intensified fantasy about masculine military prowess, a kind of romance not unlike that which animated the initial worldwide enthusiasm for the Great War, at its start, before the reality set in. Because we came to embrace and canonize these authors' stylistically modernist masterpieces, what got passed on to readers was an artificial machismo these writers were simulating.

This is especially true of Hemingway, though *Sun* still evinces a lot of male vulnerability even while it touts the hard-boiled attitude he's famous for. The narrator, Jake Barnes, is missing his penis, and he understandably cries over this when he's alone at night. But by the time you get to Hemingway's next novel, *Farewell*, a runaway bestseller, the characteristic machismo is fully realized and has nothing missing, so to speak. Traditional gender roles, completely out of whack in *Sun*, are snugly back in place in *Farewell*. In the earlier novel, the main female character, Lady Brett, is outrageous, not just one of "the chaps" but the alpha of the in-crowd, and the elitist and bigoted Jake takes some deserved licks from her as well as Robert Cohn. Jake is often back on his heels, sometimes laid out on the floor. By contrast, Frederick Henry, *Farewell*'s narrator, is essentially an action hero, and his nurse-girlfriend, Catherine Barkley, is so submissive and accommodating she actually apologizes to him for hemorrhaging as she dies in childbirth.

I'd like to say I want honesty from literature and not a con. But, practically speaking, I guess that would limit me to porn, Beckett, and little else. What I like from literature is tense, comic self-contradiction; painful but lovely uncertainty, and aesthetically pleasing confusion: just the sort of thing you get from Hemingway's *Sun*.

What does it mean to live in an era in which one is governed by one's aptitudes? To be downgraded on the basis of one's aptitudes, for failing to meet physical, mental, or performance standards, as Hemingway,

Faulkner, and Fitzgerald were in wartime, is a heavy kind of subjection. (And part of their reaction—a very ugly part—was to scapegoat disadvantaged ethnic Americans who benefited from this new type of social control and organization.) It is the sort of official rejection that leads one to postulate for oneself some kind of personal authenticity that institutions cannot appreciate or measure. Might I offer the wild hypothesis that the rise in our culture of the notion of authenticity—from art to psychotherapy to the counterculture to commerce—is absolutely tied up with the rise of meritocracy, which got its first national boost with the World War I army?

For better or worse, meritocratic methods of evaluation and assignment may be a more psychologically inescapable form of subjugation and disgrace. With race, class, or sex discrimination, the person subjected can, at least, indict the exercise of power as unjust. Meritocratic rejections are less easy to contest morally. Can one blame the military for refusing to put nearsighted or very short men in pilots' seats? It's hard for an individual to reject or deflect the rejections of a meritocratic system, even though that system will inevitably have its own arbitrariness. As Nicholas Lemann put it in *The Big Test: The Secret History of the American Meritocracy*, about our own era, "The SAT had become a powerful totem. To the taker it was a scientific, numeric assignment of worth which, no matter how skeptical one tried to be about testing, lodged itself firmly in the mind, never to be forgotten."

Yes, you could say these most famous and beloved American modernist novels represented the first wave of white male backlash art, with many more to come. Many more because, though the genie of meritocracy was put back in the bottle after World War I, it had clearly reemerged at some point and spread with a vengeance.

Now I wondered when and how. The endpoint of any Foucault history was to trace the trajectory of our forms of knowledge and power up through the present moment. (Thus, he referred to the nature of his study as "history of the present," which we had back then at Berkeley taken as the name of our little newsletter.)

Of course, racism, classism, and sexism, extreme in the World War I era, continue to be very much with us today. But it seems self-evident that we are also still living in a "regime of aptitudes"—though the army is no longer the driving force. This art of government, which seems to have extended itself all over our society, does a fairly effective, and sometimes painful, job of sorting us according to our grades, our test scores, and our résumés—and of exhorting us to identify ourselves on this basis. But I wondered: How did it happen that the army lost its dominant position in this regime, and what has that meant for American society? How did this expanding art of government impact the Vietnam era? And how did it affect those who were children then—my peers and myself?

It was beginning to nag at me that what I'd discovered about the Great War and the modernists was like the surface of a lake—and the depths involved for starters my profession's seeming taboo on research about the military. I sensed that there was a much larger story here, about American war and manpower and masculinity in the entire span of the twentieth century, which for some reason had been ignored. And, for very personal reasons that I didn't yet entirely understand but were nonetheless pushing me onward, this issue mattered to me.

Imagine my growing paranoia when I discovered that not only had the three major American Lost Generation novelists been frustrated in their military ambitions but that the two major Beat Generation novelists, William Burroughs and Jack Kerouac, had, too. Again, Burroughs failed numerous times to get into officer training, and Kerouac wanted to be a pilot but flunked the US Naval Air Force qualifying math test on calculating altitudes.

All five of these major US novelists—representing two major prose movements in American letters and the two world wars—had wanted to be combat officers, and specifically pilots. All of them had failed to do so. That was pretty striking.

That nobody had written about it was also pretty striking.

PART V

THE MYSTERIOUS ZONE

I must only warn you of one thing, [the master says]. You have become a different person in the course of these years. For this is what the art of archery means: a profound and far-reaching contest of the archer with himself. Perhaps you have hardly noticed it yet, but you will feel it strongly when you meet your friends and acquaintances again in your own country: things will no longer harmonize as before. You will see with other eyes and measure with other measures. It has happened to me too, and it happens to all who are touched by the spirit of this art.

—Eugen Herrigel, *Zen in the Art of Archery*

PART V

THE MYSTERIOUS ZONE

CHAPTER 26

The Big Wait

"Beth!" I yelled, as she opened the door and jumped out of the back seat of a moving car.

We had flown to Cleveland for my father's stone setting—it had been a year since his death. A relative of my dad's, in the driver's seat, still hurting badly, suddenly started yelling at my brother and me.

Meanwhile, Beth, who was dead set on withdrawing from her own family's destructive dramas, wasn't going to sit by and witness a berating we didn't deserve. The car was fortunately going slowly, through a hotel parking lot. She wasn't badly hurt, only scraped up a bit.

As we stood graveside later in the day, I mentioned to her that my father had changed for me in the intervening year since he died. He was very much in my dreams, visiting me in a guise different from his earthly one. At least what I thought he'd been like.

"How's he changed?" asked Beth, whose beliefs included strong and eccentric ones about the afterlife. In her afterlife, people had jobs.

"I always used to think of him," I said, "as someone that people took advantage of and walked over. A *mensch*, to use a word of his, but too nice. But maybe I had him wrong. Maybe he was a guy who said yes, and then did what he wanted." Maybe I'd missed something important about my dad. "Now he seems this powerful, mischievous spirit."

"Interesting."

"I thought he'd had, you know, normal mainstream attitudes. Now he comes and tells me things like, 'Don't worry too much about money.' Or he's driving me in an extra lane on the highway out past the shoulder that nobody else knows about. He's like a trickster character."

"That's pretty cool."

"Sometimes Foucault is in the car with him."

"Huh."

"I guess you don't have to be Sigmund Freud to figure that one out."

Beth shrugged. "I don't know. It may be more than just another father figure. From everything you've told me, I got the impression Foucault was a major trickster. And your dad was the one who introduced you to humor, wasn't he?"

I had a draft of the manuscript by the end of April, almost a month before the sabbatical ended.

Of course, nothing was in the bag. Publication was by no means guaranteed, let alone a prestige imprint—a necessity if I was going to have any chance of leveraging this book to get a new job. There were many ways even a carefully researched, innovative work could fail, and I'd already had a taste of some possibilities by the time I was sending out proposals.

One of the colleagues I'd asked to vet the book, a Lost Generation expert, had liked the manuscript so much he wanted to publish an excerpt in the journal he ran. A few weeks after he solicited the chapter, however, he came back to me, mortified. The editorial board had been divided, so intensely that publication threatened to tear it apart. He explained that some scholars felt fiercely territorial about "their" authors.

Another, more serious problem I was facing, which I tried to ignore, was that modernist scholars no longer considered the war to be relevant to the books I was discussing.

I was unpleasantly reminded of it when another colleague, likewise working on postwar writing, was putting together a panel proposal for the big, annual literary modernist studies conference and asked me to take part. I agreed, and the panel in the end included three scholars who had new books on the subject, either out or under contract. Nonetheless, the proposal was rejected, and that year, though the modernism convention included more than twenty panels, it had none related to war.

So I wasn't surprised when all the top presses I queried declined even to consider the manuscript, except one, which I understood was willing to give me a hearing because I'd published that slum book with them previously.[1]

I was entering what was for me the most psychologically difficult part of the whole process, trying to interest a publisher. And luckily, given the alternative of no press being willing to consider the manuscript, I soon found myself in the uncomfortable position of waiting, as I often did, as it sometimes seemed I'd spent my entire professional life doing, to hear back.

The sabbatical technically ended, and I passed the time on the tennis courts as well as packing up and moving to another, somewhat larger apartment in the less gang-infested neighborhood of the West Loop, thanks to money that had finally come through probate from my dad. In my mind, I was convinced that it was also beneficial to move at this point so I could have more square feet in which to pace.

After a few months of hardly knowing I was waiting, I woke one morning quite aware that I was.

"Go walk yourself," I snapped at Quilty, who was hovering near the bed.

"The sun is shining," I sternly told myself.

"Oh, boy," I thought.

One other thing Hemingway was right about—though I hated to admit he was ever right about anything—was the depression one experiences after finishing a book. What he didn't say is that the depression, for the average writer, is soon compounded by the anxiety that the book will be universally rejected. I'd been there before: days after finishing a book, I'd be trying to flee myself like a fugitive.

I could have really used at this point a Zen tennis master.

"Okay," I resolved, and dragged myself out of bed. Ready or not—and I knew I wasn't, mentally—it was time to enter official tournaments. Incidentally, the deadline I'd given myself was coming up.

---

1. Getting a hearing meant the editor would send my manuscript out to a couple experts in the field, who, for a token gratuity (around $200) but mostly out of a dedication to the profession, would anonymously review it and write reports that recommended publication or rejection.

My need for distraction was almost clinical. I slapped myself in the face.

"Huh," I mused. It was like I'd known what I was doing when I'd taken up tennis at the start of my sabbatical. If it hadn't early on given me refreshment from the strain of researching and thinking—it often enough gave me instead a different kind of intellectual strain, so that the solid intellectual ground of scholarship became an escape from the mental morass of tennis—it could now serve as an antidote to waiting.

I had no reason to be embarrassed by the thousands of dollars and hundreds of hours I'd poured into a mere hobby: it had a purpose after all.

I was so desperate I got online and signed up for the next adult USTA tournament, which happened to be on Rosh Hashanah weekend, the Jewish New Year. I wasn't very observant of the High Holidays, but on the other hand, I didn't set out each year to make a mockery of them either. If my father had still been alive, I'd definitely have lied to him about my plans.

CHAPTER 27

My First Official Tournament as a Grown Man

Almost as soon as I registered for my first singles tournament—an "open" for men forty and over—and paid the entrance fee, I started having second thoughts.

I mentioned my plans to my partner Tim, asking him to form a doubles team with me as well.

"Have you ever seen these guys play?" he said. "No thanks."

But even losing, though unpleasant, would be a diversion. Plus, I'd been preparing for this for nine months, and I wasn't going to turn tail and run, so I began instead to resign myself to a quick defeat.

In the first round, I got paired with a guy who was well below my level, and I beat him easily.

The next night it was pouring and tropically warm. This time my opponent looked like the real thing. He was around six feet one, fit, and probably weighed about 185. In the two-minute walk to the courts, he let me know that

1. He'd played Division I college tennis.
2. He was now on a team representing a big Chicago suburb.
3. He'd made it to the finals of several USTA tournaments for men thirty and over.
4. He'd yesterday beaten the third seed.
5. The only reason he wasn't a top seed himself was that he'd just turned forty, so this was his first year in the new bracket, where he had no rating yet.

We warmed up for five minutes; I could see that he wasn't bullshitting about his ability.

The courts tonight weren't open as on the previous evening: there were curtains between them. His warm-up serves had a big lateral kick.

"Maybe we should pull the curtains," I said.

"Nah. It's better this way. Then we don't have a ball coming in from another court," he said. "Last night the curtains didn't interfere."

I was a little dubious of his claim, but I let it go.

In the first game, on his ad, he hit a spin serve wide right and smack into the curtain: my racket ended up tangled in the netting. That gave him the winning point.

I wanted to kick myself. The guy—I quickly forgot his name and thought of him as Butch—had picked me out for the novice I was, and I'd allowed myself to be conned.

Irritated and rattled, I immediately demanded that the curtains be opened. Too late I realized I should have waited one more game to demand the change: so I got to serve once with the same advantage.

On the baseline, I found myself unable to find Death Cab for Cutie's "Summer Skin" in my head, the tune I'd relied on the night before to calm myself. I dropped serve, and he held again. It was all happening very fast. I'd won only a few points in three games. My shirt was soaked through. I was panting and shaking my head. He was the real thing, all right, and I *was* going to lose 6–0, 6–0 in about fifteen minutes at this rate.

During the short break after odd games, I changed my shirt.

"Get a grip," I said to myself. "This is what you'd wanted; this is what you've been preparing to test yourself against. Settle the hell down. Do what you know how to do. This guy's great and wily, but you've got skills, too. Give this a real go. Forget about the curtain trick; it's over. Probe his game; find a relative weakness and exploit it. Don't waste this chance, you dumb son of a bitch."

Though I wasn't thinking about it at the time, this little monologue was hardly specific to the sport, or sports in general. Tennis, I'd come to see, had something intrinsically valuable to it that was invisible to a spectator. Maybe what Zen was about was mastering the emotional game involved, and anger was only one major instrument in the toolkit.

Yes, this was only tennis, just athletics, and there was nothing riding on this match but my own peculiar investment. But tennis has that large mental component. The best players in tennis, and in life more generally—which is to say, the happiest people—know and accept the following:

1. Things don't always go your way.
2. Allowing yourself to be intimidated when there is no real danger is a formula for failure.
3. Some things are beyond your control so to focus on them is self-defeating.
4. The past cannot be changed so to dwell on it is worse than pointless—it's detrimental.
5. You need to shift your approach when it doesn't work and try things out until you find something that does.

Yes, these are basic philosophical principles but to recite them is one thing and to internalize them is quite another.

This time when I came up to the baseline, I took my time; as server, I could set the pace. I waited until I got the song in my head. "Children swim / . . . our summer skin." Then I tossed up the ball and punched in a good serve.

I started trying to figure out what I needed to do to take points. I experimented with different shots, and I soon spotted a small weakness in Butch's game. I wanted to pull him wide on one side then the other, and make him hit on a full run—by putting more pace on the ball and going for shots deep in the corners. Yes, I'd miss some this way, but it was the only way I had a chance.

I got him off balance a few times, and he hit some forced errors into the net and a couple out of the court. Briefly I caught his eye between points: the look of dead confidence was gone. I took the game, then broke him, then held service again. We were tied.

In that moment, I had a glimpse of what it took to compete on this level. I had a quality of focus and determination that was foreign. My nerves had gone, and my thinking was lucid, a rarity for me away from a computer or outside a classroom. I barely recognized myself.

Unfortunately, those games had taken a lot out of me—and thinking things like "I barely recognize myself" was unhelpful. I started hearing a voice telling me I simply didn't have the energy in this heat. A cramp in my calf was crimping my movement, due to nerves spiking and physical depletion. My serve got erratic again, and I dropped the next few games and lost the set.

I went to the men's room, tore off my shirt, soaked my face and head at the sink and barely toweled off. I could see my beet-red cheeks reflected in the mirror. I put on yet another fresh shirt, my third and last.

Returning to the courts, I was almost knocked over by the temperature. That voice reminded me I wilted in these conditions. I tried to tune it out. I quickly dropped some games. As we switched sides and took the break, I told myself to put everything I had into the following one. I swore at myself again and called myself more names.

He was serving. I managed to release myself. My body was at its maximum speed. A forehand crosscourt smoked out of his reach. A backhand hit on the run, down the line, for a clear winner. His second serve was jumped and then followed to net; he hit high. It was allowed to go by untouched and out. A forehand volley and again forward; he tried to pass me crosscourt, and a backhand slice was chipped out of his reach.

I'd broken his serve without his getting a point.

Exhilarated, I could serve harder. Last game I'd caught him off guard; he'd been expecting me to roll over at that point. But now he dug in too. The game got to deuce.

Then I launched a serve that painted the midline and smacked against the back wall. It was an ace, the best I'd ever seen come off my racket. He called it out. I paused. I thought about making a deal of it for a second.

The next moment, even as I was hitting the second serve, I knew I'd made another newbie mistake. I could have called over an umpire; they're standing by at USTA matches to call the lines when the players disagree. More generally again, in any struggle you find yourself in, discover or remember the resources available to you and be ready to use them. I should have argued just for the potential adrenaline rush involved and gotten the ump to change the dynamic. I needed any kind of pick-me-up. I could have used the break in play.

All this went through my mind in a split second, but it was too late.

He took the next two points and the game. The voice I wasn't listening to told me I was completely out of gas. My leg went stiff. I limped through the next two games, double-faulted on my serve for the final point, and lost the set badly.

I was disappointed, irritated, and pouring sweat. The unhappiness stuck with me until the next day. I found myself barking at Quilty and Lazarus, on our walk.

I wondered if the depth of my mood corresponded to the intensity of the struggle I'd been through. Maybe you risked such a strong reaction when you threw yourself so completely into a sports competition—something new for me as an adult.

My funk made me feel childish. For Christ's sake. Maybe the last time I'd been in a black mood over something like this was when I lost in the finals of the fourth-grade spelling bee, on a technicality. The word was "professional."

But, obviously, there was more than a tennis match at stake.

A full month after the USTA tournament I was going to realize what had gone down with me during the competition. I'd experienced my defeat as largely physical—my leg cramping, my energy draining. I knew the guy had taken a couple of points by cheating, but I didn't understand that, more significantly, he'd successfully played with my head. As a result of that unchallenged line call, my enthusiasm was deflated, my comeback short-circuited.

This was only the beginning of what I'd failed to perceive. It was amazing how much you could miss. I felt so low the day after the match because something more profound, and weird, had transpired within me.

CHAPTER 28

Going Outside My Familiar Discomfort Zone

"Thank you for your service to our country," said the man on the phone at the reception desk at the Sheraton in central Utah, as I made my reservation.

"What?" I said. "Oh, I'm not military. I—uh—just research the military."

"Well thank you for that. That's important, too."

No one outside of the profession had ever told me my work was important, and now that I thought of it, not many inside the profession had done so, either. More to the point, no one had ever mistaken me for military.

Because the big literary modernism conference wasn't interested in the connection between World War I and American modernism, I'd accepted an invitation to present my work at the Seventy-Fifth Annual Society for Military History conference—a convention entirely outside of my discipline. I realized that delivering a paper at a conference at which no literary colleagues would be present wasn't going to tell me much about how my work would be received in my field, but I kinda wanted at present to try out my ideas in public.

Most academics deliver papers at conferences not only to demonstrate professional activity on their résumés but to get useful feedback as they begin a project. I'd never proceeded in this practical way; I was always too impatient with my half-baked ideas and preferred to embarrass myself prematurely with publishers. But it was a first for me to attend a conference that was more or less professionally irrelevant.

The fact was I needed to go somewhere, shake myself out of a scholarly postpartum funk, and this invitation materialized without my doing anything. I'd contacted Nancy Ford to thank her for her extraordinary research and undervalued work; she invited me to be on a panel.

I was also vaguely curious to go because I had some unanswered questions, no longer about my project on the Lost Generation but as a result of it. In that sense the trip was potentially not entirely frivolous. What I didn't see, but perhaps intuited, was that going to Utah and hanging out with military-history scholars, some of whom were military or former military, was going to prompt me to examine my own prejudices about the armed services, about scholars, and also about myself.

Several weeks went by after the USTA match, and I'd gone down some sort of rabbit hole. My play had become at best spotty, at times abysmal: I was losing just about all of the sets I was playing, some incredibly badly. I was getting hammered by Trip in every tiebreaker.

But I also had some of the best games I'd ever played. Though I never had even these flashes of brilliance with Trip, I could sometimes decisively take some games off the best players in a club league. And then I felt ecstatic—until I lost the set and match.

I was hitting plenty of winners, but loads and loads of unforced errors. My old counterpunching game of keeping the ball in play now felt alien. The end result was that now I couldn't beat anyone. Not the better players I wanted to, nor lesser players I used to blow out with my conservative game. At times I became very emotional on the court; sometimes I almost felt like crying.

One night I played a stranger in a pickup game and forced myself to play very cautiously, breaking on every swing my vow of hitting away with confidence, just because I wanted to take one goddamn set. But after I beat the guy, I didn't feel good either.

Meanwhile, my opponent was angry over the loss. "That wasn't tennis, that was volleyball," he said.

"I've never been disqualified for playing that way."

"Your victory was hollow."

I shrugged, but uncannily the stranger was articulating what I felt. It was almost as if I'd cheated: not my opponent (he was being childish, just another jerk in a long line) but myself.

Beth observed that I was no longer telling her about my games.

"I guess I'm in a cocoon phase," I weakly jested.

My sometime partner Tim had been out of town, and when he returned, he asked me what'd been happening.

"I don't know. I'm getting weird."

"Weird*er*?" He smiled. "How so?"

"I don't seem to care as much about winning or losing anymore."

"Really? That's interesting."

Was it? If I were finally making strides, it was hard to say toward what.

I guessed what I really wanted right now—as I waited—was not simply competition and a positive outcome but to be taken out of myself, to vacation in the zone for a while.

I called up Reuel. I confessed to him I had a sense of disorientation on the court.

"This is very good," he said excitedly. "Don't you see? You're letting your Unconscious take over. It doesn't care about winning or losing, all that ego stuff. But the reason you're sometimes so emotional is that the ego is still there, of course, off and on. You're jarring deeply rooted habits, shaking yourself up where it counts; your ego's protesting." He suggested I might look at *Archery* once more and followed up with an email:

Now, you're onto something.

A passage comes to mind that I once read. It was written by a Zen Roshi who was describing his quest for enlightenment. It went something like this:

Before I set out to achieve enlightenment, mountains looked like mountains and rivers looked like rivers.

And then as I deepened my quest, mountains no longer looked like mountains, rivers no longer like rivers.

After many years of searching I finally reached a state of enlightenment: Mountains once again looked like mountains and rivers like rivers.

I'd never taken to Eastern philosophy. It seemed to me the sages were always saying impressive-sounding but annoying things like this.

However, this time it didn't seem empty. Was I suddenly able to approach Eastern philosophy because of my shamefully intense and deteriorating relationship to tennis?

If so, who cared? I felt so unhappy on the court so regularly I wondered if I was just going to quit altogether.

It had now been several weeks that I hit as hard as I could on every shot, and ended up deciding the outcome of just about every point: I either struck an unreturnable ball or a made an unforced error.

In a typical match—I usually lost, say, 3–6, 2–6—I would hit around thirty winners and sixty unforced errors. I was never going to win a match with that kind of ratio, but I was kind of enjoying myself, when I wasn't feeling mixed up or on the verge of tears.

If this were a movie, the honest-to-goodness Zen master I needed would appear at precisely this point.

CHAPTER 29

The Much-Needed Zen Master Doesn't Appear

There was something curious going on: I was losing every match by more or less the same game scores, and things progressed in just about the same way, regardless of my opponents' abilities. This wasn't exactly an achievement, but it was a phenomenon worth contemplating.

Weirdly enough, in some real way, I was no longer competing with others so much as enacting, or reenacting, a struggle with myself. I figured I was acting out a sort of script, a primeval emotional sequence that maybe had little to do with tennis.

It was easy to forget this sort of knowledge, to believe that as one grew older one was naturally freed from the treadmill of one's past. But like all freedom, it couldn't be seized once and for all, but had to be retaken again and again.

So I set out to observe my feelings in the course of a match. I was finally looking squarely at the second mental block that had long stood in my way.

My sets began with a loss of a few games.

Then I'd come back and win a few in a row. That was because, I saw, after losing several straight, I'd feel offended that my opponent was underestimating me, even though the estimation was so far completely deserved, as I'd shown no talent at all. It was then, with wounded pride, that I was able to let go.

So far, so good: decipherable even if mad.

But the rest of my performance was at yet opaque. Once I evened the score, I tended to get nervous again and lose the set in straight games. Why?

And the next set, when I only got one or two games? It made no sense, but after essentially tanking for the last few games of the first set, I would feel sort of resentful that I'd relinquished my own chance of winning. I couldn't understand the second half of my pattern—but decided I'd maybe spent enough time trying to psychoanalyze what was after all only a tennis match.

Then one day, I ran into Marco at the courts and agreed to play him, and because his behavior was an exaggerated version of the normally irritating opponent's, my feelings were likewise magnified.

True to form, Marco made a horrible call early in the first set—when I was way behind. I'd served an ace that clearly hit within the line and gave me the ad.

Then he did this thing of staring at the ground, where the ball had bounced, as if he were somehow seeing the past event, as if he were a "shot spot" machine used in pro tournaments to verify line calls. After a full fifteen seconds of looking at a phantom area on the ground—which is a long time to stare at nothing when someone else is waiting—he silently held up a finger: indicating the ball was out. I walked up toward the net and said, "No."

"It's my call; it's my call," he shrieked.

I shook my head.

Then he finally said, "I'll allow you to take the serve over."

By then I was pissed off that he was yelling in my face, and I said, "No."

"Do you think I'm cheating?" he screeched, pointing out quite rightly that he didn't need to cheat to beat me.

Though I wasn't sure what I believed, I said, "No, I think you don't always see well."

He insisted loudly on his excellent eyesight and his right to make the call, and we went round and round on this, until he accidentally let slip that he'd also bragged to his optometrist that he had perfect eyesight, on the occasion of this eye doctor telling him he needed glasses.

When I pointed out to him the implication of what he'd said, he tried to withdraw the comment, but it could hardly be taken back. Now I insisted on the point, unilaterally took it, and went on to win the game, after which we yelled at each other some more. And then I proceeded, on the strength of having whipped myself up into a mindless fury, to slash at the ball as if possessed not by a muse but a demon, won four games straight, made a rare specialty shot I'd never even attempted before, a backhand swinging volley smash, and took the lead for the first time ever against him.

But, when it came down to the last game I needed to win the set, I suddenly felt bad for him.

Standing on the court, waiting for the next game to begin, sweat coursing down my body, I stepped back from myself and watched. It was a disorienting experience. As I looked at my opponent with pity, a second self had stepped off and was shaking its head at me with a mix of wonder and pity.

Marco suddenly looked so weak and desolate standing on the baseline on the other side of the net. Yes, I was worried about Marco, who was so obnoxious almost everyone at the courts refused to play with him at all. I felt bad for Marco, who was so annoying some people at the courts would later come up to me and thank me for having screamed back at him that day. Though he was over six feet, he seemed so small and defenseless, like a bigger version of my brother when we were little.

I was a bit stunned. It seemed undeniable that I was reliving a pattern I'd established back in the late 1960s as a nine-year-old.

Then I realized something more dizzying still. This syndrome had begun even earlier, and I couldn't blame my brother for it. He was actually not manipulative but quite accommodating, a really nice guy and a gem of a brother. In his anxious accommodation, he was a lot like me.

And we were alike because as little kids we both had the sense that our mother was fragile, and we had to take care of her or she might break down, leaving us without an adult caretaker. We had to spare her suffering by taking it on ourselves because we were better able to handle the frustration of our desires, even as children, than she was able to handle any conflict, no matter how small. She gave us signals to this effect, including screaming jags that segued into mute black moods, temporary breakdowns of a terrifying nature to a child, especially when they aren't followed up by any explanation or words of reassurance. Was she one day going to have a fit from which she just didn't resurface? Would she just be gone for good? Neither of us really experienced desires as little kids. We'd quickly learned to repress them in the interests of survival.

And we both became experts at picking up the slightest signs of dismay in our mother so we could stave off a crisis.

When I was in the hospital and thought I was dying at age eight, I didn't share my fear with my mother because even then—desperately and maybe fatally ill—I felt she was weaker than me and I needed to protect her. My brother and I believed that what would devastate her would merely cause us discomfort that we could handle. Evidently even my death fell into this category.

And the way I handled my mother was how I came to treat my brother when I was nine, my girlfriends until about twenty-nine when I got a lot of therapy, and now my opponents as a middle-aged adult. I'd essentially gotten past this twisted scenario in intimate relationships. But because I'd never analyzed my habitual reactions on the tennis court, I hadn't gotten a handle on them there.

When I played opponents who would get upset if they started to lose, I backed off so they could win because, odd as it sounds, I felt as a child I could better handle adversity than my mother. I helped them beat me, so they wouldn't be devastated and break down—but in a way that didn't absolutely humiliate me in the process.

In order to improve at tennis matches, I had to come to grips with the reality that someone was going to have to lose, and I really preferred, despite my childhood training to suppress my preferences, that it wasn't me. I had to bring to the tennis courts what I had learned about handling myself as an adult—and I'd at least started to learn something.

I was just now in my midforties figuring out how to write and perhaps publish a book about a major subject, one that many people in my discipline had approached and some cared intensely about. I was going to have to be willing to step on some toes. Which perhaps involves, even when it becomes habitual, especially because it's a face-to-face encounter in tennis, a sustained kind of ferocity.

And the problem was precisely that I couldn't sustain it, not in person anyway. Relying on anger in tennis matches was a problem because it could always open the floodgates to other overheated emotions—I could slip back into really sickeningly retrograde mental states, as my opponent put on the mask of my brother's face.

"Are you playing or not?" Marco was yelling at me.

Was there some other way to get into the zone? I wondered.

"What's wrong with you? Are you in a trance?"

"I gotta go," I said, and walked off the court and picked up my bag.

"You cannot leave in the middle of the set. This is not a victory. Ah, you are a baby. You are ahead, but you are still a baby. You are afraid you will lose. You are right to be afraid. But this is very disrespectful."

Was there some way to be fiercely confident without being irrationally furious? Maybe not. I headed toward the parking lot.

"You have not won! I will tell everyone about this! The set is not over! You have forfeited! . . . I win . . . baby . . . disgraceful . . . superbaby."

Since the court didn't seem to be getting me anywhere, except down, I quit playing. I threw out another two pairs of shoes and put my tennis bag in a closet.

PART VI

SOME PROVISIONAL ANSWERS

There are moments when the inner life actually "pays," when years of self-scrutiny, conducted for no ulterior motive, are suddenly of practical use. Such moments are still rare in the West; that they come at all promises a fairer future.

—E. M. Forster, *Howards End*

CHAPTER 30

Scholarly Detective Story VIII

POSTSCRIPT ON SEEING THE VIETNAM ERA
IN HISTORICAL CONTEXT

No one mistook me for armed forces once I arrived at the Society of Military History conference in the Utah foothills: a good percentage of the participants in the halls and the meeting rooms, both men and women, were in uniform. This wasn't the crowd of English professors I was used to from the annual Modern Language Association convention.

And I had a little epiphany as I wandered around that first morning in the Sheraton Hotel on the one main street in what must have once been a small western town, wondering what in the hell I was doing there.

One of the more obvious things I hadn't noticed during my sabbatical was that what I was up to when I wasn't researching and writing, namely trying to become a strong middle-aged tennis player, had something to do with what I was writing about, once I came to realize what that was, namely masculinity. Or emasculation and the attempt to overcome it.

Unlikely as it may sound, I hadn't previously made the connection between the Lost Generation writers' traumas of being rejected or underutilized by the US Army and my own somewhat less dramatic experience of having been benched or underappreciated on my high school soccer teams. I didn't notice this connection because I was busy noticing something else.

That was the stark difference between the Lost Generation's experience of masculinity and my own, which boiled down to their relationship to the military and mine. When they came of age, they wanted to get into the army and into a war. They felt they had to—or their lives, starting with their sex lives, would be blighted.

I'd felt nothing remotely similar. Not only was there no war when I came of age, but I had no interest in going to one. My parents had had the wisdom to move into an integrated neighborhood just inside the border of a mostly wealthy Cleveland suburb, which had a superlative school system. The military offered me nothing I was interested in as a young man, such as girls and a road to career success.

In addition, I felt no pressure whatsoever to go into the army. When I graduated high school, men could still enlist in the army, but those who didn't, who gave no thought to the military, didn't have their masculinity nullified or even compromised. At twenty, I'd had to register for the draft—President Carter was considering there might be a war in the Middle East and required registration of all young men. Though I was unthinkingly "antiwar," along with most of my collegiate peers, some of whom said they wouldn't register on principle, I couldn't afford to be principled. I was on scholarship and knew that students failing to register could lose their federal aid. I hoped I wouldn't be asked to serve but didn't really worry about it too much.

I knew why there was this difference between my generation's sense of war and the military and that of the Lost Generation. The Vietnam era had changed things. Though I'd never really thought about it much before, it was now clear to me that, thanks to the 1960s antiwar movement, service in the army was no longer culturally required for masculinity, among the college-educated. You didn't have to go into the military to be a man. You could even refuse to serve in a (bad) war and retain your masculinity (which might be of a new type, the sensitive kind).[1]

---

1. Yes, the Vietnam era had changed a lot of things, except maybe the thing it was supposed to have changed. The huge resistance to Vietnam had ostensibly dissuaded the government from pursuing any more protracted ground wars for fear of another massive antiwar uprising. I remembered having heard that a lot in the 1980s and 1990s, from academics on the left.

But of course the 2000s had proved that the government hadn't been dissuaded. And that was because the government didn't expect any more huge antiwar uprisings once it got rid of the draft. The government's gambit, of ending the draft and turning to an all-volunteer force so it could conduct its wars without being hampered by mas-

The Vietnam era changed the seemingly ironclad equation of masculinity and military service, which had held sway in America from World War I through the Korean War. The men of my generation were living proof of that. Though still quite narrow, American masculinity had been miraculously opened up.

Given what I'd just gotten through discovering about World War I and the modernists, I couldn't help but wonder just how this transformation had happened—why it had been able to happen. Yes, Vietnam was a horrible and seemingly pointless war, and it was the first televised one, effectively bringing the horrors of the conflict home. Those factors were obviously a major part of the answer. But, after all my research on World War I, I sensed more was involved.

---

sive civil unrest, turned out to be correct. No mass protest against the wars in Iraq or Afghanistan had materialized.

Meanwhile, the Vietnam protests had the effect of changing the government's mind about the draft—and that was actually no small thing. The antiwar movement effectively ended it, after more than thirty straight years, from 1941 to 1973.

But relying on social and economic forces to provoke enlistments in an all-volunteer force was, really, a continuation and extension of the Vietnam-era draft practice of allowing those young men who could to find a way out of being drafted—in order for the government to avoid an even bigger civil crisis. In the end, the most common method of avoidance for students was not the student deferment. Most students graduated, and thus lost their student deferment, before the long war was over, partly because President Johnson got rid of across-the-board graduate school deferrals in 1968. The most common method was medical disqualification. Draft dodging—breaking the law, say by going to Canada—was a much less pursued alternative, and a relatively minor one, statistically speaking. College students took advantage of loopholes in the draft regulations, but the government knew this was going on and let them get away with it. The government made no effort to close those loopholes that let around five million men arrange a medical deferment and let another million men—and here being socially connected could matter—serve in safety in the National Guard. The government thus avoided a showdown with middle-class and wealthy parents that would have made the continuation of the war an absolutely drastic decision rather than simply a "painful" one.

The All-Volunteer Force made into policy the de facto practice of allowing the educated or connected to avoid the Vietnam draft through loopholes. Socioeconomically speaking, the end of the draft turned all the loopholes into a blanket exemption for everyone who had other opportunities or means enabling them to opt out of what military service had to offer.

Even though I didn't really like Hemingway, Fitzgerald, and Faulkner because they took out their military frustrations on ethnic Americans, I could sympathize with their plight as young men caught up in the wartime hysteria that equated masculinity with combat service. They didn't deserve to be emasculated—or, to use Hemingway's metaphor in *Sun*, thought of as "dickless"—just because, as a result of some minor physical or personal limitation (bad eyesight, small size, inability to command a squad of men), they couldn't be pilots or successful officers, and didn't end up as high-ranking combatants. Maybe they hadn't wanted to end up as privates in the trenches. But they weren't sissies. They'd been *sissified* by circumstance, by the zeitgeist.

Because of the Vietnam era, the men of my generation had been spared that brutal pigeonholing. Sure there were thuggish guys in my high school, soccer teammates of mine, who would have liked to walk around calling me "dickless," like they viciously called our sweet but perhaps somewhat plain-looking water girl "cuntless." But they never did, and, even if they had, it wouldn't have mattered. Though I had no interest in the military, prevailing notions of masculinity had not made me dickless; which is to say, pretty girls were nonetheless interested in me— once I grew to five feet eleven. I'm not trying to claim I was manly in the sense of brave. I clearly wasn't, for I never stood up to these kids who called me and my friends plenty of other horrible names. But I wasn't nullified as a male sexual being.

There were two viable, and fundamentally different, types of masculinity at my high school. I'd inherited a new type, invented by the antiwar movement, and the bullies in junior high and high school were inheritors of the older, traditional American masculinity. These "tough" guys were the younger brothers, sometimes literally, of the working-class men who served in Vietnam.

There was a good deal of overlap in style between the two masculine camps by the late 1970s, which made things more confusing. Whether they were sensitive and bookish (like me) or apathetic about school and violent, more or less all the guys at my high school had long hair and were interested in sex, drugs, rock and roll, and sports. Nonetheless, the differences in masculinity were absolute.

Following Hemingway's insistent and fairly elaborately worked-out genital metaphors in *Sun*, where hard-boiled, hard-drinking, bullfight-loving Jake has his penis blown off in the war on a "joke front," and nervous, irritating, boring, gets-green-at-the-bullfights Cohn is compared to a steer, a castrated bull, the implication being that he lacks balls: in high school, you might say I was ball-less but not dickless. Since perhaps that formula is not immediately lucid, as Hemingway's weird metaphor of dicklessness is not as familiar as the common trope of ball-lessness, this could use a bit of, well, fleshing out.

Hemingway asserted, in an interview with the *Paris Review* years after the novel came out, that his narrator-protagonist Jake was not castrated like a steer. Meanwhile, in a letter to Fitzgerald, he called the book: "THE SUN ALSO RISES (LIKE YOUR COCK IF YOU HAVE ONE)." Hemingway didn't imagine his narrator Jake to be, like Cohn, ball-less. The familiar implication about Cohn is that he is gutless, or suffers from an inner emasculation. And it's consistent with the general portrait of him as a Jewish neurotic who, despite his "good body," his unimpeachable boxing ability, his military school education, and his ability to have sex with Brett—that is, despite his intact physical or outward masculinity—is the most nervous person Jake has ever met off the battlefield.

Hemingway takes significant pains to set up Jewish Cohn as a foil to Anglo Jake; one of the reasons the gang of characters in *Sun* goes to the bullfights—aside from the fact that they're in a Hemingway novel and the war is over so there's no active battlefield to go to—is to make it painstakingly clear that Cohn is comparable to a castrated bull while Jake, though literally missing part of his genitals, is not.

Jake, then, doesn't lack "balls" or guts: he has an inner manliness that serves him in war and makes him generally "hard-boiled." It is evident from the novel that Jake isn't suffering from what they called in World War I "shell shock" (and what we have called since Vietnam PTSD). One way Hemingway makes this evident is to describe such a character, Brett's previous husband, Lord Ashley, who, even after the war is well over, sleeps on the floor clutching a loaded revolver.

And this, by the way, is why I think Hemingway didn't make Jake an infantry soldier who saw the gruesome action of the trenches: Hemingway isn't interested in representing, by Jake's wound, the inner loss of masculinity brought about by mechanized warfare, of the sort Lord Ashley suffers (though the critics have read it this way). Hemingway is clearly trying to represent something different, what you might think of as an "outer emasculation."

Jake has his "balls" but lacks the private part that matters to his sexually hungry true love, Brett: his "dick." This metaphorical distinction is hardly common, perhaps a Hemingway invention. Jake has suffered an outer or social loss of masculinity because of the war. And what Jake—who serves as a pilot, which is to say in the most elite wartime position—has lost, to interpret the metaphor of his missing dick, is the phallus as masculine status, as male attractiveness, as sexual viability to the opposite sex.

Hemingway had experienced something spiritually equivalent to Jake's physical loss. His penis hadn't literally been blown off, though he'd been hit in the legs by shrapnel and maybe that gave him the idea. What had happened *socially* was that Hemingway found himself feeling unfairly downgraded, and emasculated, in the eyes of women because, in the hysterical tunnel vision of the era, he was seen, as the war went on, as merely an ambulance driver, doing "women's" or "boys'" work. And it was unjust because as such he'd nonetheless had to risk his life and endure a serious war injury. Metaphorically speaking—in his own novel's terms—while Hemingway had proved himself in possession of a pretty big pair of balls, he'd nonetheless come to be seen as lacking a "dick."

Maybe it's obvious, but "mobilization wounds" of the sort Hemingway, Fitzgerald, and Faulkner experienced were only possible, the hysteria surrounding masculinity could only happen, because in the wartime era young women and older girls basically concurred with the US military in its evaluation of men. Insofar as females were attracted to the uniform, went wild at the sight of the soldier's uniform, became "charity girls" or went "khaki wacky" (a World War II term for such females), and shied away from the draft-age men who weren't in uniform, young men sought to be in uniform and in the war, and felt emasculated if they couldn't get into both. No wonder Hemingway and Faulkner (both eighteen at the start of the war) tampered with their uniforms and lied about their service, and Fitzgerald (twenty-two at the end of it) still regretted a decade later not having made it over to Europe.

In high school, I was ball-less all right (and I'd spend my thirties attempting to get my balls back), but I wasn't dickless. I'd been deemed in possession of a dick by the only experts who mattered as far as heterosexual boys in the mid-1970s were concerned: high school girls. In his late teens, Hemingway had done a hell of a lot to prove his manhood, and had ironically been deemed less than a man when it was all over.

Things were much the same in World War II as they'd been in World War I. The perennial Christmas favorite *It's a Wonderful Life*, which came out the year after that war ended, now seemed to me, after all my research, like an entire movie dedicated to the apparently controversial proposition, circa 1946, that you could live a "wonderful" and even worthwhile life as a man without going to war—in fact, while having been rejected by the army. George Bailey couldn't serve because he had a bad ear.

A lot of girls and young women had obviously stopped, in the Vietnam era, thinking of nonsoldiers of draft age, and even draft avoiders, as unmanly. They started thinking of such men as, in fact, attractively virile. "Girls say yes to boys who say no" was an antidraft slogan used by the movement; a famous—supposedly sexy—poster with that caption was produced around 1968 featuring Joan Baez. And it wasn't just propaganda; it was a reality. In the World War I era, males who tried honestly to join the army but were turned away for medical reasons, such as Katherine Anne Porter's Chuck, in her long short story "Pale Horse, Pale Rider" (1939), were seen as "rejected men," hardly men at all, undatable, but in the Vietnam era, men who faked medical exemptions were praised by female peers and got girlfriends.

It was clear to me that without female support and involvement, there never would have been a massive antiwar movement on college campuses. Young men will hold on to their masculine viability, even at the risk of their own lives. So it followed that the coed revolution in college education, largely accomplished between the Korean and Vietnam wars, was a necessary component in the mass student protest and draft avoidance. Draft-avoiding men needed to make sure they had their female peers in their camp.

But something even more basic had taken place at colleges to set the table for the Vietnam antiwar movement—and the turn away from military service. If the antiwar movement had detached masculinity from military service and associated it instead with rebellion, the nation had unwittingly made this possible by detaching status from military service.

Another reason I'd never had any interest in going into the army was that military service no longer meant a boost in social standing. The path of social opportunity for ethnic Americans and lower-middle-class kids like me was no longer through the military, as it had been during the world wars and Korea, as it had been for Gatsby. That path now lay directly through the university. You didn't need armed service and a GI Bill to go to college as a poor or ethnic kid: you needed good grades and test scores.

Between Korea and Vietnam, the universities changed their admission policies. Finally, after decades in which the military was the vanguard of meritocracy in the nation, the universities caught up and took the lead (and soon started criticizing the military for its backwardness). Universities dropped their ethnic quotas, started admitting students on merit, and offered them financial support if they needed it (no doubt the universities changed their admissions policies in response to the carrot of GI Bill money and then Cold War federal dollars). Lower-middle-class and ethnic kids in the 1960s didn't need the army to get ahead, if they could excel in high school; they were already ahead by virtue of earning college admission, and now military service was a step down in terms of status.

The structure of American opportunity had changed between the world wars and Vietnam. If it was weird to think of Gatsby as Foucault's World War I–era New Man, it was even stranger to realize that I myself was also an example of the New Man—when he was no longer so new. I wasn't devastatingly handsome like Gatsby, and I was never in a war. But like him, I came from an ethnic American family that wasn't well off, wanted at some level to change my class, had a good high school education in the Midwest, did well on standardized tests, and thus benefited from a developing meritocracy.

After my presentation about my research that first day at the Utah conference, a retired officer named Peter stayed around and talked to me. He'd been at Penn State in the late sixties and early seventies. Like Beth's father, he was a Vietnam vet who'd enlisted, but this guy had signed up while in college and became a commissioned officer.

A burly older man with a classic walrus mustache, he told me, "As soon as women saw my short, drill-team haircut, they asked me if I was ROTC, and if I said yes, that was often a quick end to a possible relationship. You were seen as a fool for *not* taking advantage of the various loopholes or deferments. I was an ROTC schmuck." (This is not to say that Peter's experience was universal for college men who enlisted or complied with the draft. Beth's father had met her mother while at community college; she was proud of his later enlistment, and there were certainly couples at four-year universities whose attitudes about service resembled theirs.)

The antiwar movement was popular with many college women, and that was in part because college women were drawn to male peers who had *status*. Crucial to the dynamic was that draft avoidance was, for a large subset up college students, no longer shameful but now a way to hold on to *it*.

As one historian of the draft put it, more or less, "During the Vietnam War, if your draft status was 2-S (deferred as a student), you were somebody; if you were 1-A, without deferment, you were a nobody." Or, as the author of *Sun* might have more succinctly put it: "If you were 2-S, you had a dick. If you weren't, you didn't."[2]

---

2. Again, these are meaningful statements in the form of overgeneralizations.

CHAPTER 31

Seeing Myself in Historical Context,
Military History Convention, Ogden, Utah

It didn't take me long in Utah to be reminded that I wasn't only nonmilitary but, like the literature colleagues from whom I liked to think I was so different, kind of reflexively antimilitary. To a not insignificant degree I shared the attitude I criticized; I carried some pretty unexamined ideas along with me to my first military history conference. Yes—and I feel ashamed, ignorant, and hypocritical—I went still believing at some level the leftist prejudice that people in the military were stupid. Even after all my research into the 1917 military—when the army was openly struggling with issues barely in the consciousness of most Americans.

At the conference I half expected to find no one interested in my work because I somehow still figured that people in the military weren't interested in literature. Peter and a bunch of other guys proved me wrong. The tiniest bit of clear thinking would have allowed me to make a distinction in advance between the thugs I'd known in high school who became grunts and the types of college-educated young men and women who eventually became officers.

It was totally fitting—for my accidental education—that the convention included a ballroom dinner at which Rick Atkinson, a popular military writer, read from his new book, during the course of which he explained that the famous World War II acronyms SNAFU (situation normal: all fucked up) and FUBAR (fucked up beyond all recognition) were just the two best known of about twenty-five such acronyms, all of which he quickly went through, including SUSFU (situation unchanged, still fucked up), FUMTU (fucked up more than usual), TARFU (things are really fucked up), and the memorably specific JANFU: joint army-navy fuckup.

The Left hardly invented the idea that the military was bumbling and incompetent. That notion was popularized, if not invented, by World War II GIs, not only "the greatest generation" but the most gloriously profane to date, who had to slog through all the mistakes cooked up by a US military command that, despite the innumerable fuckups, helped win a war that the country and its allies couldn't afford to lose.

When I thought about it, it was obvious why the military was associated with bungling and would always be: because *its* mistakes often involved fatalities. No matter how much literary academics fucked up, nobody got hurt, except in the way boredom and especially delusion are varieties of injury. But when the army screwed up, people on your side died.

I can only hope that Peter and the other officers who showed so much interest in my talk, because they were educated and in particular versed in the works of Hemingway, had come to listen to it with prejudice against me as a literary professor: say, that I was a leftist crackpot. Probably they didn't have such prejudices—even when they saw I had the middle-aged male hipster haircut. They probably figured if I was at the military history conference I wasn't an idiot filled up with stupid leftist ideas about the military. Only I sort of was.

In any case, I was something of an oddity for them. It turned out I was the only lit professor there, and, by the second morning of my stay, the apparent, absolute oddity of this meant that total strangers, some in military uniform, were coming up to me and referring to me as "our literary guy." I'd never been so warmly received at a conference before: I was treated like a mascot or a VIP from a distant, exotic, madcap foreign country that people had heard about but never visited. (I've again and again found that, within the academy and even the humanities, the work of my discipline is viewed by professors of other fields as hermetic, irrational, and humorously bizarre.)

Peter and a few other military and ex-military guys who were employed in educating the army's officer corps invited me out for drinks;

I heard war and mobilization stories about Vietnam and the Gulf War, none of which I remembered too clearly because I was quickly drunk. Rather, and maybe because I was drunk, I started having some weird, yet very lucid, thoughts.

"Here I am," I thought, in a hotel bar at a military history conference, "drinking with soldiers and vets, living my adolescent Hemingway dream." That fantasy was nonsensical and meant nothing to me now.

No, I felt something else. Sitting and talking with these military and ex-military scholars, some of whom had recently seen action in Iraq or Afghanistan, others of whom had fought in the Gulf or Vietnam, it was hard to believe I'd ever seriously thought of intellectualism and scholarship as antithetical to manliness. Not only had that been a wrongheaded idea of mine; it'd been mostly a lie, a comforting delusion I soothingly told myself after the screwup of my oral exams.

For the first time, I understood that the rebellious, bohemian artist phase in my early thirties had not been a masculine recoil from an academic world I found "nerdy" and was therefore ambivalent about, but an injured retreat from an academic world I thought I was meant for but was ambivalent about me. I wasn't uncomfortable being a scholar; I never had been. Rather, I'd been uncomfortable failing as one.

Sure, I had some issues left over from my lack of confidence and poor showing during secondary school sports, but these feelings of self-doubt were reactivated when I found some of my Berkeley English professors incomprehensible—to my math- and science-trained mind. Maybe I'd wanted to redshirt on the Cal soccer team because I was already feeling for the first time in my life like a dumb jock.

As I downed a fifth or sixth beer, I remembered a hot-tub party my first year at Berkeley. Afterward, as I was showering with the host's girlfriend, for some reason—it *was* California in the early 1980s—she'd said to me, staring, "How can you be a graduate student with a body like that?" And my main thought was, perhaps missing her drift, "Maybe I'm not smart enough to get a PhD."

Yeah, I'd thought a lot about trying out for the Cal soccer team. Also for the first time in my life, I was lifting weights. I'd never wanted to play soccer or any other sport as an undergrad at Amherst, and that was because I was kicking ass academically there. When I almost failed my orals, I felt pretty "dickless"—and that's when I felt the need to prove I had balls.

Now I saw it: saw what it was I most profoundly had in common with Hemingway and company and why I could mysteriously understand them. It wasn't cryptic any longer, and I wasn't having an attack of Hemingitis fever either. There was nothing glorious here at the SMH convention drinking beers with military officer professors. In central Utah. And no pretense. It didn't even have to do with my rekindled interest in tennis.

I finally glimpsed how miserably like the Lost and Beat Generation writers I was: in our painful experiences of status demotion, of failure or rejection or disappointment—theirs at the hands of the military, mine in the university—and our attempts to compensate by self-delusion or rebelling. They had wanted to be stars in the military and thought they could be because of their exalted ethnic and class and collegiate backgrounds. I'd wanted to be an academic star and thought I could be because I'd been a scholarship kid at an elite college, entered Berkeley as one of a couple of PhD students granted a full ride for the first few years, and then was asked by Foucault to work with him on a book.

They'd ended up angry at the US Army, and their books for the next ten years were filled with offhand cracks about the military: its officers, training camps, ideology, and bureaucratic language. I'd been pissed off at academia, so I decided to give it a serious go as a bohemian novelist, and I was, all these years later, still in my mind reflexively slagging on the institution, colleagues, scholarship, even teaching—pretending to think the academic literary endeavor was fundamentally preposterous, of little interest to anyone and better left behind, when I obviously felt it was worth devoting my entire career to.

The irony in all of this was that because I'd begun to fail where it really mattered to me, in my professional status, my scholarly career, I also began to develop a sensitivity to the experience of failure that all these years later allowed me to recognize the mortifying experience of the Lost Generation writers, even though in their 1920s masterpieces they did such a masterful job of covering it up and transposing it.[1] The day

---

1. These experiences of shame are, by the way, much more obviously represented, and

I almost failed my orals and stowed away those military papers out of disgrace—because I hadn't begun to see how the Lost Generation writers had "lost out" in the brand-new era of aptitudes ushered in by the World War I military—was the day I began to undergo a similar experience, during a sort of second era of aptitudes, when the universities had gone meritocratic. My own disappointment would eventually allow me to identify their experience for what it was, and to finally pull out those military papers again and make good use of them.

That once empty phrase from Foucault that I'd walked around repeating to myself back in the early 1980s now brimmed over with meaning for me. If I was a New Man because, like Gatsby, I'd benefited from the developing American meritocracy, the phrase had also taken on another, personal significance. I was in addition trying to become a New Man who, unlike these Lost Generation writers, wasn't trying to con anybody, least of all himself. Quite apart from whether my book got published, I wanted to become honest with myself, as opposed to cynical, angry, and proud of some hip specialness or artistic "authenticity" that it was pretty to believe in as a compensation for my meritocratic failures.

I was very drunk indeed.

---

with almost no transposition, in their earlier 1920s works: Hemingway's "A Very Short Story," Fitzgerald's *The Beautiful and Damned*, and Faulkner's *Soldiers' Pay*.

CHAPTER 32

A Zen Master in Wrigleyville?

Back in Chicago, I saw something at the Waveland courts that I probably wouldn't have noticed before. Now I was transfixed.

I hadn't played in weeks. Though I'd quit tennis for the moment, there didn't seem any harm in going to the courts alone, not to play but to teach myself how to hit a stroke I'd always lacked, the topspin backhand.

Leaves from the nearby trees were sprinkled over the courts. Regularly impatient or in a hurry when I had a game, I'd have been content to kick some of the leaves out of the way, brush some others aside with my racket, and play on a partially leaf-strewn court.

There was a guy several courts away who had a completely different response. He made a functional broom from materials lying around.

I'd seen this man a few times but hadn't given him much thought. He was the Asian guy that Marco had mocked as a "superbaby"—for only rallying and often with much weaker players. (His being Asian wasn't in itself something unusual; I'd played plenty of guys from the Far East.)

He constructed a very effective broom from scratch. He made it out of twigs and thin branches that had also been dropped by the nearby trees, and he found some vine-like greenery down by the lake to tie them all together. That took about five minutes, and then in another ten he'd cleaned the court completely. Because the broom was short, he swept with knees deeply bent and moved about something like a traditional Russian dancer.

By this time I'd walked over to him.

"I've never seen that before," I said.

"People make brooms and sweep this way in Malaysia," he answered. "I'm Chong," he said. He was waiting for his partner; he'd come early to clean the court.

I didn't understand why it made such an impression on me, but I was soon to find out.

A week later, we met on the courts and rallied. Chong hit hard and rarely missed. I also noticed that it was very comfortable practicing with him.

The third time we were playing, he asked me, as we took a water break, if I'd like some advice on my strokes.

Chong was not the first person who had made such an offer. More like the hundredth. Often, hitting partners would ask and then comment on your game without waiting for your reply or even taking a breath.

"Do you know what you do wrong? You fail to . . . ," etc.

It was another variety of one-upmanship, an opportunity for a scrap of domination. After numerous such experiences, I'd learned to head people off before they could get a second sentence out. "Hey, I don't care," I'd snap. "Worry about yourself."

There was something about the way Chong asked that made me react differently. Sure, I sensed that he liked to play teacher. Beth, who was even more sensitive to men's tendency to assert expertise in everything around them, would have been suspicious of him.

But he'd posed the question and then waited silently for my reply. He was, in contrast to most male tennis players, polite and soft-spoken. As much as anything, the timing was right: I'd come out to Waveland on my own to work on my fundamentals. And here was a person who was offering to help me. You didn't have to idealize someone to learn something from him.

So I said, "Sure."

"You seem to me very fast. But with your backhand you take a step back to field the ball, rather than stepping toward it."

"Yeah?"

We continued hitting, and I watched myself doing exactly what Chong described. The pros often take the ball incredibly early, as it's rising or on the "short hop." Most club players generally hit the ball after the apex of the bounce, as it's moving more slowly.

It took me numerous sessions with Chong to break this bad habit of mine. Our rallies became different.

One afternoon, in the middle of one of these sessions, I realized I was in the zone. Probably we both were. And I hadn't gotten there through anger, or even competing in a match. There *was* another way in.

Chong seemed to intuit my experience just from watching me.

"Singles partners are involved in a dance that both participate in creating," was the way he put it to me that day at the net.

I stared at him, mute.

After all the macho posturing I'd encountered on the courts, it was an arrestingly poetic statement. It took real masculine confidence for an American male tennis player—yes, he'd been born in Malaysia, but he'd lived in the United States for decades—to say something that sounded so patently unmanly.

Later, I grasped that anger was perhaps the easiest, most accessible way, into the zone. Zen and anger are not generally seen as connected, but the link is quite simple.

Why does anger work? Entering the zone is about turning off one's nearly constant worry, or one's attempt to cautiously control one's actions and their outcome. Worry is the psychological dross that necessarily accompanies the desire to maintain control and avoid all unpleasant consequences. But this sense of conscious control is illusory; rather, one is simply in the grips of worry.

Anger is one way to stop worrying. One cedes the illusion of conscious control to raw feeling; one puts a powerful emotion in charge. The magic in this is not the anger per se, but the fact that one has given control over to something other than one's intentional, worrying mind. It might even be considered a first step in the spirituality of faith: trust in something besides one's anxious thinking.

And, though a step in the right direction, it's a crude one. I'd already found that ceding control to anger had its problems and limitations.

After several sessions taking the ball early both forehand and backhand, I was eager to bring this newly developed style of playing to other courts, and to games, especially with Trip. But I found I couldn't do it.

For some reason, without Chong, I'd mechanically revert to my old habit of taking backhands on my back foot. I seemed to have a special private game with him that I couldn't reproduce elsewhere.

It was frustrating and hard to understand. Maybe I didn't feel at ease enough playing with strangers to call on the kind of focus and intensity I engaged in with Chong. There was too much psychological static, you might say, that came from their barely concealed hostility and anxiety over possibly losing. But was this the case with Trip?

And then, to top it off, such experiences took me back a step. When I played with Chong again, I'd find that I'd regressed some; it would take a while to regain my new form.

I was embarrassed.

But he was not surprised.

"I can see you've been off-hitting in your old way," Chong said to me on one of these days, smiling. "You must have been playing out of harmony."

"Harmony?" I thought.

One day I asked Chong if he'd played with Marco or Theodore.

"No, never."

"But you know who they are?"

"Yes, I know them. I say hello to them. But just from watching them, it's evident to me I would never want to hit with them."

"I understand. But wouldn't it be sweet to beat them in a match?"

"I don't think it would be pleasant at all. Why would it?"

"Because it would bring them down a peg, even for a moment."

"I'm not sure it would, even for a moment. They would find a way to rationalize. But why do you care? That's not the right reason to play someone. It's disrespectful."

"But they deserve disrespect."

"It's disrespectful *to the game.*"

"What do you mean?"

"You could not create a dance with them."

I guffawed—the idea of creating a dance with Marco or Theodore was so ludicrous.

"If it's not a dance," Chong went on, "then what's the point? Yes, I can beat them, but I already know that."

"But they don't know it. Or at least they don't believe it."

"I'm sure they believe a lot of things that aren't true."

"Yeah." I had to give him that.

"What do I care what they believe? And even if I beat them, I might not win," said Chong.

"You mean you'd compromise yourself by coming down to their level?"

"Possibly, but I meant I might not win because they could cheat," he said, not so cryptically.

"It's not Zen to put up with players who are obnoxious," Chong declared, one day as we were walking off the courts to the parking lot. It was the first time either of us had referred to Zen. It occurred to me that coming from Malaysia, Chong might have been raised Buddhist. He went on: "It's Zen to avoid them."

It was all very tantalizing—Chong had shown me a different way into the zone. I wasn't entering in the freedom of rage, but in the trust of fellowship.

But would that mean I had to forgo competition—and rally only with people who were not obnoxious? Would it work to compete against people whose behavior was just mildly irritating? Was Trip one of them? And what about Chong himself? I knew Beth would have found Chong's oracular manner annoying.

"So tell me why you don't play matches anymore," I said to Chong, a few days later.

"There is a reason professional matches have umpires—and even spectators. All of these things are there to ensure that the match remains tennis. And still sometimes it devolves into something less, a grudge match won by breaking rules and 'psychological warfare.' Meanwhile, we amateurs don't have these things. I have to call the lines, stop the point if it is out; I have to wonder about whether you are calling the lines correctly. This is all interference. It clearly detracts from our presence. We can't immerse ourselves as we do when we hit to each other."

Presence?

Chong was implying that it just wasn't possible, given the limitations in amateur competitions, to have "sufficient presence." I wasn't ready to accept that.

It wasn't hard for me to imagine that unsportsmanlike conduct of other tennis players had helped convince Chong to give up match play.

But I also recognized that he had made a choice to limit his self-exposure. He no doubt had his reasons for doing so, which I couldn't begin to guess as I knew next to nothing about his personal life. However, to a limited degree, I could appreciate the opinion of Marco on this issue, even if I was repelled by his abrasiveness. Chong's decision only to rally didn't, for me, make him a "baby," but he was almost certainly sparing himself a battle with his ego. Whereas that was something I was instinctively seeking out.

CHAPTER 33

Playing Tennis against Pilots and Matadors

The next time I was about to play a match with a new partner—a really big guy named Kim whom I'd met on an online tennis site—it occurred to me I could simply ask him ahead of time, right out, if he could deal with not winning. The question would function like the presence of officials, or spectators. The guy would be much less inclined to throw a tantrum or cheat, I reasoned, once he maintained that he would control himself. There would be something deeply unmanly about losing your shit after saying you wouldn't.

It felt weird, but suddenly I found myself saying to a tall, perfect stranger, as we stood across from each other at the net, "Well, um, do you think you can handle it if you lose?"

I was ready for him to snap back something along the lines of, "Of course I could. But I'm not gonna lose."

However, looking down at me from his six feet three height, his face sort of fell, and he said instead, doe-eyed with shame, "No, I don't think I could."

"Okay," I said. "Well, let's just rally then."

"Yeah, that's better."

I hurried back to the baseline.

I continued to post requests for games on the Chicago tennis website.

I was now describing myself, based on Chong's estimation, as a 4.0+

215

USTA player—though that description was more than a bit hypothetical. I'd yet to prove it.

One day, I got an email from a guy named Martin who described himself as an Austrian pilot for Cargolux, the cargo branch of Luxembourg airlines. He was on a two-day layover in Chicago.

In person, he turned out to look and sound like a knockoff of Arnold Schwarzenegger; though not as big as the Terminator, he was clearly a weightlifter, in tip-top condition, with huge biceps and shoulders and tremendous thigh muscles almost overhanging his knees. In warm-ups, I saw his game resembled his fitness.

After a while, I asked him if he wanted to play sets, and though it seemed hardly necessary, I reeled out my now usual caveat that I didn't want to play if he was one of those guys, all-too-frequent in my recent experience, who couldn't handle losing.

He looked over at me, dismayed.

So I told him about one of my absurd encounters, to defuse the awkward situation I'd created.

"'One-ball' indeed," he murmured in his mild, middle-European, Arnold-like accent. He smiled.

So did I. Could this actually work?

I hit hard in warm-ups, taking the ball early. Of course, it was easy to do it in practice.

He won the racket spin (like a coin toss) and got ready to serve. The first two points went by quickly. I was going for strong returns right off his fast serve, and missing.

On the next point, I got the ball back, but by letting up some. He put it away on the next shot. "Damn," I thought.

On the baseline, waiting for the next serve, I centered myself. "I can do it," I thought, suddenly calm. "He's here from overseas. We'll play this one time, and he'll fly off forever. There'll be no lingering disgrace even if I hit every ball out. I'll never see him again ... But that's not even it. There's no belligerence or desperation coming from him, nothing weird. It's all fine. He flew the plane over here himself for Christ sake. If you can't do it now, it's on you, not him."

It was like diving off the high board. And just like that, I was airborne. The next thing I knew, we were having monster points that sped by superfast, and I was hitting hard, leaning into the ball, going for shots.

It was happening. And realizing it didn't bump me out of the mood.

He won both sets by two games, and I was panting, but that was because he was a higher-skilled player—at the 4.5 level at least.

"Thanks," I said, at the net.

"Yes, that was great," he said.

"Good luck." I put out my hand.

He shook it. "Wait," he said. "What are you doing tomorrow?"

"You don't have plans?"

"Well, I do . . ." He told me that it was such a good contest that he preferred to cancel them, to spend his other day in the United States playing a rematch.

"Okay," I said.

The next day he won again. But it was another beautiful match.

I couldn't help thinking, as I watched him walk off the court, on his way to his Lakeshore hotel and then eventually back to *his* plane—"This is apparently what I've wanted since I met Chong, to play competitive tennis with international aviators on a midweek layover. Of course! My research on Hemingway and those other amazingly talented jack-offs from the Lost Generation should have told me: I need to compete with pilots and air force captains and matadors and former college football and hockey players, Olympic runners, or retired professional soccer players. Men who are confident about their masculinity and have nothing to prove in that regard. It's funny how you don't know exactly what you want until you have it."

I would actually come to play with men who fit all of these descriptions, except that of matador.

CHAPTER 34

Sweeping Myself Clean

Something wasn't right with Chong. He was now faltering first in our rapid-fire exchanges.

I was old enough to understand that, outside of the movies, the world wasn't graced with the odd Zen master who just happened to haunt your neighborhood playing fields, simply looking for apprentices whose games they could selflessly turn around.

"Is everything okay?" I started. "You seem off."

"You're very kind to keep hitting with me. You're obviously better."

I shook my head. "I don't think so," I said. "Anyway, I'm the one who should be thanking you. You've given me a lot, and, frankly, I wish I could give you something."

"Oh, but you have," he said. "You don't know that?"

"No," I said.

Chong explained that a year ago, his partner of twenty-five years had died of a sudden stroke. "The time I met you, I was using tennis to escape and recover from the loss of her. I was never very good, and with a lot more free time decided to improve my ability. You have provided a good steady 'sparring and dance' partner. It has been comforting. You definitely can blow me away, but I know you take a lot off to cut me some slack. My tennis has improved and I have something to look forward to."

"I don't cut you slack, and I can't blow you away."

He shrugged. "Losing someone that loved you and also thought you were special was hard. Also being around her made me feel smart because of her intelligence. You also have that quality, and being able to talk 'Zen' talk with you is something I cherish. These kind of conversations are not really what many people get. It is rare that people react favorably to it. Being able to connect to each other and talk about our quest in life with you is special. This I missed not having my partner around, and so you have filled the void."

I nodded. "I'm glad. But you're just having a hard time these last few weeks."

"You're right about that. I am feeling stuck. I need to make a big change. In a few weeks, I am moving to Hong Kong for a while."

Chong was leaving, but at this point I felt I might be able to put his teachings into practice, even with someone who didn't fly a plane. I was going to play with Trip yet again—but with a difference.

By now I knew precisely why I was always hamstrung with him. It was pretty simple: though he didn't engage in the uglier ploys of gamesmanship, his total control of what we did on the court at every moment not only gave him a decisive psychological edge, but me a psychological stumbling block.

Maybe his approach was Zen of a sort, but if so, it was more akin to the angry approach that I'd previously practiced. His was based on subjecting the other person to his routine, almost blotting out his presence rather than harmonizing with him. He was perhaps comparable to a hermit—who maintained his peace of mind by keeping others at bay. Of course, tennis competitions couldn't be played on one's own, so Trip needed a partner to be there physically. But his iron routine did its best to keep you not only at a distance from him but subordinated to his will.

Given this realization, I'd asked myself, was it craven to allow myself to be thus subjected? Wasn't he another obnoxious player I should simply avoid?

This was a judgment call. Though he was involved in gamesmanship, I'd decided that his brand wasn't unbearable, because it didn't involve his making bad line calls and running at the mouth.

From my time with Chong I understood that, having made a conscious decision to continue playing with Trip—not just carrying on out of habit or convenience—it became my responsibility not to feel put upon by his routine or impatient with the wait involved. Rather, I had to embrace it fully. I had to harmonize with his idiosyncratic program. I'd already come to the same conclusion regarding the publisher's time-consuming process for evaluating a manuscript—and I no longer felt I was waiting.

The day we were supposed to play, I got to Waveland before Trip arrived, and I went out to an empty court at the back, closer to the lake, which was a bit more private. Usually, while waiting like this, I'd suit up in preparation: change my glasses to "rec specs," tape my thumb, put on my tennis gloves. I'd hit some serves. Make a phone call.

But today I suddenly found myself doing something I'd never done before, something I didn't even understand as I did it. It was impulsive; my body surprised me.

It spontaneously took up an unfamiliar posture, a pose, as one might do in yoga, which I had almost no experience of. I found my head was bowed slightly; my hands were touching, and my knees were bent, as they might properly be on a low groundstroke. I was also almost but not quite saying something in my head, something alien; I'd never heard myself think this way before. Maybe it was partly the weather, the full blooming of spring at last, some unaccustomed warmth from the May sun. Perhaps it was also because I felt fed up with my evasions, my absences on the court, the kind of underachievement I'd experienced so many times with Trip.

But more than exasperated, I suddenly felt I could be free of all that. The voice in my head wasn't coherent; it wasn't mostly words. I thought something along the lines of, "Let me put aside myself, my concerns, my tentativeness. I will play at the top of my game, no questions asked, no anger needed, no shame should I lose in that way. The outcome doesn't matter most; the most important matter is the spirit of play. I surrender to that spirit and put aside all hesitations and personal feelings. I am not here; I dissolve into the game which is somehow both dance and duel."

Only later did I realize that I'd been praying.

Shortly thereafter Trip arrived.

We warmed up. He was going through his unbending routine. As we rallied, I was taking the ball earlier, and, because he had less time, he was making more errors.

I knew Trip well enough to know that his on-court persona was one of absolute detachment, no matter what went down. I could have hit balls so hard that they burst into flames, and he wouldn't have said a thing. He would merely have picked up a fresh, uncharred can.

Then he turned to serving.

He tossed in his high, loping spin serve—his second serve—and I smashed it past him for an unreturnable winner. His expression didn't change; he probably figured the return was a fluke, as I'd never done it before. This serve had given me constant trouble in the past because it bounced above head height. If I let it. Taking it early changed the challenge and reduced it considerably. I had to react faster, but I was contending with a shoulder-high ball—in my strike zone.

I slammed it past him three more times. And now brief flashes of dismay appeared on his face.

I was at this stage already in competition mode, as I knew I had to be. There was no time, in the seven-point tiebreaker we were about to play, "to work my way into the set." Whenever that short competition started, my engines had already to be revved at full throttle. I'd probably have less than five minutes to show what I could do.

I had the benefit of knowing exactly what we'd be doing if not exactly when. Yes, he insisted on total control of the proceedings, but for the first time there was no irritation or alienation on my part, as I'd decided to consider his routine mine.

Trip announced that the tiebreak would begin. We spun a racket, then we were playing. I continued to take the ball early, went for my shots, retrieved his serve from the absolute closest spot possible. It was all over very quickly. I'd finally beaten him—the point score was 7–3— and done so decisively.

The tennis completed, Trip, according to his iron rules of behavior, could become again the relaxed hippie he wanted to be off the court. He could speak.

"Good game," he said.

The next time we met, a week later, Trip began his warm-up with his usual complete nonchalance.

Confident after my win the previous time, I was even more focused. During the rallying phase of our warm-up, he came to net, and I took the backhand so early and with my knees so bent—the right knee almost touching the ground—that the crosscourt passing shot zipped by him too quickly for him even to react. He tried the same thing again, with the same response from me.

"That's a really awesome shot," someone said. It was a young man on the next court. He was maybe college age, and he'd apparently stopped playing to watch us.

It was a nice thing to compliment a stranger, and rare enough among tennis players, so I wanted to say something. But I found I could barely manage a grunt in response. I felt rude, but talking to another human being at this point would have pulled me out of the spiritual socket I was plugged into. I could say something afterward if he was still around; that was the best I could do.

It was then it occurred to me that something important was happening. I was in the zone *in a competition mode*, but I wasn't angry. And thinking about it didn't expel me from it. I felt I could continue to hit all out and not miss.

When we turned to practice serves, I was again creaming his second serve for winners. But then, when he turned to his fast flat first serve, he put the ball in my forehand wheelhouse, and I slammed it back out of his reach. Again, he didn't have time to move.

"Wow," said a voice that was very familiar. But I couldn't place it. Not in my current headspace. Nor could I shift my focus to examine the small crowd of spectators that had gathered.

"Out," Trip called.

My ball was well in, so for a moment I didn't understand. Was he making that joke players sometimes made when you hit a clear winner—calling it out in a pastiche of cheating as a last resort? But it was totally uncharacteristic of Trip to joke this way on court. This would be his putting himself in a momentarily subordinate position, something he'd never done.

"The serve," he yelled. "My serve was out."

Ah. He was calling his serve out to negate my winner, which would have made more sense had the tiebreak begun. He wanted to wipe away my return because it devalued his serve. The call also covered for his not having been able to move for it.

"Huh. Looked good to me," I mumbled.

"It was out," he barked.

I shrugged.

Then he went on serving.

It was now time for the tiebreak.

Trip shook his head. "I'm finished for today," he said. "Thanks," he offered.

He'd done this before. Was he simply not in the mood for a tiebreak today? Or was it that he didn't want to risk losing a second tiebreak when winning was looking anything but sure?

I got my answer as we walked off the court.

Another player—an older guy, not bad but significantly weaker than either of us—called to him. "Hey, Trip, you want to hit?"

"Sure," Trip said. "You wanna play a tiebreak?"

I was a few paces behind him, and I couldn't imagine he'd forgotten I was there. On the contrary, he wanted me to hear him. Why wasn't he embarrassed? That was harder to figure. It felt to me like he was admitting he'd forfeited.

I could only guess he was trying to make a power play. Desperate to reestablish dominance, he may have imagined he was denying me tiebreak privileges with him, and I would feel excluded.

"Hey, buddy." It was the familiar voice again. Now I could place it.

I turned around. "Bobby! Good to see you."

We embraced.

"I saw the whole thing."

"I *thought* I heard you before."

"I can't get over it," he said.

"What's that?"

"You've gotten so much better. You take the ball early now. Like that guy Warner. You're a match for him now."

"That might be going a little far," I said. Warner was above a 4.5 USTA.

Bobby shook his head. "You're different too. You used to get so angry all the time. I was expecting you to explode there on that call."

I continued to hit fairly regularly with Trip, but he never proposed another tiebreak. The subject was never again broached, and we never competed again.

I'd stumbled across the fundamental paradox of Zen: the less you worried about the outcome the better the outcome was.

Once you began to focus on the outcome—once you started to get ashamed, or anxious, or proud—your game took a noticeable dive. And there was no way to cheat here. You could pretend you weren't thinking about the outcome when you were, but your game would reveal the truth.

It's not that you didn't care; it's that you needed to focus on the point being played. You replaced worry with trust: confidence in your body's abilities and the efficacy of that focus.

(The same was true, and much more obviously so, of scholarship, and writing in general. The more you concerned yourself with what you thought publishers wanted, and tailored your work to please, the less original and valuable it was. If I'd been writing with agents or editors in mind, I would never have produced and published anything remotely resembling the two books, a monograph and a novel, that had so far made my career.)

Though I didn't realize it at the time, the catalyst to my unexpectedly praying before what turned out to be my first victory and last tiebreak with Trip was not the sun or even my own frustration, both of which I'd experienced many times before. Chong had shown me the way months ago, and he'd no doubt shown me quite unintentionally: for he'd done so that day he made a broom and swept the court of leaves.

The thing about Zen that was so weird was that it really *couldn't* be transmitted in words. In a revealing portion of *Archery*, the German novice, frustrated with his inability after months and even years to understand the experiential approach of the Japanese master, brings him a book of Zen philosophy, hoping that he and the master will then be able to use the text as a guide and talk things through.

The master's response after he reads a few pages is something like, "I don't understand this at all."

Chong could have talked my ear off about humility and receptivity, and it wouldn't have helped because it lacked the magnetism of an action. Even better, he wasn't so much trying to teach me anything as he was just being himself: yes, expressing to me his better way of hitting backhands, but also just modeling a kind of being in the world that was different.

His cleaning the courts was hardly meant as a demonstration for me; it was just his reacting in his particular way to the situation. But his patiently taking time to sweep, his humble gathering of branches and twigs, his almost deferential squatting to brush the courts because the broom he made was short: these all communicated an attitude that struck me deeply. His actions were charismatic, and they captivated me, because they were so shockingly unconcerned with typical poses of masculinity.

To be sure, I had watched *Kung Fu* as a child and enjoyed samurai movies as an adult; I had read and reread *Archery*. But I imagined the "gentle warrior" was, if not an Asian myth, a thing of the past. True, I had never traveled to the Far East, but I'd been in a number of other countries, on three continents, and also on a lot of tennis courts. Wherever you went on earth, seemingly independent of culture, it seemed you found most men were macho jerks. I'd actually met very few men in any setting who were remotely spiritual—Foucault being an exception.

It was as if—though I hardly thought this on the day I met Chong or later when I suddenly bowed my head for the first time before a competition—he and I had enacted an allegory that early spring day. The leaves were bits and pieces of ego, and I would have been content to bump into them as I played; so what if they interrupted me, interfered some. I didn't see it as important. Even though I experienced them as a nuisance, I was too busy to take the time, too self-important and proud to clean the courts—if I thought about it at all, I'd feel it wasn't my job to sweep; it was someone else's; it should be done for me; I was above all that.

I was in any case too unobservant of my surroundings to realize that all the materials I needed to make a perfectly usable broom were also strewn around me. The twigs and vines that Chong picked up and melded together were also, in the metaphor, other bits and pieces of human spirit available if one took the time to gather them and arrange them, which might be used to enact changes within oneself.

Several weeks later, on that afternoon when I spontaneously prayed, I did the exact same thing, but now psychologically. I took time; I bent down; I humbled myself, and I swept myself clean of ego before I touched the racket.

CHAPTER 35

Jekyll and the Dragon

More than a few years later, I was no longer driven by anger or even harmony. I could feel myself poised to level up again. My accomplishments against Theodore and Trip had receded in the rearview mirror as modest achievements in some faraway past. But I knew the stages in leveling up would still be the same: I would find myself initially intimidated and stymied by a new opponent I simply could not beat, then I would try to figure out how I might beat him anyway, next I would recommit physically as well as mentally, and then, if it was possible, I would somehow finally best him, much to the surprise of everyone involved, including myself.

My most extreme case of this pattern came against a guy named Johnny whose opponents called him, not in jest, "the Dragon." He often referred to himself, not much more modestly, as "Superman." A former college soccer player, ten years my junior, he had serious skills (he'd made the transition from soccer some years ago, with lots of high-quality, expensive tennis coaches), was a beast of fitness, and possessed the habit of unrelenting focus that only trained and coached college athletes have. He was operating at a consistent 4.5 USTA level.

We played every week, at least once a week, and, in the first two and half years, I took a grand total of three sets off him. We'd played maybe 125 times. I suppose many people would have simply given up and found other, more appropriate partners, whom they could sometimes beat; the players who called him the Dragon hadn't stopped playing him either, but they *had* given up trying to win. They accepted that they would lose to him—and very, very occasionally pull a single set. I had not. Even after going something like 0–125 against him, I planned to turn the tables. "Nobody beats Keith Gandal 126 times in a row," I said to myself.

First of all, I had to get in better shape. Much better. One thing that helped me in this project was a new, crazy, fantastic, one-day, eight-hour, start-to-finish, single-elimination tournament at the indoor-in-winter courts everyone called the Bubble. The tourney was sponsored by a local legend by the name of Eric. Eric was from Guyana or French Guyana and grew up in the States. He was a businessman and a tennis player, owned property, and had one thing in common with that most famous of names connected with Guyana, Jim Jones. Eric had the charisma, smarts, and speaking chops to succeed as a cult leader. I had never met anyone with the civic-mindedness of Eric: in this regard, he was like a character you would only find in a film. *Field of Dreams* comes to mind: "Build it and they will come." He did not work at the Bubble or for the Parks District; he just saw an opportunity to mobilize these agencies for his own civic ends. There was no money to be gained. His idea was simple, and no one else would have had it or, having had it, done anything about it. Eric had decided to create a tennis community—where talented amateur players of different ages and levels and races and ethnicities and genders would get to know each other personally. The "Bubble Invitational" tournament was part of that project.

Even though I was unceremoniously dispatched in the first round of that tourney, I played about four hours of tennis that day, as the proceedings included two warm-up rounds that didn't count and ideally prepared players to be in top form when play began in earnest. It didn't work that way with me: I'd totally spent myself, physically and emotionally, in the practice sets, so that I was dead in the water by the time I stepped onto the match court.

But it was a great way to kick start a serious fitness program. After that shock to the system, which came at the end of winter, I committed, for the first time in my adult life, to doing some kind of hard cardio workout every day. Riding a bike did not qualify as intense enough—though I let myself slide occasionally if I did twenty miles. On days when I wasn't playing tennis, I was running up a hill. It was an eighth of a mile at a 10 percent grade. At first, it winded me just to walk it. Soon, I was doing the whole thing at a clip, without stopping.

The mental adjustment I needed in competing against Johnny was likewise clear, but no less demanding. I'd gotten habituated to losing. I had to wipe out the memory of the last few hundred sets. This sounds impossible, and it is. But I didn't really need to do that. More precisely, what I needed to do—and this is harder to put into words—was to steal back time I had unconsciously ceded to him. Because I had become fazed by his prowess—because I was shell-shocked by all the lost points and games and sets and matches—I quite literally experienced his shots as faster than they actually were. Bizarre, no? Not really. This is a common phenomenon in tennis. The way it worked, at the microtemporal level, was this: I experienced a minishock each and every time his ball approached me. That miniconvulsion wasted—I don't know exactly—some nontrivial fraction of a second. I therefore had less time than was actually available, pure and simple. I had to short-circuit my minipanics.

The Denzel thriller *Man on Fire* does a nice job representing this phenomenon—and showing a way to overcome it. The girl-child character, Pita (played by Dakota Fanning), is the fastest swimmer among her peers. But she loses every race because she is the slowest off the blocks into the water. And she is slow off the blocks because the gunshot that starts the race shocks her each and every time. Her minipanic eats up a crucial fraction of a second. Creasy (Denzel) has to completely habituate her to the sound of the gunshot—through repetition—so that she no longer convulses and loses that thin but significant slice of time. I didn't have a Creasy drilling me, but I had a knowing voice in my head that found ways to reassure me of the temporal reality and restore my tranquility of mind in the face of Johnny's shots.

With this mental adjustment and the amelioration of my physical fitness, I was able to become competitive with him. I began to take sets off him regularly. One of our matches was observed by his other opponents who'd dubbed him the Dragon. They were stunned to see me giving him so much trouble.

Then I started to win matches. It was now his turn to be shell-shocked. He went into a mental tailspin, so I was able to go on a winning streak that lasted for weeks. Six months after the Bubble Invitational, in the late summer, I beat him in straight sets, and I actually "bagled" him— took the first set six-love. At one point in that set, I'd whipped a hard forehand he didn't try to play, though it was within his reach. I asked him what was up. "I couldn't even see it," he said. He now had Pita's problem.

After that set, he told me, "I have to take time off. I'm not enjoying tennis anymore. It feels like a job." It occurred to me, without any need for reflection, that his enjoyment was intimately connected to winning. In the second set, he got up 2–0. When I tied it up 2–2, he repeated, "I need to take time off." When I took the set, he said nothing.

He did take time off. When he returned to playing, he battled for a few months, but then started to pivot once more toward despair. One day in February, after I took a first set off him, he started to talk doomfully again. "I need to take time off again." "This is no longer fun." Etc.

It was nice to turn the tables after all the hammering he'd given me over the last thirty-six months. But my ultimate aim was not to crush his spirit entirely—and this was partly for selfish reasons: over the last few years now, he was my most reliable opponent.

So I began, spontaneously, to coach him up. I was stern with him: "This is harder now because you're facing an opponent who has gotten in much better shape from a year ago. Yes?" (It was odd to talk about myself in the third person.) "Your attitude is a problem. First, you have to drop the negative talk. No more of that. All right? No more." I hadn't spoken this way to humiliate him, but I still wasn't sure how he'd take it. It was possible he'd strike out.

Surprisingly, perhaps, he did not take it badly at all, but rather responded as if I were his coach. "All right," he said.

I must have sensed that, as a former college athlete, he would respond to coaching behavior. He did better in the second set, and took it.

It was an odd, somewhat confusing experience being at once his opponent and his coach. I did this double duty each time we played for the next few weeks. The confusion came in for the obvious reason that my loyalties were split. I was trying to help him defeat me. I gave him pointers on how to defeat his opponent (who I also was). I didn't know whose side I was on. But I knew this was only temporary, and I was happy to do it, or mostly happy: I knew what it was like to feel down and defeated. I was giving him a push, to get his mental engines restarted, and then he could run on his own. Like the way they would start up a car or a plane in the old days, by cranking it, or start a toboggan in an Olympic run.

I ran into his two other opponents one afternoon during this period. One was complaining that "the Dragon" was crushing him again. (Even in the depths of his crisis, Johnny had never started losing to them, but he wasn't winning as decisively.)

I smiled—I was still invested in him as my charge.

"Why are you smiling?" the guy asked.

I wasn't going to tell them that I'd been coaching their Dragon. Like I said, I wasn't looking to humiliate him. I hadn't ever told them even about my improved results with him. All they knew about me and Johnny was that, for about a year, I'd been giving him trouble on the court. And whatever else he might have told them, but I assumed this was precisely nothing.

"The Dragon . . . ," I said, by way of covering for my smile. "It's funny."

The guy said, "You don't see him as a dragon?"

"I guess not anymore," I said. "It reminds me of a line from that movie *Jacob's Ladder*. When you're dying but are afraid of death, you feel pursued by devils. But when you stop being afraid of dying, the devils turn into angels. . . . He's not a dragon. Yes, he can fly and swoop. But Johnny—he's a dove."

They shook their heads. "You're crazy," the guy said.

In a rare moment of earnest instruction in my upbringing of my daughter (who I have purposefully left out of this story completely), I explained to her that, in the real contests of life, you don't lose until *you* give up. This is not a very deep insight for an adult, but she was maybe eight at that point. The reason I was rarely earnest with her, beyond the fact that I am rarely earnest with anyone I care about (earnestness usually being boring after a short while for all present, and often enough a subtle form of manipulation and oppression), is that I felt from the get-go that what a father says is much, much, much less important than what he models. I didn't want to model earnestness too much, as irony and humor are much more sanguine modes generally: I thought it important to model mood. My parents modeled anxiety and defeat and near-panic, which are pretty nonfunctional states of mind, and hard, for a child marinated in them for years, to shake. I think the most profound thing Norman Mailer ever wrote was that "totalitarian" powers "render populations apathetic" through "the destruction of mood."

In my experience, what wins tennis matches, when your partner is your match or better, is your irrepressible mood and your refusal to let it be destroyed.

During the first annual Bubble Invitational, Eric had called me aside because I got into a loud spat over scoring protocols during the first match with a young man probably twenty-five years my junior. Looking back on it, I can see that it was highly unnecessary, given that this was a warm-up round and the scores didn't matter.

"Come here," he ordered me.

"Oh, come on," I said.

"Come here," he repeated. And pointed to the floor in front of him.

He *was* the tournament director, and I *was* kind of spoiling the tournament's congenial mood.

I trudged over. "Wha-at?" I said, with the mock innocence of a schoolboy. "I didn't do anything. What did I do?"

"Look around you at all these people," he said to me, in a very paternal way, which I had obviously asked for.

I did.

"So . . ."

"Everyone here knows what you're like."

"They do?"

"Yes."

"What am I like?" I asked. There was some genuine curiosity at this point: it is interesting to find out how one is perceived. It's usually shockingly different from one's self-image.

"You present as all nice and charming. But then, on a dime, you can turn 180 degrees and go off into this extreme hostile dark mode. You are like Jekyll and Hyde."

I thought about that. "That's a fair description."

A year later, as the second annual Bubble Invitational approached, I ran into Eric and Johnny.

Eric said to Johnny, "You know, there are a number of people who wanted me to exclude your pal Jekyll here from the tournament. But I said, 'Oh, no. Jekyll's a colorful character. Jekyll's got to be there. He has to be part of it.'"

"Thank you," I said. I'd pretty much forgotten the trouble I'd caused the year before and was kind of surprised that other people hadn't. I was eagerly looking forward to the second annual. It wouldn't be much of an exaggeration to say that I'd been preparing for it for a year: I'd begun my most recent tennis overhaul after last year's marathon where I'd bombed out in the very first round. I'd won just one game. I wanted to do better. Much better. I was hungry to do so. I felt primed.

Yes, my initial motivation for rededicating myself to physical and mental fitness had been to end my two-year losing streak against Johnny. But once that was accomplished—and it was actually accomplished, rather rapidly, in a matter of weeks—I began to focus on this other challenge. It was a huge test: as Eric had put it to me in the run-up to the first annual: when you play this tournament, you'll understand Johnny is not such a big deal. Naturally, it had been hard for me at that point to look past the behemoth of Johnny that stood in my way. But that hadn't been the case for eleven months.

(By the way, it may seem strange that, after losing consistently to Johnny for two years, I was able to turn things around so fast. Or to put it another way, if that were possible, why hadn't I done it earlier? But that's how things often work, in sports, in scholarship, and in everything else. Shakespeare answered that sort of question for all time in *Hamlet* and then again in *Lear*: "The readiness is all." "The ripeness is all." Taking Prince Hamlet's predicament: it's hard to kill the king who happens also to be your uncle and stepfather. Yes, it would have saved a lot of lives and aggravation to have pulled it off in acts 1, 2, 3, or even 4. But Hamlet's just not up for it yet. And then suddenly he's ready in act 5. You have to be in the right state of mind, and, well, we have less control over our mentalities than we like to admit. One's mood is a fragile and mysterious animal. For some obscure reason, I'd only then been ready, after two and half years of defeats, to level up.)

I was on a roll in the lead-up to the second annual—and I knew I had to be peaking, if I hoped to do, not just a little bit better, but a lot better. Johnny had had a time with me the last couple of weeks. So had Robert, another regular 4.5 USTA partner of mine (a 5.0 player in his prime, he was, at my age, by far my oldest opponent). Let me put it this way: both had gotten uncharacteristically, microscopically gifted in their line-calling abilities the week previous—with Robert suddenly doing a version of the phantom shot-spotting that Marco had done to me, and with Johnny claiming a key shot of mine was "out by a millimeter or two." With Johnny, a teaching pro named James who was giving lessons to Johnny happened to be watching our third set tiebreak, and he noted to me, after Johnny departed, victorious, that that key shot of mine, one of the most devastating inside-out forehands I felt I'd ever hit in my life, was in fact just as beautiful as I thought, and not the garbage it got chalked up as—a point in his column that put him over the top.

Then the next week, in another coincidence, both Johnny and Robert had lost their shit with me. Robert had gotten so angry with me when I hit five "lucky" shots in a single game where I'd broken him that he totally snapped and yelled at me for a solid five minutes. "You alternate between unforced error and lucky winner: wild miss, lucky winner; wild miss, lucky winner. This is no fun. We never have a rally. I never got to play a ball." Then he told me never me to call him again and stomped out. I'd been taking his serve more or less from the service line because, though it was highly spun or sliced, it was quite slow—and I decided the best tactic was to just rely on my reflexes to bunt it back, making some errors but getting some drop-shot winners that way. I think most male players cannot help but take it as a personal insult when you don't show them "the respect" of standing back on their serve.

James the pro had been on hand to witness that event as well, as he was giving a lesson on the next court. "Can it really still be just luck if you hit five of them in one game? When does it stop being luck?" I asked him. He shook his head and shrugged. Then Johnny, well, Johnny hadn't totally lost his shit, but when I questioned his call on a serve that he said was a foot out—*because* he said it was a foot out when it was at most an inch or two out—he gathered up the balls and ended the match for the day. (I didn't think he was intentionally cheating; I thought it was just coming too fast right at him for him to get a read on it.) To Johnny's credit, he later apologized. (I never heard from Robert again.)

"You sure you won't participate in the tournament?" Eric said to Johnny.

"By tournament time on Sunday, I'll be drunk, as I am every Sunday by 5:00 p.m.," Johnny said, not even tempted.

"Okay," Eric said. He shot me a knowing glance. I knew he thought Johnny's "disinterest" was a face-saving move. Eric took his tournament seriously, and who could blame him. It was a huge undertaking involving around thirty-two players—as they have in the lesser professional tournaments.

Like I say, I was ready for the tournament. I figured that if, in the same week, *both* Johnny *and* Robert were fudging line calls, it indicated more about me than about them. And I figured that if, in addition, in the same week, *both* Johnny *and* Robert had, without precedent in each of their cases, stopped the match and walked off the court, it again indicated more about me than about them.

Johnny and Robert were not roommates whose lunar rhythms had synched through proximity; they didn't know each other. I was the big, consistent force in the equation that had brought them, as it were, into quantum entanglement. It was as a result of what I was doing in the two-week build-up to the tournament that twinned them: they would have been quite amazed if they had shared notes and discovered their synchronicities. It was uncanny: horror-show material or psychophysics. They were being flipped by me, and in just the same way.

Yes, the signs were there that I was peaking. I was raring to go. I had just at the right moment stepped up my game again. As Oscar the tennis sage might have put it, I was at this moment able to play beyond my ability. And like Shakespeare said and repeated, the readiness is all; the ripeness is all. Now, I just had to sustain my mood for another forty-eight hours.

It wasn't a trivial task: I would soon be in the presence of around thirty other competitors, a number of whom were at a higher level than I was or, to put it another way, many of whom were much better players than me on any given day. How could I possibly do really well and go deep in this tournament where I was without question outclassed by many of them? Well, it wasn't any given day: it was one day. Think of Cinderella: she had the help of magic until midnight. So did I. But, as with her with a little help from a fairy godmother, it was up to me to forget about my usual poverty and lowliness: to wear my rags like a ball gown and ride that pumpkin like a carriage.

The second annual took place on the last day of winter. I arrived at the Bubble early, around 4:30 p.m., as everyone else did per Eric's instructions. There were already twenty-five players in the building adjacent to the courts: the waiting room. Most were men; a few were women. As a veteran of last year's tourney, I had a much better idea of how to handle an all-day and -evening tournament.

Last year, I had dragged my heavy winter coat around for four hours from court to court; this year, I brought a lock to put it in a locker.

In the men's locker room, I ran into a stranger who was about my age. He was not there for the tournament; he was some kind of out-of-town coach who was there to instruct some players in another special Sunday evening event that was overlapping with Eric's. Luckily for me, he had a sense of humor, and was happy to talk to me—maybe because he had never been to the Bubble before and knew no other men there (he had come there with a woman colleague). The encounter with this man, whose name I forget—maybe it was Sam or Steve or Sebastian—might seem tangential to the event of the tournament and hardly worth mentioning. But it was not.

You see, I was trying to maintain my mojo here, and it wasn't clear how I was going to do that with twenty-five players waiting, some of whom were unquestionably better players than I. Now I knew, at least for the initial moment. It was good to jabber nonsensically, but I didn't necessarily want to talk to my friends or acquaintances. One of them, one of Johnny's other opponents who called him the Dragon, was around, in, and out the locker room. I could sense that this guy George was nervous, and felt green; this was his first Bubble Invitational. We rallied sometimes (just hit, never played matches), and I was happy to offer him some general pointers on Eric's tourney. But because he was nervous, his energy didn't offer me anything: it could have drained me some. This was not the time for me to play coach to someone else: it wasn't the mood I needed. It was too serious.

I wanted to be loose. Feel free and light. Yes, I could have played off him as a "straight man," and gently ribbed him, but I liked him and didn't want to use him that way. Steve or Sam was good for my needs, and our relationship was totally reciprocal with no inequality. We both wanted to blather to feel comfortable at what were for both of us strange events, and his not being in the tournament meant I wasn't in competition with him, nor did he need my help. His very tangential-ness was what made him the perfectly fitting companion for the moment.

I'd never put my things in a locker at the Bubble before, and the lock I brought didn't fit the locker. I didn't want to be burdened with my coat again this year, so I needed an alternative.

I realized my problem in the midst of changing clothes. I headed out to the waiting area, where thirty players now milled around—I was shirtless. Manning the reception desk, where the staff handed out courts and took money, was a young woman I knew, Patty. I knew that you weren't supposed to be shirtless outside the locker room, as did Eric, who was looking at me across the crowded room, with a little consternation. It was his tournament; I was breaking a facility rule that could have, he told me later, gotten him in trouble.

"What is he doing now?" he was thinking.

I crossed my arms on my chest and covered my breasts with my hands—as Cinderella might have done if she were in my precise situation.

Some people were pointing and laughing.

Eric said, though I was too far away to catch his words, "Keith isn't wearing a bra tonight, it seems."

I asked Patty if I could borrow a lock.

Yes, she could lend me hers.

How kind. How nice to have a fairy godmother.

Just one caveat: she had to leave, with her lock, at midnight (actually 10:30 p.m.). As Cinderella, I was used to that sort of thing.

All of this nonsense was very good. Perfect for the loose mood I apparently wanted. The answer to Eric's question, "What is he doing?" was: feeling my way into the right relationship to my peers and the event.

Now suited up and my coat deposited, I came out of the locker room dressed and ready to hit the courts, my equipment all there and in order. (I'd just this week had my favorite racket restrung—I'd happened to break my strings with Johnny just the week before.) By the way, I had recently felt my way, as well, into a lower tension on my strings. Looser strings give you more power, which I wanted, at the expense of some control: think of a trampoline. I'd been experimenting with going down in tension, little by little, for months. At the beginning of my tennis comeback,

I'd been stringing at fifty-seven pounds of pressure; that's what the manufacturer recommends. My rackets were today strung at forty-seven.

In the waiting area, Eric approached me with the signup sheet, a list-in-progress from which he would make the seeds and determine who played whom. I was wearing a backpack stuffed with two rackets, a few towels, some changes of shirt, some tape, a couple pairs of weightlifting gloves, some snacks, and so on; I was clutching a bag full of half a dozen drink bottles, and had on my "rec specs" (which were for distance vision only and not trifocals). Eric held out the clipboard, but with only one free hand, my bag balanced over one shoulder, and unable to see close up in focus given my specs, I was not sure how to manage to print my name. Having gotten all geared up, I didn't feel like putting everything down, taking off my glasses, and so on. Everyone had written their first and last names. Searching for a shortcut, I said to Eric, "Can I just sign in as Jekyll?" It was only six letters.

"You can sign in as whoever you want," he said.

I took the pen in my fist and sketched out, "JEKYLL" (all caps). Eric looked at his signup sheet, as did I. At the bottom of twenty-some rows of neat, clean, uniformly small print was a huge, John Hancock–sized scrawl that meandered across several lines; it looked more like the scratchings of an animal than the handwriting of a human being. Then he turned away and walked to the next person.

Warm-up hitting began, four players to a court. The year before, at the first annual, I had several times asked Eric when I would be playing my first practice match. This year, I did not ask him even once. There was no point in asking, except to prepare oneself mentally and physically, but I was already prepared. And asking him would have interfered with my mental preparation. I knew the ropes from last year.

George came up and complained to me after a while about the waiting around. He looked at his watch. "We've been here for an hour, and I have yet to play. This is chaos. I don't have all night." I understood, having felt the same exact way at last year's invitational, but this time, I did have all night. It didn't matter to me if I played the next minute or, actually, never played at all. To give George a chance at even minor success, because I could feel from his words that his chances had already diminished significantly, I explained the challenge facing Eric, with seven courts to dole out and three rounds of sixteen matches to place, before there were any eliminations. "It's inevitably chaotic," I said.

As I had done in playing Trip, with his elaborate and somewhat irritating ritual, I completely gave myself over to the proceedings, which were entirely in the hands of someone else. But Eric had made it work last year in the end, and I trusted he would this year as well. But if he couldn't, he couldn't. When he or his assistant Terry finally summoned me onto a practice round court for a miniset (first to three games), I was completely ready. I had no idea—none—how long I'd waited, partly because I hadn't been waiting.

My first match was against a charming African-French guy named Pierre, whom I'd met through Eric. He had been a psychoanalyst in Paris and had studied with Lacan. He was the only tennis player with whom I talked about Foucault, whom he'd read but never met. I'd never played against him. Last year, though I understood the practice matches couldn't result in elimination, I also knew they still counted in a significant way: Eric used the results to determine seeding, and thus whom you would play in the first live round. The better you did in the practice rounds, the higher you were seeded and thus the weaker the player you were initially matched against. Last year, I'd tried hard to win and put a lot of energy, physical and emotional, into the contest. I'd gotten into a screaming match; it had all been a colossal waste at the time (though it was serving me well now, having earned me a nickname). This year, I'd decided that much more important than the seeding was to maintain my mood and energy. It was so much more important, in my view, that, by comparison, the seeding basically mattered not at all. I played four games against Pierre; I was loose and won three of them. I didn't expend much energy. We shook hands.

It was quite a while until I was summoned again, though I have no clear concept of how long, for what was supposed to be a second warm-up round. I found myself on the court with a big Italian guy named Federico, who was 20 years younger than me. I'd played Federico a few times, and once in the last few months. We'd played one set, and I'd edged him out 7–6. I didn't love playing with him because he was moody—a little pouty. But it didn't matter because this contest didn't count: this was a second warm-up round. No, wait; Eric was telling me that this was my first live round. "Okay." It still didn't matter. I could beat him—I'd just have to drown out his slightly whiny, victim-ish energy because I didn't want to be affected and infected moving forward . . . Wait, Eric was telling me a mistake had been made. I hadn't had my second warm-up round. Perhaps because I hadn't asked Eric or Terry even once when I would be playing next, they had forgotten about me. But soon I found myself on the court with a guy named Jeremy, who was the one other player there who hadn't completed the practice rounds.

The runner-up in last year's tourney, Jeremy was the favorite this year to win. (Last year's winner was away.) Jeremy and I really got along—and always had a lot of laughs. He worked as a personal trainer. He was a 5.5 USTA player, maybe higher. Fifteen years younger than me, he was in inhumanly good physical condition; given his job, he spent six to eight hours a day doing athletics. A couple of years ago when we'd played fairly regularly (and he wasn't yet this good), he usually skunked me, but one blustery, early spring day, with rain threatening, I'd taken a set off him 6–0. I'd adjusted to the difficult conditions better than he did. After the set, he picked up my tennis bag and mimicked looking through it.

"What's up?" I said.

"I'm looking for your copy of *Winning Ugly*," he responded, smiling. "I know you must have the book in there."

That, again, was Brad Gilbert's book, which is about how you can sometimes beat players who are better than you, something Gilbert occasionally achieved against Connors and McEnroe.

"Actually, I do own the book," I admitted. "But since I've memorized it, I don't feel the need to carry it around any longer."

He'd never forgotten that day; neither had I, and we often needled each other about it. "Ooh, that was an *ugly* win." "Have you been bageled much lately?" That sort of thing.

Because we were the last warm-up match, and partly because he was favored to win the tournament, we had a lot of fellow players watching our little practice contest. I like when people are watching—not only because it guarantees I won't allow myself some pathetic emotional regression. As is probably already evident to the reader, I'm also a shameless ham.

This time we were playing first to win four games. I served well the first game and won. Having run a bit in the process, I told myself, "No more of that. I've used up my quota for this stage." I'm not saying I could have beaten Jeremy; I'm saying that after one game, I wasn't trying to do anything but stay loose and conserve energy. I tried some trick shots, one of which ended comically badly: a leaping backhand drive volley sent the ball to the top of the back curtain on a fly. But I also made one, where I feigned dashing across court as he prepared to swing on an overhead, only to stop stock still in place: the ball came right at my feet and I punch-shoveled it over his head with a nonchalant-looking backhand flip of the wrist. The crowd liked it. After I lost the miniset 1–4, a fellow competitor I didn't know named Nick came up to me, and told me he liked watching me play. "You have an entertaining game," he said. By this point, I was so deep into channeling the Robert Louis Stevenson character that I didn't even think, "Well, they don't call me Jekyll for nothing."

I went into the fieldhouse and joked around with the janitor for forty-five minutes. I told him most of a long story of a night on Bourbon Street when, among other things, a woman in a bridal party—I knew because the bride was in a bridal gown—had, unprovoked, grabbed my crotch in the middle of the street. (Dear reader: please excuse the obscenity of the anecdote. Tricksters are notoriously and inappropriately sexual, and I was deep, deep in embodying the trickster at this point.)

"Should I have reported it to the police?" I asked Tyrone.

"I'm afraid the police wouldn't necessarily have taken it very seriously. 'Dude,' they probably would have said. 'Welcome to the French Quarter. This is why people come to Bourbon Street from all over the country. People are very, very drunk here. You're how old—in your forties? Fifties? You've been touched up by a pretty twenty-two-year-old woman. Y'all have had the ideal experience. Now get the fuck out of here and treasure it. Oh—and tell your friends about it. We love tourists in N'awlins.'"

I ended up with a bye in the first live round, God knows why. (If you have less than exactly thirty-two players, then a few are going to get a pass in the first round.) It might have been because I did fairly well, after all, in the warm-up sessions. I beat Pierre soundly, and he wasn't a bad player. I got a game off Jeremy to start, and most likely Jeremy dropped no games in his first practice set. But I didn't know why I got a bye, and

I still don't. I never asked; apparently, Jekyll accepts good luck and bad on its face.

Eric came up to me and told me I was playing Jim; it was a super set, first to seven games. Jim was an excellent player and fifteen years younger than me; though I had never played him, his reputation at the Bubble was well known. Johnny had played him a number of times, and, I remembered, been thrilled one day to get a set off him.

I had actually tried to play with Jim myself. I'd asked Jim to play with me, and he'd politely put me off. I'd then even gone on to write him a rather pathetic text telling him that I'd improved a lot in the past year, and he could have that vetted by Johnny. He didn't write back, and I didn't blame him. Really good players like him were always being asked to play, and I had a pretty lousy reputation as a player. And not only had I crashed out of last year's tournament in the first round, having won only one game; I had also alienated several people—hard to know how many—and had a pretty lousy reputation as a person as well.

Anyway, we were standing in the alleyway between rows of courts, and I said to Eric, "Okay. Jim, huh? Jim is a good player."

"He is a good player," said Eric. "But he can be beat." Then he walked away.

I said out loud, not exactly to myself alone, since others were also in the alley, and, actually, it wasn't exactly like it was just me speaking either, more like Jekyll through me: "Eric says I can beat Jim. Maybe not in so many words. But he has strongly implied it. Jim is a good player, but Eric is telling me I should beat Jim. If Eric is telling me to beat Jim, then I will beat Jim. I guess I have to beat Jim."

And then I went out to the court and beat Jim.

That makes it sound like it was easy. But in a sense it was. I had gotten myself in the zone before stepping on the court. Things are pretty easy when you're in the zone. I was so loose that I played exceptionally well. I hit such unexpected, high-level winners that Jim more than a few times threw up his hands in his dismay. Actually, the gesture—made with one hand toward the spot where the ball landed and went by—was like brushing off a reality he couldn't quite credit but had nonetheless to count in the score. It was something like the body language of equivalent of: "Oh, come on! You've got to be kidding me. Give me a break." I beat him 7-4.

It was easy to beat Jim because all the hard work had been done before the match. I'd gotten in very good shape, starting almost a year ago; cut my teeth competing against skilled players such as Johnny and Robert; built my confidence on numerous good wins against them and other good players; in the last couple of weeks sucked in their cheating and their tantrums as delicious little cocktails. I was drunk on these and other trifles. Then I'd engaged in all these trickster shenanigans that night.

I maintain that if you can actually say to yourself, in an audible voice, with conviction, within earshot of other random people standing around, what I said to myself outside the court that night about beating Jim, you are going to beat Jim. Unless Jim has meanwhile tapped into some pretty extraordinary mojo of his own. If you can get yourself into such a state, you've managed to fully neutralize the worrying mind that is actually your biggest obstacle on the court: bigger than your opponent (unless you are outclassed by a good half-point or more on the USTA scale)— because, more effectively than your opponent, your doubting mind trips up your body's natural power, grace, and instinct. On any normal day, I would lose to Jim. But I think it's clear that I had made this day extremely abnormal for me.

After I rolled over Jim, Eric presented me with a choice. Given that I was older than most of the other players, I could either continue in the main invitational tournament, or move into separate "senior" shadow tourney, which would have its own semifinal and final. There were two other senior players left in the mix. One I didn't know and the second was Johnny's other partner who spoke of him as the Dragon. I'd played him many times in the past, and I'd lost only once.

"I'm staying in the main draw," I said to Eric. What did Jekyll care about a trophy?

"All right," Eric said. He explained that my quarter-final opponent in the invitational, Dirk, had just retired, due to a pain in his knee. He had left and gone home. I was kind of disappointed that he had: I'd been looking forward to a grudge match of sorts.

Dirk was a guy I had played with the year before—generously, I thought—all through his rehabilitation of his knee. But then when he got better he'd announced to me that he didn't have time to waste playing the likes of me, as he prepared himself for some USTA tournaments. Dirk was a great player, no doubt. But the likes of me? I didn't understand; we'd never played a match. I thought: you were injured.

"We played 7 sets, and you lost them all," he said to me.

We had? You'd kept a tally? Jesus. Shades of Trip. I didn't bother to enlighten him to the fact that no one tries fully when the other person makes a big deal that they're rehabbing, wears a huge brace, and is hobbling.

So I was even a little sorry he had forfeited and taken off while I was playing Jim; I might have liked to needle him a bit before he left, given his odd way of thanking me. I might have said something like, "Well, now that your knee is injured again, perhaps you can waste the time playing me again."

Anyway, my next opponent, in the semifinals, was a man called Sean. I'd met Sean, through Jeremy, still the favorite to win, at the previous invitational. As with Jim, I had in recent months texted Sean to ask if he wanted to play. He wrote back a polite text explaining that there was a misunderstanding: he was a tennis pro who gave lessons for a living, and he only played people of the caliber of Jeremy for free; he implied but did not say that I could pay him his hourly fee to play me. He was in fact, I later found out, giving lessons to Johnny, and was still doing so.

His response was not only polite but reasonable; I took no offense. I had had no idea how accomplished he was. I hadn't realized he was a teaching pro; nor did I know when I texted him what I'd subsequently learned from Johnny: as a younger man, he had actually played on the Challenger circuit (one level beneath pro) and had on one occasion come just one match victory away from qualifying to play in a pro tournament! He had been ranked in the top fifty among male Canadian players, and he had also been invited to try out for the Irish Davis Cup team. That meant that in his prime he'd been at the USTA level of around 6.0 or 6.5. The pros are at 7.0. (It's an exponential scale: the skill difference between 1.0 and 3.0 is small; that between 4.0 and 6.0 is gigantic.)

Well, the upshot of all of this, I figured, was I was going to get to play him for free after all.

After a thirty-minute rest period, we hit the court. Sean was an inch or so taller than me and ten years younger. His serve was still near professional grade; it was over 110 mph. He played a serve-and-volley game. I'd never faced a serve remotely as good as Sean's—except for that one night at the Chicago Midtown Tennis Club when the teaching pros played us. Nor had I ever faced anyone who served and volleyed remotely as well, except once, also during that team experience. One night I had the privilege of playing a set against a 6.0 player named Ivan. It was like trying to play against a freight train; no matter what I did, he came relentlessly forward until he put away the ball. I lost the set 6–0 in maybe fifteen minutes. I barely got a handful of points.

Things started out with Sean much the same as they had against Ivan. Sean served first, and I went down 5–0. It all happened very quickly. Jim had been a 4.5 USTA; Sean was operating, I had no doubt after five games, at the 5.5 level (somewhere between 5.5 and 6.0). What this translated to in practical terms was that Sean's shots were coming at and back to me, not only more consistently, but at a significantly faster pace. He was taking further time away from me by following his serve to net. His volleys were sharp and deep, the best I'd ever experienced firsthand. All in all, I had fantastically less time to get in position to hit my shot. I'd stepped again from the mortal world of club players into that which you saw on television.

And as in professional tennis, there was an audience. As I've mentioned, I enjoyed that. The loudest was the man Nick, the guy who'd complimented me way back in the practice round against Jeremy—"You have an entertaining game." He was rooting very hard—for Sean. It was a little hard to understand the intensity of Nick's investment. Were they related? Lovers? Oh, right: Sean no doubt gave Nick lessons. Nick was here to support his teacher; Sean was normally always supporting *him* (for money, true, but still). Here was Nick returning the favor. That was sweet; I was touched. (I was a teacher after all.)

Sean didn't seem to need much in the way of support, but it was nice that a spectator cared so much. And, really, why shouldn't someone root for Goliath over David for a change? It *was* a bit tiresome that people always rooted for the underdog. As Jekyll, I rather liked the absurd piling on of adversity.

There was only one moment it bothered me: when Nick cheered yet another winning volley of Sean's that happened in this one anomalous case to a be a mishit. It looked like a perfectly planned drop shot by Sean, but you could hear that my ball, returned with so much zip, had actually caught the edge of his frame, and the drop shot was unintentional. As I came to retrieve the ball, I had to pass near Nick, who was still cheering, and actually cheering louder than he'd cheered before, this incredibly impressive but sheerly accidental placement of the ball. And I felt I had to say something. Maybe I was concerned that Sean could misinterpret this raucous, orgiastic cheering of a fortunate goof-up as mockery. I knew Nick didn't mean to poke fun at his teacher, whom he was earnestly trying to support. But maybe I felt I had to say something for another reason. Maybe I thought Nick was actually losing rational perspective as he went absolutely apeshit over the spectacle of his 5.5–6.0 USTA, former Challenger circuit, former top fifty player in Canada coach so far shutting out someone who was, well, at a significantly lower level, to put it mildly.

I feel the need to say something more about the exponential USTA grading scale here—for non-tennis enthusiasts, if any are still reading—to appreciate just how significantly lower: because 4.5 doesn't sound that much smaller than 5.5. It's just one point, etc. As people who understand tennis and this scale would know: a true 5.0 player will beat a 4.5 player 6–0, 6–0, no question. A 5.5 player will beat a 5.0 player by the same score line. Sean was at least that 5.5 player, maybe more. So Sean was not my absolute superior; he was my superior's absolute superior. He was my boss's boss. If I, say, was the undersecretary of state for European affairs, Sean was the secretary of state. That's why, quite reasonably, he didn't want to hit with me or play matches against me "for fun." There was no fun it in for him, unless there was money in it.

But I need to say a bit more, because the one-point difference between 4.5 and 5.5 is so much greater than that between 3.0 and 4.0; remember, again, we're working here on an exponential, as opposed to a linear, grading scale. To visualize the math involved in exponential scales, let's say, for example, the numeric difference between a 3.0 and a 4.0 player is $e^{3.0}$ versus $e^{4.0}$ (I'm using the "e" of the natural log here to a degree arbitrarily, simply because it's associated with exponential scales): a quality difference in tennis play of around 35 "tennizens" (I'm making up a word to mean something like "particles of tennis ability"). Then, working on the same exponential scale, the difference between a 4.5 player and a 5.5 player is $e^{4.5}$ versus $e^{5.5}$, a raw difference of approximately 155 tennizens, more than four times as many as the difference between 3.0 and 4.0. One hundred fifty-five is a lot of tennizens, my friend.

But to get back to my walking near Nick. I wasn't sure why I felt the need to say something to him. It's not always easy to know why you do things, especially when you're being inhabited by a trickster spirit you barely understand. To be sure, I was surely influenced by my awareness of the dramatic *tennistential* difference between Sean and myself. Anyway, I said, "This guy's volleys are incredible, but just now you're cheering a mishit. Just so you know."

I went to the bench.

To win even a single game, I had somehow to kick up my own abilities—starting in the next two minutes. Could I? A few years ago in that team practice, I hadn't gotten a single game off Ivan. No big deal. I was better now.

Plus, I sort of had Nick's obliviousness to my usually lower level to spur me on: I guess I had so impressed him at some point in the evening that he seemed to think I too was a former Challenger player, a former secretary of state. And to a degree my usual level, which was a shade or more below 4.5, didn't really matter anymore: God knew what level I was at at this strange moment—or more to the point, could be at shortly—some six hours into my shape-shifting experiment, fresh from my strong victory over Jim, and poised to make one more fierce, musical leap upward. There is only one way to understand why Nick didn't feel he was being a totally unsportsmanlike prick in loudly rooting for a bobcat over a rabbit, Tom over Jerry, a monster truck against a VW Bug: what Nick saw as he watched wasn't a competition between David and Goliath, but, rather, a contest between his awesome, beloved coach Sean and the maybe slightly sinister Red Baron. (Yes: Eric later told me that Nick referred to me that evening and from that day on as "the Red Baron"—my rec specs look a bit like old aviator goggles; I had a mustache, and that night I randomly wore a red shirt and shorts.)

On the changeover, I turned my mind to the question of possible tactical shifts.

On Sean's serve. Fact: my returns weren't bad; some were quite hard hit, but he was such a great volleyer, it didn't matter in terms of the outcome. Analysis: as long as he could reach the ball, he was putting it away, or hitting a good enough volley to put it away a shot later. Ergo: I had to stop returning crosscourt—and instead hit exclusively down the lines out of his reach. Easier said than done, but at least I had a plan.

On my serve. Fact: I was getting points on the first one, but never on the second. Analysis: my finesse or second serve just wasn't good enough to give a guy of his caliber trouble: not nearly enough kick or slice. Ergo: I could only hit first serves.

I served the next game—all hard, first serves—and I held. I'd finally won a game. I was down 1–5. We were playing a superset up to 9.

Then he was serving again. His serve was so fast, it was definitely a challenge trying to hit it down the line. I called a first serve of his long that just missed; it was close, but I thought out. Hard to see because it was so rapid.

He came to the net and maintained that it was in. "Look," he said. "I can see that you're calling the lines fairly and giving me the benefit of the doubt. So no complaints, Keith." Indeed, I had purposefully called nothing out that wasn't blatantly out. "But that was definitely in. I'm absolutely sure. I'm 100 percent positive."

"I guess if you're that sure," I said.

By then Terry, Eric's assistant, had walked onto the court and up to us. Starting with the semifinals, as Eric had explained, he and Terry would be serving as umpires—just in the case of a disagreement. "It was out," Terry said.

Sean didn't apologize; he hardly shrugged. He went back, prepared to take a second serve. Needless to say, this was a weird moment. Soon enough, he won the game. I was down 1–6 now.

I didn't know what I thought. Looking back on it, there were a variety of possibilities. Was he cheating on purpose, or was he rather so fiercely determined to win decisively that he was "seeing things" the way he wanted them to be? (That was essentially how the teaching pro James described Johnny's calling my in-ball out in the heat of the tiebreak that day.) Why not give me the benefit of the doubt here, given that he was a much better player and also already crushing me? But maybe he sensed, despite the box score, that I was a threat and he needed to start fighting over line calls, especially after I'd finally taken a game. Was he trying to fuck with my head? Should I confront him?

At the time, I didn't really think any of these things. Instead, and perhaps counterintuitively, my instant and unreasoned decision was to henceforth play every ball that was even near the line—and only call one out if it was grossly out. Whether he'd meant to fuck with my mind or not, he had done so by stopping the flow of play and taking my focus off the game. My only chance to win games, let alone beat him, was to preserve my white-hot state of mind. I couldn't afford to be stopping and having discussions. I couldn't play line judge and have chummy discussions with him and the organizers—and also play at the extreme level I needed to. Perhaps needless to say after all I've said before: I was in the zone. The zone had requirements: I needed to respect the place or leave it.

I lost the next game on my serve, again in part because my focus had been damaged. I was now down 1–7. He served again, and held again. He was a game away from the set.

Now Eric had been watching, serving as "umpire" along with Terry. He stopped the match for a moment—his serious face on. "Keith, you seem to have misunderstood. Let's get something clear. Terry and I are not calling the lines. You have to call the lines. We only chime in if there's a disagreement."

I knew why he was saying this. I was playing serves—and other shots—of Sean's that weren't in. "I understand," I said.

He looked dismayed. I walked away.

"This is it," I said to myself on the changeover. "Gotta kick into overdrive now. You can do it. You started to, only you got waylaid."

I held my serve again.

I was now down 2–8. It was a miserable score line, but I was at this point heartened. Forgetting about the first five games I lost before I acclimated and made a plan, the score of the last few games was 2–3. Quite a different story. And I'd played a couple of those games slightly distracted. Not only had I held twice, I'd managed to return a massive first serve of his down the line for an exquisitely timed winner in probably the best shot I'd ever hit. I knew I was improving dramatically; it was a totally different match now. The only problem was that I was running out time. I had no more games to give.

In the next one, on his serve, I played my best game of the tournament—and quite simply the best of my life. I hit three more down-the-line service return winners, including a high backhand down the line from the ad court—this sort of "redirection" shot on a high backhand, especially of a serve (the fastest shot you get), is one of the most difficult in tennis. It requires not only perfect timing but also strength. It was even better than the previous best shot of my career made two games ago. I fended off four match points—on the ad side of course, the more difficult side to defend because it was easier on that side for him to serve to my backhand—but on the fifth, he won the contest: 9–2.

Sean and I shook hands. (In the weeks to come, when I'd run into him coaching Johnny, he would treat me with a new and profound respect.)

Nick had watched the whole thing. He came over and congratulated me.

Terry came up to me. We had been rally partners off and on for years (he was seventy-one, and didn't play matches anymore). "I'm very impressed, Keith. I've never seen you play at anything like that level," he said. "I didn't know you could. And I didn't know you had that sort of grit in you."

I thought: I didn't know either.

Eric also talked to me. He was upset. "You played six or seven serves of his that were out. Why? That's a lot. It could easily have made the difference. You might very well have won."

I shrugged.

"I think you could have beaten him."

"You should have told me that before the match," I said. "Then I would have." I didn't even smile. It was 11:30 p.m. I'd been at the event for seven hours.

Sean lost to Jeremy in the final. In fact, Jeremy crushed him. It was an unusual result in their rivalry.

Jeremy texted me a day after: "Made a nuisance out of yourself I see. Gandal Tennis 101. <Wink emoji>. Thanks for the help."

Eric said to me a week later, "You shocked people. You were terrible last year. And a jerk. You were the surprise of the tournament."

"I think I'm still a jerk," I said.

"But now they fear you too," he said.

A week later, Eric told me he had had a trophy made for me. It was of heavy glass and quite elegant. The engraving read:

**Master's Singles Finalist
Keith "Jekyll" Gandal.**

CHAPTER 36

Coming Back to What We Love

"Was that so bad?" Beth asked, polishing off a glass of champagne.

She had organized a party for me, to commemorate the publication of the monograph. The last guests departed, the gathering finished, she was teasing me because, according to her, I'd never previously celebrated any of my achievements.

"It was wonderful," I said. "Thank you for forcing me." I opened the door of the bedroom where the dogs had been banished on account of overexcitement. Lazarus and Quilty for sure hadn't been to a book party before. They bounded in and started nosing around for spilled food.

The scholarly manuscript had faced a final stumbling block to publication: one of the reviewers loved it, but the other rejected it after a single, somewhat peevish page, which wound up by saying, "I would be happy to provide more specific[s] . . . at a later date." This was weird as such "specifics" actually constituted a review. Generally, one negative response sinks a project. Fortunately for me, the editor, Shannon McLachlan, to whom I'll always be indebted, made a judgment call, decided this insufficient review could not "determine the fate of the book," and sought a third reader to "break the tie." The third review was overwhelmingly enthusiastic.

"I couldn't have done it without you," I said to Beth.

"I'm glad I could help."

"Do I do the same for you?" I meant her doing well in premed studies.

"You do."

Of course, neither of us was guaranteed a positive outcome where it "mattered most": she hadn't yet gotten into medical school, and I didn't have a new job offer. But something else, something immeasurable, mattered now, maybe just as much.

"I don't know if I've fully turned a corner. But it felt right to celebrate," I said. "I've wanted to do a book like this for twenty-five years."

I'd dedicated it to Foucault and my father. And also to Beth.

"I'm proud of you, Keith."

"I'm proud of you," I said.

"And it's wonderful the way you've gotten to love the dogs," Beth said. "I didn't expect you would."

"I'm a changed man, maybe. I do love them." I looked around the room at the almost-empty glasses, a smattering of uneaten appetizers, and other detritus of the party. "Can we clean up later?"

"Yes. Let's do something else first."

I took her hand.

"Quilty and Lazarus will have a field day with the leftovers."

"Ah, let 'em," Beth said. "They've helped too."

It had been a year of metamorphosis. I thought I was entering tennis for some recreation, and I got revelation. I thought I'd gotten in it for the physical exercise, and I experienced a kind of psychic exorcism. I thought with my scholarly research I was simply proving something to the academic world, trying to become a player, but it was also a way to discover something personal, which had meaning only to me. I learned prayer.

It's an old story and a familiar one, but it seems it's one that you're fated to learn and relearn if you learn anything: I went to take on opponents, and I took on myself. It's a story whose broad outlines I knew from my encounters with sickness and with intimacy. It is something I'll presumably learn again (unless my life ends unexpectedly and suddenly) in experiencing dying. I will have to get to know it, make it personal, be honest with myself, and stretch to the limits of my abilities—perhaps beyond. My initial, conscious goals to perform at a certain level in tennis matches and to land a new job had been subsumed by the challenge of being a better, happier human being.

A big part of the lesson was that thinking, cogitation, was a tool. Though crucial, it wasn't the supreme authority. It didn't have the answers. You needed to use your mind to figure out how to gain access to and make use of the wisdom of your body, your emotions, your dreams. Give the mind too much importance and control, and you never met these wisdoms that were latent and waiting for you, gifts that were yours but could remain wrapped and unopened for your whole life unless you let yourself find your way to them. If you allowed your mind too much authority, it shut you off from the resources you needed to get along on the playing field, at work, in relationships, in your craft—and to move along in them.

But give it too small a place and you career along without the benefit of steering, unable to change direction until you crash into something, or someone. I'd learned a faith that there was a way, resources within and without you could encounter, draw on, gain from: not a blind faith, but a directed one; not a relinquishing of thought, but a utilization of it. Not that it was ever easy to balance these things.

Of all the evident things I didn't see about myself during this period, the connection for me between my tennis play and my scholarly detective work was the hardest to believe I'd missed. Tennis, like the military papers and the research project it implied, was something I'd set aside earlier in my life and had now picked up again, decades later. Every time I'd moved, I'd brought those boxes of documents with me, and I'd always kept a racket on hand as well. I hadn't noticed the latter because rackets are light and thin and can be jammed almost anywhere.

And not only had I previously put both tennis and this research aside, I'd put them aside for the same reason: self-doubt. I'd dropped these two things that were important to me at moments when my confidence was at a low ebb. In the case of tennis when I was thirteen, my parents had recently divorced; my mother had just remarried a man I didn't get along with, and, meanwhile, I found myself in a junior high classroom that was alien and hostile, where all the kids were rich and white, and material things mattered. With the research, Foucault had died, and I'd almost flunked my orals. I'd turned from tennis to soccer, my brother's sport, and, in a similar way, I'd switched from this military-themed project to one on the literature of the slums, a topic one of my professors had at least broached in class. When in doubt, I preferred to follow to a certain extent, rather than continue to pioneer.

But again with both, I'd kept them on ice for decades, never throwing them out and, without knowing what I was doing, protecting them by packing them away at the dangerous moments when they were threatened. I never planned the comebacks detailed in this story, but something in me instinctively knew to hold on to these things, and it wasn't true that I held on to everything.

I think I'm hardly the only person who comes to detest what he once loved and might still love. Some of our loves are permanently poisoned, turn completely into hates, and cannot be recouped. When we lose for good the things we once loved and might still love, we are protected, but also diminished.

Middle age, though difficult in many ways, including a reduction in natural physical fitness and a heightened consciousness of the reality of death, is also potentially a period of deeper self-assurance—based on experience and achievement. Ideally, you can have the confidence to do things that you are drawn to but that other people, and maybe even you yourself, find embarrassing at your age. Embarrassment is an unavoidable stage in the Zen journey.

Yes, a lot of us break from our families, their expectations of us, and their worldviews when we leave home at eighteen or so. But in the confidence of middle age, you can continue the job. You can arrive at a point where you are finally able to stop following in—or even looking over your shoulder at—the big and safe footsteps of your "older siblings" and peers as well, make a clean break, and take off in directions that are absolutely your own. You might also find that your hatred for certain things that were once meaningful to you has diminished some, allowing you to get back to what you love.

Epilogue

After a couple of years of making applications without success, I wondered if even a handsomely published book concerning dead white male writers, masculinity, the military, and war could in fact land me the kind of job I'd hoped for in today's academic climate. "Why didn't you focus on any women authors?" was a question I was asked at one interview, basically an academic equivalent of "When did you stop beating your wife?"

"You've written a *man*ograph!" a not exactly supportive colleague later quipped. "That's just not going to fly in this day and age."

But then one almost fantastical, final stroke of luck changed the playing field. For the first time in my twenty years of checking the professional job list, a position came up on the grid for a scholar / creative writer: a research scholar, with a lit PhD and monographs, who'd also published a book-length creative work. (Literature and creative writing programs typically have separate faculties.) The job call was even more specific to my situation: it was for a "senior faculty member who is a dually accomplished Creative Writer and an Americanist." It was for a job at the City College of New York in Harlem, a place I'd always wanted to be, and where I'd in fact previously interviewed, more than fifteen years before. For a good five minutes, I read the short ad over and over again, finding it literally too good to be true. Perhaps only a couple handfuls of people in the world qualified. I managed to get that job.

Beth's excellent premed record was spoiled by the MCAT, which turned out to be all-important in the application process. Her score essentially limited her to med schools in the Caribbean. Unlike an unmarried Faulkner in his late teens who was willing to go to standard-less Canada to get into the war, she decided living abroad for years—and apart from me—wasn't a sacrifice she was willing to make to become a doctor. The decision wasn't difficult for her, but I knew the meritocratic "failure" would be. She would have a kind of life crisis: maybe not right away, but almost inevitably. I got ready for it.

During my last month at my old job, various colleagues who'd learned about my good fortune gave me their parting thoughts. One of my favorites, a truly talented writer and a friend, came up to me in the hall, gave me a big hug, and whispered in my ear, "Fuck you."

Along with the dogs, Beth and I moved to New York City, where neither of us had ever lived for any length of time.

Bibliography

As a procedure for lightening the weight of causality, "eventalisation"...
works by constructing around the singular event analysed as process a "polygon"
or rather a "polyhedron" of intelligibility, the number of whose faces is not
given in advance and can never properly be taken as finite. One has to
proceed by progressive, necessarily incomplete saturation.

—Michel Foucault

I've detailed only the most dramatic research thread in the forego-
ing story. In executing this research project and producing the peer-
reviewed and scholarly monograph that came out as *The Gun and the
Pen: Hemingway, Fitzgerald, Faulkner and the Fiction of Mobilization* (New
York: Oxford University Press, 2008), I consulted dozens and dozens of
texts on a wide range of topics; the aim was to reconstruct the historical
context of the famous Lost Generation novels. And then I consulted a
whole further set of topics and slew of books to understand how and why
the meaning of the military and of masculinity had changed in the Vietnam era; the academic, peer-reviewed article on the subject appeared
as "Why the Vietnam Antiwar Uprising? The Confluence of Scholastic
Meritocracy and Cold War Mobilization in a New Student Class." *Telos*
150 (2010): 9–26.

My research and analytic methodology was derived from that of
Michel Foucault, and specifically his later work. He had coined a notion

of historical "saturation" (which I was attempting to use) and expressed it as specified in the epigraph to this bibliography, using a metaphor from geometry: imagine your subject as a point (my subject was the 1920s literary masterpieces of the Lost Generation) and build around this point a "polyhedron of intelligibility," with each face of the polyhedron standing for another historical development and functioning as another window or lens through which to view that point. The more such faces or windows you look through onto your subject, the more you "saturate" your subject historically. By the way, these faces of the polyhedron, or the windows of intelligibility, are theoretically endless (and if you could multiply the faces of the polyhedron forever, you would approach a sphere surrounding your point), so you have to figure out which are the most important ones.

To put works of literature in their historical context in this method is, as you can imagine, research-intensive, involved, inductive, and slow-going, and you are hardly guaranteed any glamorous or trendy results. You are neither sycophantic of the authors nor arrogant about the literature or the world. This historical approach is absolutely unrelated to the kind of deductive literary criticism that begins with an overarching theory about history, society, or literature—such as Marxism or deconstruction—and then finds "another example" of, say, the "domination of the bourgeois class" or the way a "text deconstructs (or fundamentally contradicts) itself" and thus proves to be "irreducibly ambiguous." You don't know what you're going to find. But if you put in the time and legwork and also get lucky and, yes, even imaginative, this historical-contextualizing process is a way to bring a work of literature to life and to animate its era. At least it is for me.

Below I list the various historical windows through which I looked at my literary subject, as well as the texts consulted in order to construct each window, each lens or aspect of the historical context. And I list them more or less in the order in which these windows or aspects come up in the book, or become relevant to the discussion. (Some texts would appear under more than one window, and in general I've listed the text according to my principal use of it.) Next, I've listed the various historical windows through which I gazed on a second subject here: my generation's changed attitude toward the military and altered sense of masculinity.

SUBJECT 1. THREE LOST GENERATION MASTERPIECES

F. Scott Fitzgerald. *The Great Gatsby* (1925). New York: Scribner, 1992.
Ernest Hemingway. *The Sun Also Rises* (1926). New York: Scribner, 1986.
William Faulkner. *The Sound and the Fury* (1929). New York: Vintage, 1956.

Window: (Some) Literary Criticism on the Lost Generation Writers or Modernism

John W. Aldridge. "Afterthoughts on the Twenties and *The Sun Also Rises*." *New Essays on "The Sun Also Rises"*, ed. Linda Wagner-Martin. New York: Cambridge University Press, 1987. This is the article in which Aldridge set forth the mystery discussed, as well as commented about the mountain of critical literature on Hemingway and that there was nothing new to say about Fitzgerald or Faulkner.

John W. Aldridge. *After The Lost Generation: A Critical Study of the Writers of Two Wars* (1951). Whitefish, MT: Literary Licensing, 2012.

John Barth. "The Literature of Replenishment: Postmodernist Fiction." *The Atlantic*, January 1980.

Malcolm Bradbury. *The Modern British Novel*. New York: Penguin, 1995.

Malcolm Bradbury and James McFarlane. *Modernism*. Harmondsworth: Penguin, 1976.

Peter Brooks. *Reading for the Plot: Design and Intention in Narrative*. New York: Knopf, 1984.

Matthew J. Bruccoli. Introduction, *New Essays on "The Great Gatsby"*, ed. Bruccoli. Cambridge: Cambridge University Press, 1985.

Stacy Burton. "Rereading Faulkner: Authority, Criticism, and 'The Sound and the Fury,'" *Modern Philology* 98.4 (May 2001).

Stanley Cooperman. *World War I and the American Novel*. Baltimore: Johns Hopkins University Press, 1967.

Malcom Cowley. Introduction, Sherwood Anderson, *Winesburg, Ohio*. New York: Viking, 1960.

Thadious Davis. "Reading Faulkner's Compson Appendix: Writing History from the Margins." *Faulkner and Ideology: Faulkner and Yoknapatawpha* (1992), ed. Donald Kartiganer and Ann J. Abadie. Jackson: University Press of

Mississippi, 1995.

Marianne DeKoven. *Rich and Strange: Gender, Modernism, History*. Princeton: Princeton University Press, 1991.

Bram Dijkstra. *Evil Sisters: The Threat of Female Sexuality and the Cult of Manhood*. New York: Knopf, 1996.

Scott Donaldson. "Hemingway's Morality of Compensation." *Modern Critical Interpretations: Ernest Hemingway's "The Sun Also Rises"*, ed. Harold Bloom. New York: Chelsea House, 1987.

Ann Douglas. *Terrible Honesty: Mongrel Manhattan in the 1920s*. New York: Farrar, Straus, and Giroux, 1995.

Rachel Blau DuPlessis. *Writing beyond the Ending: Narrative Strategies of Twentieth-Century Women Writers*. Bloomington: Indiana University Press, 1985.

Leslie Fiedler. *Love and Death in the American Novel*. New York: Stein and Day, 1966.

Alan Filreis. *Modernism from Right to Left: Wallace Stevens, the Thirties, and Literary Radicalism*. New York: Cambridge University Press, 1994.

Paul Fussell. *The Great War and Modern Memory*. New York: Oxford University Press, 1975.

Maxwell David Geismar. *Writers in Crisis: The American Novel, 1925–1940*. New York: Hill and Wang, 1966.

Sandra M. Gilbert and Susan Gubar. *No Man's Land: The Place of the Women Writer in the Twentieth Century*. Vol. 2, *Sexchanges*. New Haven: Yale University Press, 1989.

Gerald Graff. "Babbitt at the Abyss." *Tri-Quarterly* 33 (1975).

Gerald Graff. "The Myth of the Postmodernist Breakthrough." *Tri-Quarterly* 26 (1973).

Carla Kaplan. "On Modernism and Race." Review essay, *Modernism/Modernity* 4.1 (1997).

Karen Keely. "Sexuality and Storytelling: Literary Representations of the 'Feebleminded' in the Age of Sterilization." *Mental Retardation in America: A Historical Reader*, ed. Steven Noll and James W. Trent. New York: NYU Press, 2004.

Marcus Klein. *Foreigners: The Making of American Literature*. Chicago: University of Chicago Press, 1981.

Julia Kristeva. "Oscillation between Power and Denial." Trans. Marilyn A. August. *New French Feminisms*, ed. Elaine Marks and Isabelle de Courtivron. Amherst: University Massachusetts Press, 1980.

Roger Lewis. "Money, Love, and Aspiration in *The Great Gatsby*." *New Essays on The "Great Gatsby"*, ed. Matthew J. Bruccoli. Cambridge: Cambridge University Press, 1985.

John Liman. "Addie in No-Man's Land." *Faulkner and War: Faulkner and Yoknapatawpha, 2001*, ed. Noel Polk and Ann J. Abadie. Jackson: University of Mississippi Press, 2004.

Eugene Lunn. *Marxism and Modernism: An Historical Study of Lukacs, Brecht, Benjamin, and Adorno*. Berkeley: University of California Press, 1982.

Wendy Martin. "Brett Ashley as New Woman in *The Sun Also Rises*." *New Essays on "The Sun Also Rises"*, ed Linda Wagner-Martin. New York: Cambridge University Press, 1987.

Sean McCann. *Gumshoe America: Hard-Boiled Crime Fiction and the Rise and Fall of New Deal Liberalism*. Durham: Duke University Press, 2000.

Louis Menand. *Discovering Modernism: T. S. Eliot and His Context*. New York: Oxford University Press, 1987.

Walter Benn Michaels (the mentor I refer to simply as Walter). *Our America: Nativism, Modernism, and Pluralism*. Durham: Duke University Press, 1995.

Laura Mulvey. "The Original 'It' Girl." *Novels for Students*, ed. Marie Rose Napierkowski, vol. 4. Detroit: Gale, 1998.

Michael North. *The Dialectic of Modernism: Race, Language, and Twentieth-Century Literature*. New York: Oxford University Press, 1994.

Claudia Roth Pierpont. "A Society of One: Zora Neale Hurston, American Contrarian." *New Yorker*, February 17, 1997.

Tony Pinkney. "Editor's Introduction: Modernism and Cultural Theory." *Modernism and Mass Politics: Joyce, Woolf, Eliot, Yeats*, ed. Michael Tratner. Stanford, CA: Stanford University Press, 1995.

Ruth Prigozy. Afterword, F. Scott Fitzgerald, *The Beautiful and Damned*. New York: Signet, 2007.

Michael Reynolds. "False Dawn: *The Sun Also Rises* Manuscript." *Modern Critical Interpretations: Ernest Hemingway's "The Sun Also Rises"*, ed. Harold Bloom. New York: Chelsea House, 1987

Edward Said. *Beginnings: Intention and Method*. Baltimore: Johns Hopkins University Press, 1975.

Bonnie Kime Scott. Introduction, *The Gender of Modernism: A Critical Anthology*, ed. Scott. Bloomington: Indiana University Press, 1990.

Paul Smith. "The Trying-Out of *A Farewell to Arms*." *New Essays on "A Farewell to Arms"*, ed. Scott Donaldson. Cambridge: Cambridge University Press, 1990.

Michael Szalay. "Modernism's History of the Dead." *A Concise Companion to American Fiction, 1900–1950*, ed. Peter Stoneley and Cindy Weinstein. Oxford: Blackwell, 2008.

Michael Szalay. *New Deal Modernism: American Literature and the Invention of the Welfare State*. Durham: Duke University Press, 2000.

James G. Watson. "Faulkner and the Theater of War." *Faulkner and War: Faulkner and Yoknapatawpha, 2001*, ed. Noel Polk and Ann J. Abadie. This is the critic who recognizes that Dalton Ames is a World War I vet.

Gay Wilentz. "(Re)Teaching Hemingway: Anti-Semitism as a Thematic Device in *The Sun Also Rises*." *College English* 52.2 (February 1990).

Raymond Williams. *The Politics of Modernism: Against the New Conformists*. London: Verso, 1989.

Window: The New Woman and the Twenties

Dorothy M. Brown. *Setting a Course: American Women in the 1920s*. Boston: Twayne, 1987.

Carolyn Johnston. *Sexual Power: Feminism and the Family in America*. Tuscaloosa: University of Alabama Press, 1992.

Jean V. Matthews. *The Rise of the New Woman: The Women's Movement in America, 1875–1930*. Chicago: Marco R. Dee, 2003.

James R. McGovern. "The American Woman's Pre–World War I Freedom in Manners and Morals." *Journal of American History* 55.2 (1968).

George E. Mowry. *The Twenties: Fords, Flappers, and Fanatics*. Englewood Cliffs, NJ: Prentice-Hall, 1963.

Ellen K. Rothman. *Hands and Heart: A History of Courtship in America*. Cambridge, MA: Harvard University Press, 1987. The quotation from the postwar study of female adolescents comes from this book.

Warren Susman. *Culture as History: The Transformation of American Society in the Twentieth Century*. New York: Pantheon, 1984.

Window: World War I Sexual Revolution, Soldiers, and Charity Girls

Records of the Military Intelligence Division, 1900–1950 (165.1) in Records of the War Department General and Special Staffs (Record Group 165), National Archives, College Park, MD. It is in this set of papers, which I consulted on a return trip to the Archives made in 2007 to look at the documents Nancy Ford had discovered and used in her book, that I found the letter from the concerned citizen in Scranton, PA.

Allan M. Brandt. *No Magic Bullet: A Social History of Venereal Disease in the*

United States since 1880. New York: Oxford University Press, 1985.

Lloyd Brown. NPR radio interview. "National Museum of Marine Corps Dedication: World War I Veteran Reflects on Service." November 10, 2006, http://www.cnn.com/TRANSCRIPTS/0611/10/cnr.05.html (accessed March 9, 2017).

Nancy K. Bristow. *Making Men Moral: Social Engineering during the Great War.* New York: NYU Press, 1996. The quotation from the Commission on Training Camp Activities is in this book.

Mark Thomas Connelly. *The Response to Prostitution in the Progressive Era.* Chapel Hill: University of North Carolina Press, 1980.

Linda Gordon. *The Moral Property of Women: A History of Birth Control Politics in America.* Urbana: University of Illinois Press, 2002.

Linda Gordon. *Woman's Body, Woman's Right.* New York: Viking, 1976.

Mary E. Odem. *Delinquent Daughters: Protecting Adolescent Female Sexuality in the United States, 1885–1920.* Chapel Hill: University of North Carolina Press, 1995.

Ruth Rosen. *The Lost Sisterhood: Prostitution in America, 1900–1918.* Baltimore: Johns Hopkins University Press, 1982.

Daniel Scott Smith. "The Dating of the American Sexual Revolution: Evidence and Interpretation." *The American Family in Social-Historical Perspective*, ed. Michael Gordon. New York: St. Martin's, 1978.

Kendall Taylor. *Sometimes Madness Is Wisdom: Zelda and F. Scott Fitzgerald.* London: Robson Books, 2002. The quotation from Zelda is from here.

Andrea Tone. *Devices and Desires: A History of Contraceptives in America.* New York: Hill and Wang, 2001.

Kevin White. *The First Sexual Revolution: The Emergence of Male Heterosexuality in Modern America.* New York: NYU Press, 1993.

Window: Homosexuals and the Army

B. R. Burg. *Gay Warriors: A Documentary History from the Ancient World to the Present.* New York: NYU Press, 2002.

David F. Burrelli. "An Overview of the Debate on Homosexuals in the U.S. Military." *Gays and Lesbians in the Military: Issues, Concerns, and Contrasts*, ed. Wilbur J. Scott and Sandra Carson Stanley. New York: Aldine de Gruyter, 1994.

Francine D'Amico. "Race-ing and Gendering the Military Closet." *Gay Rights, Military Wrongs: Political Perspectives on Lesbians and Gays in the Military,*

ed. Craig A. Rimmerman. New York: Garland, 1996.

Randy Shilts. *Conduct Unbecoming: Lesbians and Gays in the U.S. Military, Vietnam to the Persian Gulf.* New York: St. Martin's, 1993.

Window: US Mobilization Policy and Army Personnel Methods, Including the Intelligence Tests

Papers from the National Archives, College Park, MD: specifically, papers from the Records of the Committee on Classification of Personnel (407.5.2) in the Records of the Adjutant General's Office (Record Group 407), the Committee on Psychology, the Committee on Provision for the Feeble-Minded, and the Medicine and Related Sciences Division of the National Research Council. These were the papers I lugged copies of around for twenty-some years and in which I found the quotations about the intelligence testing program and the methods for selecting captains in the training camps.

Rod Andrew Jr. "Soldiers, Christians, Patriots: The Lost Cause and Southern Military Schools, 1865–1915." *Journal of Southern History* 64.4 (1998).

Raymond E. Fancher. *The Intelligence Men: Makers of the IQ Controversy.* New York: Norton, 1985.

Stephen Jay Gould. "Carrie Buck's Daughter." *Natural History* 7 (1984).

Stephen Jay Gould. *The Mismeasure of Man.* New York: Norton, 1981.

David M. Kennedy. *Over Here: The First World War and American Society.* New York: Oxford University Press, 1980.

Daniel J. Kevles. "Testing the Army's Intelligence: Psychologists in World War I." *Journal of American History* 55 (1968). This is the secondary source that Gould and Kennedy worked from.

Alan M. Osur. *Blacks in the Army Air Forces during World War II: The Problem of Race Relations.* Honolulu: University Press of the Pacific, 2005. Here's where I got the information on African American scores on the intelligence tests.

Nina Ridenour. *Mental Health in the United States: A Fifty-Year History.* Cambridge, MA: Harvard University Press, 1961.

Robert M. Thorndike and David F. Lohman. *A Century of Ability Testing.* Chicago: Riverside, 1990.

United States, Adjutant General's Office. *The Personnel System of the U.S. Army.* Vol. 1. Washington, DC, 1919.

United States Army in the World War, 1917–1919. Vol. 16, *General Orders, GHQ, AEF.* Washington, DC: Center of Military History of the US Army, 1992.

U.S. Army Personnel Manual, November 1, 1918.

Window: Immigration Restriction and the Intelligence Tests

Carl Brigham. *A Study of American Intelligence*. Princeton: Princeton University Press, 1923.

Congressional Record—House. Vol. 65, part 6, 68th Cong., April 2, 1924, 5440. Washington, DC: Government Printing Office, 1924.

Congressional Record—Senate. Vol. 65, part 6, 68th Cong., April 8, 1924, 5824. Washington: Government Printing Office, 1924.

Congressional Record—Senate. April 1924, 5941.

David J. Goldberg. *Discontented America: The United States in the 1920s*. Baltimore: Johns Hopkins University Press, 1999.

Senator Lodge. "Must Guard Our Gates: The Necessity of Restricting Immigration to Our Shores." *New York Times*, March 17, 1896.

Mark McGurl. *The Novel Art: Elevations of American Fiction after Henry James*. Princeton: Princeton University Press, 2001.

Ronald Schaffer. *America in the Great War: The Rise of the War Welfare State*. New York: Oxford University Press, 1991.

US Bureau of the Census. *Historical Statistics of the United States, Colonial Times to 1957*. Washington, DC, 1960.

Robert M. Yerkes. *Psychological Examining in the U.S. Army. Memoirs of the National Academy of Sciences*, 15. Washington, DC: Government Printing Office, 1921.

Window: Ethnic Americans in the World War I Army

Records of the Military Intelligence Division, 1900–1950 (165.1) in Records of the War Department General and Special Staffs (Record Group 165), National Archives, College Park, MD.

Congressional Record—Senate. Vol. 61, part 1, 67th Cong., May 2, 1921, 916–917. Washington, DC: Government Printing Office, 1921.

Nancy Gentile Ford. *Americans All! Foreign-Born Soldiers in World War I*. College Station: Texas A&M University Press, 2001.

Rabbi Lee J. Levinger. *A Jewish Chaplain in France*. New York: Macmillan, 1921.

Robert A. Rockaway. "Hoodlum Hero: The Jewish Gangster: Defender of His People, 1919–1949." *American Jewish History* 82.1–4 (1994–95).

Richard Slotkin. *Lost Battalions: The Great War and the Crisis of American Nationality*. New York: Henry Holt, 2005.

Window: African Americans and the World War I Army

Arthur E. Barbeau and Florette Henri. *The Unknown Soldiers: Black American Troops in World War I*. Philadelphia: Temple University Press, 1974.

Byron Farwell. *Over There: The United States in the Great War, 1917–1918*. New York: Norton, 1999.

Jennifer Keene. *Doughboys, the Great War, and the Remaking of America*. Baltimore: Johns Hopkins University Press, 2000. It was this otherwise excellent book that claimed the army personnel committees moved too slowly, in compiling their test results and qualification cards, for the pressing needs to assign recruits in the first few days of service, but it's a tribute to Keene's integrity as a historian that I was able, on the basis of the documents I had in my possession, to convince her otherwise.

Jennifer Keene. "Raising the American Expeditionary Forces: Early Decision Making in 1917." *Battles Near and Far: A Century of Overseas Deployment*, ed. Peter Dennis and Jeffery Gray. Canberra: Army History Unit, Department of Defense, 2005. It is here that Keene talks about the army's initial plans for African American recruits.

Window: Ethnic and Jewish Quotas at Universities

Charlotte G. Borst. "Choosing the Student Body: Masculinity, Culture, and the Crisis of Medical School Admissions, 1920–1950." *History of Education Quarterly* 42.2 (2002).

David Brooks. *Bobos in Paradise: The New Upper Class and How They Got There*. New York: Simon and Schuster, 2000.

Theodore Dinnerstein. *Anti-Semitism in America*. New York: Oxford University Press, 1994.

Edward C. Halperin. "The Jewish Problem in U.S. Medical Education, 1920–1955." *Journal of the History of Medicine and Allied Sciences* 56.2 (2001).

"Harvard's Jewish Problem." *The Jewish Virtual Library*. http://www.jewishvirtuallibrary.org/jsource/anti-semitism/harvard.html (accessed July 26, 2007).

Jerome Karabel. *The Chosen: The Hidden History of Admission and Exclusion at Harvard, Yale, and Princeton*. New York: Houghton Mifflin, 2005.

Window: Conceptions of Ethnicity and Whiteness in the Era

Karen Brodkin. *How Jews Became White Folks and What That Says about Race in America*. New Brunswick, NJ: Rutgers University Press, 1998.

Matthew Frye Jacobson. *Whiteness of a Different Color: European Immigrants and the Alchemy of Race*. Cambridge, MA: Harvard University Press, 1998.

David R. Roediger. *Wages of Whiteness: Race and the Making of the American Working Class*. London: Verso, 2007.

Window: World War I General Information, Casualties, and Epidemics

John M. Barry. *The Great Influenza: The Epic Story of the Deadliest Plague in History*. New York: Viking, 2004.

John Whiteclay Chambers, ed. *The Oxford Companion to American Military History*. New York: Oxford University Press, 1999.

J. P. Clark. "Modernization without Technology: U.S. Army Educational and Organizational Reform, 1901–1911." Seventy-Fifth Annual Society for Military History Meeting, Weber State University, Odgen, UT, April 18, 2008. This is where I learned that, in the era immediately before World War I, American officers were taught about the supposed human ability to prevail over machine gun fire.

Edward M. Coffman. *The War to End All Wars: The American Military Experience in World War I*. New York: Oxford University Press, 1968.

Alfred W. Crosby. *Epidemic and Peace, 1918*. Westport, CT: Greenwood, 1976.

Nancy Gentile Ford. *The Great War and America: Civil-Military Relations during World War I*. Westport, CT: Praeger International Security, 2008.

Daniel Malloy Smith. *The Great Departure: The United States and World War I, 1914–1920*. New York: McGraw-Hill, 1965.

Richard B. Stolley, ed. *Life: Our Century in Pictures*. Boston: Little, Brown, 1999.

Window: General Military and Civil-Military Studies

Stanislav Andreski. *Military Organization and Society*. Berkeley: University of California Press, 1968.

Samuel P. Huntington. *The Soldier and the State: The Theory and Politics of Civil-Military Relations*. Cambridge, MA: Belknap Press of Harvard University Press, 1981.

Window: Biographical Information on the Lost Generation Writers

Carlos Baker. *Ernest Hemingway: A Life Story*. New York: Scribner, 1969.

Matthew J. Bruccoli. *Some Sort of Epic Grandeur: The Life of F. Scott Fitzgerald*. New York: Harcourt Brace Jovanovich, 1981.

Peter Griffin. *Along with Youth: Hemingway, the Early Years*. New York: Oxford University Press, 1985.

Samuel Hynes. Introduction, E. E. Cummings, *The Enormous Room* (1922). New York: Penguin, 1999.

Frederick R. Karl. *William Faulkner: American Writer: A Biography*. New York: Weidenfeld and Nicolson, 1989. I refer to this author as Faulkner's major biographer.

Donald Jones. "Newspaper Job in Toronto Launched Writer's Career." *Toronto Star*, June 18, 1977. Here's where I got the Gregory Clark quotation about Hemingway.

Townsend Ludington. Chronology, John Dos Passos, *Novels 1920–1925*. New York: Library of America, 2003.

Arthur Mizener. *The Far Side of Paradise: A Biography of F. Scott Fitzgerald*. Boston: Houghton Mifflin, 1951.

Michael Reynolds. *Hemingway: The Paris Years*. Cambridge, MA: Basil Blackwell, 1989.

Michael Reynolds. *Hemingway's First War: The Making of "A Farewell to Arms."* Princeton: Princeton University Press, 1976.

Michael Reynolds. *The Young Hemingway*. Oxford: Blackwell, 1986. Reynolds was apparently the biographer who exposed Hemingway's lie about infantry service and tall tale of his wounding.

Lillian Ross. "Hemingway Told Me Things." *New Yorker*, May 24, 1999.

Window: Other Literature by the Principal Authors

William Faulkner. *As I Lay Dying* (1930).

William Faulkner. *Flags in the Dust/Sartoris* (1929).

William Faulkner. *Soldiers' Pay* (1926). New York: Liveright, 1997. This is Faulkner's first novel, where I got the quotation about the "big circus" of the "hysterical" wartime moment.

F. Scott Fitzgerald. *The Beautiful and Damned* (1922). New York: Signet, 2007.

F. Scott Fitzgerald. "The Crack-Up" (1936). *The Art of the Personal Essay*, ed. Phillip Lopate. New York: Anchor Books, 1995. It's in this essay that Fitzgerald regrets that he didn't play football in college or get sent over to Europe during the war.

F. Scott Fitzgerald. "I Didn't Get Over" (1936). Referenced in Arthur Mizener, *The Far Side of Paradise: A Biography of F. Scott Fitzgerald*. Boston: Houghton Mifflin, 1951.

F. Scott Fitzgerald. *This Side of Paradise*. New York: Scribner, 1920.

Ernest Hemingway. *A Farewell to Arms* (1929). London: Granada, 1980.

Ernest Hemingway. "A Way You'll Never Be" (1933). *The Complete Short Stories of Ernest Hemingway*. New York: Scribner, 1987.

Ernest Hemingway. "In Another Country" (1927). *The Complete Short Stories of Ernest Hemingway*. New York: Scribner, 1987.

Ernest Hemingway. "A Very Short Story." *In Our Time* (1925). New York: Macmillan, 1986.

Ernest Hemingway. "Soldier's Home." *In Our Time* (1925). New York: Macmillan, 1986.

Window: Contemporaneous Literature by Other Authors

Hervey Allen. *Toward the Flame: A Memoir of World War I* (1926). Lincoln: University of Nebraska Press, 2003. This is one of the uncanonized World War I American literary works that give the sort of horrific account of the war that is missing from Lost Generation novels (the others are below by Boyd and March).

Sherwood Anderson. *Winesburg, Ohio* (1919). New York: Viking, 1960.

Isaac Babel. *Collected Stories*. New York: Penguin, 1994. Babel's narrator character in his masterpiece *Red Cavalry* (1926), set in the Bolshevik post–World War I Polish campaign of 1920, is most of all worried about killing others, so he goes into battle with an unloaded gun.

Djuna Barnes. *Nightwood* (1936). New York: New Directions, 1961.

Thomas Boyd. *Through the Wheat: A Novel of the World War I Marines* (1923). Lincoln: University of Nebraska Press, 2000.

Willa Cather. *One of Ours* (1922). London: Virago, 1986. Cather interestingly uses the phrase "new men" to describe American soldiers in this novel.

Blaise Cendrars. *The Astonished Man* (1945). London: Peter Owen, 2004.

E. E. Cummings. *The Enormous Room* (1922). New York: Penguin, 1999.

John Dos Passos. *One Man's Initiation: 1917* (1920) and *Three Soldiers* (1921). *Novels, 1920–1925*. New York: Library of America, 2003.

Robert Graves. *Good-Bye to All That: An Autobiography* (1929). Norwell, MA: Anchor, 1958.

James Joyce. *Ulysses* (1922). New York: Penguin, 1980.

William March. *Company K*. New York: Smith and Haas, 1933.

Henry Miller. *Tropic of Cancer* (1934). New York: Grove, 1961.

Katherine Anne Porter. *Pale Horse, Pale Rider: Three Short Novels* (1939). New York: Harcourt, Brace, 1964.

Siegfried Sassoon. *Memoirs of a Fox-Hunting Man*. London: Faber and Faber, 1928.

Siegfried Sassoon. *Siegfried's Journey, 1916–1920*. Vol. 3. New York: Viking, 1946.

Nathanael West. *The Day of the Locust* (1939). Alexandria, VA: Time-Life, 1982.

Edith Wharton. *A Son at the Front*. DeKalb: Northern Illinois University Press, 1923.

Virginia Woolf. *Mrs. Dalloway* (1925). New York: Houghton Mifflin, 1990.

Window: Literary Theory

Nina Baym. "Melodramas of Beset Manhood: How Theories of American Fiction Exclude Women Authors." *American Quarterly* 33.2 (1981).

Didier Eribon. *Michel Foucault*. Trans. Betsy Wing. Cambridge, MA: Harvard University Press, 1991. Here's where I got the information about Foucault's late opinion of his *The Order of Things* (1966), and this is also the book that contains the photo of me as a young man with Foucault.

Michel Foucault. "Questions of Method: An Interview with Michel Foucault." *Ideology and Consciousness* 8 (Spring 1981). This is where Foucault discusses the method of "constructing . . . a 'polyhedron' of intelligibility."

"Foucault and the Prisons: An Interview with Gilles Deleuze." *History of the Present* 2 (Spring 1986). This is the interview Paul Rabinow did, with my assistance.

Keith Gandal. "Michel Foucault: Intellectual Work and Politics." *Telos* 67 (Spring 1986). This is the article I researched in Paris in 1985.

Gavin Jones. "Poverty and the Limits of Literary Criticism." *American Literary History*, 15.4 (December 2003). This is where I learned that my *The Virtues of the Vicious: Jacob Riis, Stephen Crane and the Spectacle of the Slum* (Oxford University Press, 1997) was one of three books on the subject of literature and poverty written by a literature professor in the last thirty years.

Julia Kristeva. *Powers of Horror: An Essay on Abjection*. Trans. Leon S. Roudiez. New York: Columbia University Press, 1982.

David Macey. *The Lives of Michel Foucault: A Biography*. New York: Pantheon, 1993.

James Miller. *The Passion of Michel Foucault*. New York: Simon and Schuster, 1993.

Eve Kosofsky Sedgwick. *Between Men: English Literature and Male Homosocial Desire*. New York: Columbia University Press, 1985.

Mark Seltzer. *Henry James and the Art of Power*. Ithaca: Cornell University Press, 1984.

SUBJECT 2. MY GENERATION'S ATTITUDE TOWARD THE MILITARY AND SENSE OF MASCULINITY

Window: Works by Beat Novelists

William Burroughs. *Junky* (1953). New York: Penguin, 1977.

Jack Kerouac. *On the Road* (1957). New York: Penguin, 1999.

Kerouac. *Vanity of Duluoz: An Adventurous Education, 1935–46* (1968). New York: Penguin, 1994.

Window: Biographical Information on the Beat Novelists

Ann Charters. *Kerouac: A Biography*. New York: St. Martin's, 1994.

Barry Gifford and Lawrence Lee. *Jack's Book: An Oral Biography of Jack Kerouac*. New York: Penguin, 1978.

Allen Ginsburg. Introduction, William Burroughs, *Junky*. New York: Penguin, 1977.

Dennis McNally. *Desolate Angel: Jack Kerouac, the Beat Generation, and America*. Cambridge, MA: Da Capo, 2003.

Barry Miles. *William Burroughs: El Hombre Invisible*. London: Virgin Books, 1993.

Ted Morgan. *Literary Outlaw: The Life and Times of William S. Burroughs*. New York: Henry Holt, 1988.

Gerald Nicosia. *Memory Babe: A Critical Biography of Jack Kerouac*. Berkeley: University of California Press, 1994.

Window: The Vietnam Antiwar Movement and the Changing Image of the American Soldier

Philip G. Altbach, ed. *Student Political Activism: An International Reference Handbook*. Westport, CT: Greenwood, 1989.

Christian Appy. *Working-Class War: American Combat Soldiers and Vietnam*. Chapel Hill: University of North Carolina Press, 1993.

Paul Berman. *A Tale of Two Utopias: The Political Journey of the Generation of 1968*. New York: Norton, 1997.

Mark Edelman Boren. *Student Resistance: A History of the Unruly Subject*. New York: Routledge, 2001.

Robert Buzzanco. *Vietnam and the Transformation of American Life*. Oxford: Blackwell, 1999.

Charles Chatfield. Review of Kenneth H. Heineman, *Campus Wars: The Peace Movement at American State Universities in the Vietnam Era*. *American Historical Review* 99.2 (April 1994).

James Kirkpatrick Davis. *Assault on the Left: The FBI and the Sixties Antiwar Movement*. Westport, CT: Praeger, 1997.

Charles DeBenedetti and Charles Chatfield. *An American Ordeal: The Antiwar Movement of the Vietnam Era*. Syracuse: Syracuse University Press, 1990.

DeBenedetti. Review of Nancy Zaroulis and Gerald Sullivan, *Who Spoke Up? American Protest against the War in Vietnam, 1963–1975*. *Journal of American History* 72.1 (June 1985).

Alexander DeConde. *Student Activism: Town and Gown in Historical Perspective*. New York: Charles Scribner's Sons, 1971.

Joan Didion. "Slouching towards Bethlehem." *Slouching towards Bethlehem*. New York: Washington Square, 1981.

James Fallows. "What Did You Do in the Class War, Daddy?" *Washington Monthly* 7.8 (October 1975).

Adam Garfinkle. *Telltale Hearts: The Origins and Impact of the Vietnam Antiwar Movement*. New York: St. Martin's, 1995.

Kenneth H. Heineman. *Campus Wars: The Peace Movement at American State Universities in the Vietnam Era*. New York: NYU Press, 1993.

Rhodri Jeffreys-Jones. *Peace Now! American Society and the Ending of the Vietnam War*. New Haven: Yale University Press, 1999.

Peter S. Kindsvatter. *American Soldiers: Ground Combat in the World Wars, Korea, and Vietnam*. Lawrence: University Press of Kansas, 2003.

Christopher Lasch. *The Culture of Narcissism: American Life in an Age of Diminishing Expectations*. New York: Norton, 1978.

Calvin B. T. Lee. *The Campus Scene: 1900–1970*. New York: David McKay, 1970.

Jonathan Lighter. "Michael Herr's LURP Tale." *War, Literature, and the Arts*, 28 (2016). wlajournal.com. The description of the LRRP's qualifications is quoted here.

Brad Lucas. *Radicals, Rhetoric, and the War: The University of Nevada in the Wake of Kent State*. New York: Palgrave Macmillan, 2006.

Norman Mailer. *The Armies of the Night: History as a Novel—The Novel as History*. Signet: New York, 1968.

Elizabeth Walker Mechling and Jay Mechling. "Vietnam and the Second American Inner Revolution." *Cultural Legacies of Vietnam: Uses of the Past in the Present*, ed. Richard Morris and Peter Ehrenhaus. Norwood, NJ: Ablex, 1990.

Charles C. Moskos Jr. *The American Enlisted Man: The Rank and File in Today's Military*. New York: Russell Sage Foundation, 1970.

John Mueller. "Reflection on the Vietnam Antiwar Movement and on the Curious Calm at the War's End." *Vietnam as History: Ten Years after the Paris Peace Accords*, ed. Peter Braestrup. Washington, DC: University Press of America, 1984.

Joseph B. Perry Jr., Meredith Pugh, Eldon Snyder, and Elmer Spreitzer. "Patterns of Student Participation in a Free University." *Youth & Society* 3.2 (1971).

John Clark Pratt, ed. *Vietnam Voices: Perspectives on the War Years, 1941–1975*. Athens: University of Georgia Press, 1999.

Willis Rudy. *The Campus and a Nation in Crisis: From the American Revolution to Vietnam*. Madison, NJ: Farleigh Dickinson University Press, 1996.

Robert Self. "Last Man to Die: Vietnam and the Soldier as Citizen." Unpublished ms., 2008.

Melvin Small. "The Doves Ascendant: The American Antiwar Movement in 1968." *South Central Review* 16.4 (Winter 1999–Spring 2000), special issue: "Rethinking 1968: The United States and Western Europe."

Barbara Tischler. "The Antiwar Movement." *A Companion to the Vietnam War*, ed. Marilyn B. Young and Robert Buzzanco. Oxford: Blackwell, 2002.

Tom Wells. *The War Within: America's Battle over Vietnam*. Berkeley: University of California Press, 1994.

Nancy Zaroulis and Gerald Sullivan. *Who Spoke Up? American Protest against the War in Vietnam, 1963–1975*. Garden City, NY: Doubleday, 1984.

Window: The Draft, Student Deferment, Army Testing

Lawrence M. Baskir and William A. Strauss. *Chance and Circumstance: The Draft, the War, and the Vietnam Generation*. New York: Knopf, 1978. Here's where I got the quotation "If you're 2-S, you're somebody."

George Q. Flynn. *The Draft, 1940–1973*. Lawrence: University Press of Kansas, 1993.

James M. Gerhardt. *The Draft and Public Policy: Issues in Military Manpower Procurement, 1945–1970*. Columbus: Ohio State University Press, 1971.

M. H. Trytten. *Student Deferment in Selective Service: A Vital Factor in National Security*. Minneapolis: University of Minnesota Press, 1952.

Window: The Military and the Spread of Meritocracy to Universities, Meritocracy in General

Kenneth Arrow, Samuel Bowles, and Steven Durlauf, eds. *Meritocracy and Economic Inequality*. Princeton: Princeton University Press, 2000.

John Lewis Barkley. *Scarlet Fields*. Lawrence: University Press of Kansas, 2012.

Bill Bishop. *Big Sort: Why the Clustering of Like-Minded America Is Tearing Us Apart*. New York: Houghton Mifflin, 2008.

Richard Brookhiser. *Way of the Wasp: How It Made America, and How It Can Save It, So to Speak*. Florence, MA: Free Press, 1992.

D. Stanley Eitzen and Janis E. Johnston, eds. *Inequality: Social Class and Its Consequences*. Boulder, CO: Paradigm, 2007.

David A. Goslin. *The Search for Ability: Standardized Testing in Social Perspective*. New York: Russell Sage, 1963.

Richard J. Herrnstein. *I.Q. in the Meritocracy*. New York: Little, Brown, 1973.

Mika LaVaque-Manty. *The Playing Fields of Eton: Equality and Excellence in Modern Meritocracy*. Ann Arbor: University of Michigan Press, 2009.

Nicholas Lemann. *The Big Test: The Secret History of the American Meritocracy*. New York: Farrar, Straus and Giroux, 1999.

Robert I. Lerman. "Meritocracy without Rising Inequality: Wage Rate Differences Are Widening by Education and Narrowing by Gender and Race." Washington, DC: Urban Institute, September 1, 1997.

Rebecca S. Lowen. *Creating the Cold War University: The Transformation of Stanford*. Berkeley: University of California Press, 1997.

Suzanne Mettler. *Soldiers to Citizens: The G.I. Bill and the Making of the Greatest Generation*. New York: Oxford University Press, 2007.

Keith W. Olson. *G.I. Bill, the Veterans and the Colleges*. Lexington: University Press of Kentucky, 1982.

Olson. "A Historical Analysis of the G.I. Bill and Its Relationship to Higher Education." Cooperative Research Project S-436, US Department of Health, Education, and Welfare, Office of Education, 1968.

C. Ornstein. *Class Counts: Education, Inequality, and the Shrinking Middle Class*. Lanham, MD: Rowman and Littlefield, 2007.

Peter Schrag. *Decline of the WASP*. New York: Simon and Schuster, 1971.

Michael Dunlop Young. *Rise of the Meritocracy, 1870–2033: An Essay on Education and Equality*. London: Thames and Hudson, 1958.

Window: African Americans, World War II, and Veteran Involvement in the Civil Rights Movement

John Dittmer. *Local People: The Struggle for Civil Rights in Mississippi.* Urbana: University of Illinois Press, 1995.

Timothy B. Tyson. *Radio Free Dixie: Robert F. Williams and the Roots of Black Power.* Chapel Hill: University of North Carolina Press, 2001.

Robert F. Williams. *Negroes with Guns* (1962). Detroit: Wayne State University Press, 1998.

Neil A. Wynn. *The Afro-American and the Second World War.* London: Paul Elek, 1976.